# RISK AND RESISTANCE

How did women come to be seen as "at risk" for HIV? In the early years of the AIDS crisis, scientific and public health experts questioned whether women were likely to contract HIV in significant numbers and rolled out a response that effectively excluded women. Against a linear narrative of scientific discovery and progress, *Risk and Resistance* shows that it was the work of feminist lawyers and activists who altered the legal and public health response to the AIDS epidemic. Feminist AIDS activists and their allies took to the streets, legislatures, administrative agencies, and courts to demand the recognition of women in the HIV response. *Risk and Resistance* recovers a key story in feminist legal history – one of strategy, struggle, and competing feminist visions for a just and healthy society. It offers a clear and compelling vision of how social movements have the capacity to transform science in the service of legal change.

AZIZA AHMED is Professor of Law and the N. Neal Pike Scholar at Boston University School of Law. She writes on the intersection of gender, health, science, and law.

CAMBRIDGE STUDIES IN LAW AND SOCIETY

Founded in 1997, Cambridge Studies in Law and Society is a hub for leading scholarship in socio-legal studies. Located at the intersection of law, the humanities, and the social sciences, it publishes empirically innovative and theoretically sophisticated work on law's manifestations in everyday life: from discourses to practices, and from institutions to cultures. The series editors have longstanding expertise in the interdisciplinary study of law, and welcome contributions that place legal phenomena in national, comparative, or international perspective. Series authors come from a range of disciplines, including anthropology, history, law, literature, political science, and sociology.



A list of books in the series can be found at the back of this book.

CAMBRIDGE STUDIES IN LAW AND SOCIETY

# RISK AND RESISTANCE

*How Feminists Transformed the Law and Science of AIDS*

*Aziza Ahmed*
*Boston University School of Law*

CAMBRIDGE
UNIVERSITY PRESS

CAMBRIDGE
UNIVERSITY PRESS

Shaftesbury Road, Cambridge CB2 8EA, United Kingdom

One Liberty Plaza, 20th Floor, New York, NY 10006, USA

477 Williamstown Road, Port Melbourne, VIC 3207, Australia

314–321, 3rd Floor, Plot 3, Splendor Forum, Jasola District Centre,
New Delhi – 110025, India

103 Penang Road, #05–06/07, Visioncrest Commercial, Singapore 238467

Cambridge University Press is part of Cambridge University Press & Assessment,
a department of the University of Cambridge.

We share the University's mission to contribute to society through the pursuit of
education, learning and research at the highest international levels of excellence.

www.cambridge.org
Information on this title: www.cambridge.org/9781108485500

DOI: 10.1017/9781108751605



When citing this work, please include a reference to the DOI 10.1017/9781108751605

First published 2025

*A catalogue record for this publication is available from the British Library*

*A Cataloging-in-Publication data record for this book is available from the Library of Congress*

ISBN 978-1-108-48550-0 Hardback
ISBN 978-1-108-70721-3 Paperback

*To Jason, Zoya, and Reza*
*To my parents*

# CONTENTS

# ACKNOWLEDGMENTS

This book would not have been possible without many fellow travelers in the world of AIDS activism. Beri Hull, Patricia Nalls, Promise Mthembu, Jennifer Gatsi-Mallet, Meena Seshu, and many others lead national and international feminist movements on HIV and AIDS, sex work, and harm-reduction. Their perseverance and creative activism compelled me to begin to document the story of social movements and those involved who were not receiving due attention for the work they were doing to remake the world around them.

I should have known instantly that Terry McGovern, the brave, no-nonsense, and down-to-earth person I respected so much, had already transformed the delivery of welfare, ensured access to legal services for people living with HIV (when few others would), and fought and won struggles around housing, discrimination, and disability. I am grateful to Terry for allowing me to document her activism and legal work. I am grateful to Maxine Wolfe for allowing me to explore her personal archive at the Lesbian Her Story Archives. This book would not be possible without her careful documentation of the activism she and others engaged in. I thank Sarah Schulman for her permission to utilize the ACT-UP Oral History Archive. Thanks also to Margaret McCarthy and Nima Eshghi for sharing personal materials with me. Thanks to Gail Pheterson for help interpreting the COYOTE archives.

I moved into academia in 2010 and began to take seriously the project of documenting the relationship between law, politics, public health, gender, and science. I desperately needed help in making sense of my observations and research. Janet Halley and Libby Adler saw possibility in me and my scholarship and helped nurture it with deep intellectual mentorship, a shared sense of irreverent humor, and a lot of food. They taught me how to be an academic, allowing me to stumble and grow along the way. Libby's clear-sighted and careful scholarship has been a constant inspiration. Janet's ability to look beneath a text and behind spoken words is a constant reminder of how to listen, read, and think. I am deeply grateful and always indebted to them.

Early on in my career, Duncan Kennedy offered me the opportunity to do a reading year with him. That year and my interactions with Duncan since have shaped my own ability to apply and think through theory in the context of my work and this book. I will always be grateful to Duncan for his time, presence, and mentorship in my academic life.

Sheila Jasanoff invited me into the world of science and technology studies and her specific mode of engaging science, technology, and society (STS). It provided a vocabulary for many of my own intellectual instincts and friendship with many like-minded people. This book reflects the influence of a body of work she and STS have cultivated over decades as well as her deep support and engagement with my work. I am grateful, too, to Ben Hurlbut for both his feedback and friendship.

My life in academia, and my academic work, shifted when I met Guy-Uriel Charles. Guy has read multiple drafts of this book. His deep and insightful feedback, always delivered with a dose of laughter, has helped me to clarify the contributions of this project and deepen the ideas within the book. I am so grateful for his intellectual mentorship and his guidance at many different points in my career. To know Guy is a gift. Through Guy I encountered a new world of brilliant, generous, and kind scholars, many who have been willing to endlessly discuss this project with me. I especially thank Franita Tolson, Bertrall Ross, Rick Banks, Luis Fuentes-Rohwer, and Timothy Lovelace for their feedback and support.

Michele Goodwin has been a constant source of motivation and inspiration for this project. This book reflects my engagement with Michele's visionary scholarship, her ability to build community, be a public intellectual, and engage in activism. She has supported this project from its inception with her encouragement and continues to do so. I am so grateful to her for this support and am deeply indebted to her for the space she has created for many of us in the academy.

I thank David Kennedy for his support of my scholarship and for building a community that nurtures critical thought. Through this community I have met many of my interlocutors, friends, and fellow travelers who have read versions of this book and provided support along the way. I am especially grateful to Dan Danielson, Kerry Rittich, Vasuki Nesiah, and Karen Engle. Their rich scholarship, support, and friendship helped me to understand how to think and engage in critical legal scholarship. Over a series of lunches, I gained the incredible insights of Lucie White which helped me think about how to frame this book.

At Northeastern, Karl Klare and Lucy Williams provided mentorship, friendship, and support. Their iSERP (International Social and Economic Rights Project) network provided a space for valuable feedback. At different points, Karl sometimes intentionally, and other times unintentionally, taught me a great deal about how to think with clarity and purpose. I cherish those moments.

Colleagues at Northeastern University also helped me to think through the ideas in this book and I am especially grateful to Brook Baker, Shalanda Baker, Daniel Medwed, Wendy Parmet, Patricia Williams, Serena Parekh, Nima Eshghi, Suzanna Walters, and Kathy Abrams. The Law and Political Economy network has been a rich and generative space for academic exchange and I am thankful to have been included. I am especially grateful to Amy Kapczynski for her support and feedback on this project.

I presented numerous versions of this work in the Vulnerability and Legal Theory Workshops hosted by Martha Fineman. The ideas presented in this book bear the imprint of thinking with and alongside her work.

During my time as a Law and Public Affairs (LAPA) fellow at Princeton University, I received wonderful feedback from the LAPA community and in particular Paul Frymer, Jessica Eaglin, Lewis Grossman, and Sarah Stazack. Melissa Murray traveled from New York to Princeton to give me comments on an early version of my book proposal and I remain grateful for this early substantive feedback.

I benefitted from feedback at many faculty workshops and conferences. I am grateful to the faculty at Brooklyn Law School, Emory University School of Law, University of Virginia Law School, University of Kentucky Law School, University of California, Irvine, University of Pennsylvania Law and History Workshop, the Health Law Workshop at Harvard Law School, and American University Washington College of Law.

So many friends and colleagues in the academy have read chapters, heard versions of book talks, and helped to shape this book with their feedback. I am especially grateful to Amna Akbar, Helena Alviar, Chaz Arnett, Sameer Ashar, Swethaa Ballakrishnen, Paulo Barrozo, Khiara Bridges, Dorothy Brown, Courtney Cahill, Vignetta Charles, Amy Cohen, I. Glen Cohen, Kevin Davis, Nomita Divi, Gregg Gonsalves, Priya Gupta, Jasmine Harris, Erin Hassleberg, Eisha Jain, Terence Keel, Stephen Lee, Aya Gruber, Liz Sepper, Terence Keel, Charlie Peevers, Naomi Cahn, Craig Konnoth, Maya Manian, Stu Marvel, Serena

Mayeri, Zina Miller, Seema Mohapatra, Kim Mutcherson, Osagie Obasogie, Shaun Ossei-Owusu, K-Sue Park, Charlie Peevers, Rachel Rebouché, Brishen Rogers, Teemu Ruskola, Liz Sepper, Hila Shamir, Matiangai Sirleaf, Karen Tani, Chantal Thomas, Philomila Tsoukala, Alvaro Santos, and Lindsay Wiley. I owe Darren Rosenblum particular thanks for helping me make necessary connections within the AIDS Coalition to Unleash Power (ACT-UP) for me to complete my archival work.

Early in my career Sofia Gruskin, Nancy Krieger, Ali Miller, and Mindy Roseman provided opportunities to think critically about public health – the imprint of those lectures, conversations, readings, and their work are in this book. At various times over the past few years, as I was working on this book, they each took the time to provide feedback and much needed encouragement.

At my current institution, Boston University, many colleagues have been helpful to my own thinking and work. Linda McClain and Jim Fleming have been enormous supporters, mentors, and colleagues. Linda McClain's encouragement helped propel this project forward. I am also grateful to my colleagues Zohra Ahmed, Madison Condon, Julie Dahlstrom, Steven Dean, Stacey Dogan, Jon Feingold, Woody Hartzog, Nicole Huberfeld, Gerry Leonard, Karen Pita Loor, Steven Koh, Andy Sellers, Erica George, Ngozi Okidegbe, Sadiq Reza, Chris Robertson, Anna di Robilant, Sarah Sherman-Stokes, Kate Silbaugh, Jessica Silbey, Robert Tsai, and Ron Wheeler for taking the time to discuss ideas related to this book with me.

I have been lucky to work under the leadership of deans who have supported my work. I thank Emily Spieler, Jeremy Paul, Bryant Garth, Austen Parrish, and Angela Onwuachi-Willig for their support.

Veena Dubal's deep curiosity about the world is a source of inspiration for me. Her scholarship serves as a unfaltering reminder that learning and writing are a way of doing politics. I hope I am as good a friend and interlocutor to her as she is to me.

Friends who are not in the legal academy provided support in innumerable ways. As I was researching this book, I recruited Caroline Jones who traveled with me to places she never expected to go. I am so glad she came with me and even more so for her consistent friendship. Sapna Desai housed me on numerous trips to India, listened to me discuss this project, and encouraged me not to lose my things. Her brilliance and curiosity always push me to think in new ways. My dear friends from law school are an everlasting source of fun and encouragement, especially Kiran Singh, Deepika Bains, and Michele Leung. Alan Ricks lent his incredible talent to generate ideas for the cover design. I am deeply grateful to him for taking the time to do this. Dedicated leaders in the AIDS movement including Vivek Divan, Mandeep Dhaliwal, and Nazneen Damji inspired me to keep working at this book.

When you are a transplant to a city, friends become family, and in turn are subject to constant book updates. I am grateful to Diya Kallivayalil, Divya Errabelli, Jasmine Hanifi, Nathan Yozwiak, Justin Steil, Ana Munoz, Tara Pedulla, Mark Pedulla, Cristina de la Cierva, Ana Feingold, Lily Song, and Andres Svetsuk for opening their homes to our family.

Thank you to the editors at Cambridge University Press including John Berger and Matt Gallaway who have shepherded this book over the finish line. Thank you to Sandy Banks for her editorial work and to many research assistants who worked with me along the way.

As I have written this book, my parents have been a constant source of support. My mom, Noorbanu Ahmed, will fly in at a moment's notice just to make sure we are all eating enough. She insists that I use her presence to write. My dad, Abdul Rehman Ahmed, is always interested in the substance of my writing and his intellectual curiosity and desire to learn has always been an inspiration for me. Noureen Miller and Sara Holman have allowed me to talk about this book project for years and provided constant encouragement. I am grateful to them for their laughter, love, and support. Ryan Miller and Todd Holman got stuck with me as a sister-in-law but I lucked out with them. Peta-Gay Jackson Booth, Eric Booth, Julian Jackson, and Bert Jackson provide a family away from my own.

I began this book when my daughter was a few months old. I continued to work on it through the birth of my son during the COVID pandemic. As I complete writing this book now, my sweet Zoya has just finished reading her first "chapter book" and my little Reza is beginning to identify letters. I wonder if they will read this book one day? I hope, if they do read it, that they see themselves in the stories of people who saw possibility despite an impossible set of circumstances; I hope they see their own place in changing the conditions of the world.

For more than two decades, Jason and I have been juggling some version of life, writing, newborns, pandemic, teaching, diapers, snacks, lunches, dinners, school, and more. But never once has Jason hesitated to stop and take a moment to encourage me in a moment of doubt, to read a draft, to check-in, or to listen. Have I even said thank you once? Thank you, Jason, for everything.

I dedicate this book to Jason, Zoya, and Reza. And to my parents, for their constant support.

Chapter 1 reproduces text from Social Movements in the Struggle for Redistribution written for the Law and Political Economy Blog as well as text from Feminism, Law, and Epidemiology in the AIDS Response in Governance Feminism: Notes from the Field (Janet Halley et al eds., 2019).

Chapter 4 builds on work and research developed while writing *The Public/Private Divide in Public Health: The Case of COVID-19*, 90 Fordham Law Review 2541 (2022) (with Jason Jackson); *Race, Risk, and Public Health*, 21 Columbia Law Review Forum 47 (2021) (with Jason Jackson).

Chapter 3 "Rugged Vagina's" and "Vulnerable Rectums": The Sexual Identity, Epidemiology, and Law of the Global HIV Epidemic, Columbia Journal of Law and Gender 1 (2013) and Feminism, Law, and Epidemiology in the AIDS Response in Governance Feminism: Notes from the Field (Janet Halley et al eds., 2019).

Chapter 5 reproduces work in *Trafficked? AIDS, Criminal Law, and the Politics of Measurement*, 70 University of Miami Law Review 96 (2015), *Addressing HIV/AIDS at the Intersection of Anti-Trafficking and Health Law and Policy*, in Revisiting the Law and Governance of Trafficking, Forced Labor and Modern Slavery (P. Kotiswaran ed., 2017), and *Feminism, Power, and Sex Work in the Context of HIV/AIDS*, 34 Harvard Journal of Law and Gender 225 (2011). The chapter builds on work developed in *Transnational Law and Global Health: Abortion and AIDS*, in The Oxford Handbook on Transnational Law (Peer Zumbansen ed., 2021).

# A NOTE ON METHODS

This book is a genealogy of AIDS told through the stories of feminist social movement actors that engaged in restructuring our understanding of AIDS and its outcomes.[1] I take genealogy to mean an "analysis that traces how contemporary practices and institutions emerged out of specific struggles, conflicts, alliances, and exercises of power, many of which are nowadays forgotten."[2] How has the past created the conditions for our contemporary management of disease? My attempt, in keeping with scholarly undertakings of genealogy, is to show how transformations in law and science interact with and are coproduced by contingent and shifting claims of individuals and institutions.[3] In the tradition of science and technology studies and critical legal theory, from where I draw much inspiration for this book, I offer an account which seeks to show how taken-for-granted ideas – science and law as objective and neutral sites of fact-finding – are disrupted to shift the material distribution of resources.[4]

This book is focused on social movement activism on AIDS from approximately 1982 until 2013. Though I am not a historian, much of my work for this book was conducted in the archive. Though for this project, the "archive" must be defined broadly. Not only did I visit traditional archives, cultivated by libraries and nonprofits, including the Harvard Schlesinger Library, Lesbian Herstory Archive, the Smithsonian Museum, Office of NIH (National Institutes of Health) History and Stetten Museum, the ACT-UP Oral History Project, and the Gay Men's Health Crisis, I also spent time in the personal files of activists and advocates. I visited their offices and photocopied personal files and photographed pictures of memorabilia and images. I wanted to be sure I could capture the moments I was writing about with all of their complexity and contingency.

Because this book centers law and legal struggle, I have also read and drawn on hundreds of legal documents, including regulations of administrative agencies, party briefs filed to the court, amicus briefs, court decisions, congressional hearings, regulations, and supplementary information to regulations spanning the course of at least fifty years.

I supplemented the archival and legal research with oral interviews with lawyers, members of ACT-UP, people living with HIV, and government officials. Where accounts of a moment in time differed between an individual account and one on paper, I have noted that in the footnotes. I also relied on the oral histories banks including the ACT-UP Oral History Project and the NIH Oral History Project.

When I began this book I was struck by the invisibility of women in the broader scholarly and public understandings of HIV and AIDS. In most accounts, AIDS was and is a disease of gay men, one that was bravely fought and won. A reader could be forgiven for walking away from this literature thinking that there were few women involved in AIDS activism and that AIDS was now a thing of the past. This sat in stark contrast to the world I was witnessing in which women and girls around me had HIV in large numbers, they had contracted HIV in recent years, they were still struggling to access basic care and treatment.

Contributing to the erasure of women from historical accounts of AIDS is their absence from the archive: Many women did not have the infrastructure necessary to save documents as they tried to survive. Most women diagnosed with HIV in the 1980s have now died; they are unable to give oral histories or tell their own stories. In writing this account, I often reflected on the work of Saidiya Hartman, who has written about absence of Black women and queer people, in the archive, the invisibility of people we knew existed, for whom we can only find "fragments of a life".[5]

In this genealogy of AIDS, I have tried to recover those stories that are lost or are quickly being forgotten, to tell a history of AIDS that shows how the entire legal structures, of nations, of cities, of agencies, and the scientific rationalities of risk that underpin them, were transformed by groups of unexpected people whose activism reverberates through the global response to HIV and AIDS.

# INTRODUCTION

## "Women Don't Get AIDS, They Just Die from It"

In 1987, Patricia Nalls sat at the kitchen table in her new apartment planning her funeral and waiting for the phone to ring.[1] This was not the life, or death, she expected. For years she had been happily married and living in the suburbs. She had two beautiful children – each a blend of her Indo-Guyanese and her husband's African American heritage. They were thriving and happy. And she was pregnant with a third. While her husband had injected drugs in the past – it was in the past. His frequent illnesses were dismissed by doctors as a cough, the flu, and allergies. It wasn't until one protracted hospital visit, when his body seemed to be withering away, that he was finally tested for HIV. His shocking diagnosis didn't allow time for the family to process.

Patricia's positive test result came shortly after her husband's diagnosis. Her youngest child, born a few months later, was immediately diagnosed with AIDS. Patricia's daughter and husband died within months of each other. As Patricia planned her own funeral, she mourned the loss of her child and her husband. She grappled with the reality that her own fate would mirror theirs.

Patricia also worried. Her children, who did not have HIV, would long survive her. She worried about their future and who would take care of them when she died. She was struggling financially and afraid to disclose to her family why she was unable to work. She was alone.

Patricia did not know any other women living with HIV. Like most people in the United States at the time, she didn't think women could even get the virus. To her, and nearly everyone else, AIDS was a disease associated with gay men and people who injected drugs. On one visit to the doctor, tired of feeling so isolated, Patricia asked her physician if she was the only woman in America living with AIDS. She was surprised when her doctor reassured her there were others. Desperate to make contact with these women, she installed a landline in her home, a financial stressor for her but worth it for the possibility of connecting with other women living with HIV. Patricia pasted signs at her physician's office asking women living with HIV to call her. Then, she waited.

To her amazement, her phone began to ring. And ring and ring again. She spoke to women who were living in secrecy and fear. They shared their stories of living with HIV, their desire to protect their children, and their inability to get support. Before long, the women began to regularly meet. Together, they supported each other in doing the unthinkable: Putting on a brave face to drive their children to school in the morning, only to return home to make arrangements for dealing with sickness and death.

Patricia began to encourage the women who called her to pool resources. They took turns driving each other's kids to school, babysat during doctor's appointments, and shared food stamps so that the children could eat. When a woman fell ill, the others took her children in; without that, the kids could be lost to child protective services and sent to live with strangers.

To them, the AIDS response itself excluded women and ignored their particular needs. In the late 1980s, no one was talking about women and AIDS. The few services that existed felt alienating: Children were not allowed to board the buses that picked up AIDS patients to take them to doctor's appointments. Because of this, women with few childcare options often missed their checkups. Support groups designed for men had little to offer women who were caring for sick children while they themselves were unwell. Food programs only provided food for people living with AIDS, not for their children. Women starved so their children could eat.

Heartbroken, Patricia watched her friends as they became weak and succumbed to death due to AIDS-related complications. She watched as children were lost to the foster system, the lucky ones taken in by family or friends. And she battled her own health challenges – but she did not die. She is still alive today. Her survival is the remarkable outcome of a feminist struggle that altered the regulatory and scientific landscape on AIDS.

* * *

Fifteen years after Patricia asked her doctor if she was the only woman in America living with AIDS, the United Nations Joint Program on HIV and AIDS (UNAIDS) declared that women were the fastest growing group of people living with HIV. The epidemic had been "feminized."

AIDS was not supposed to impact women in large numbers. In the 1980s, when confusion and death reigned, scientists and epidemiologists chased hypotheses about the disease: Was it a gastrointestinal virus? A pneumonia? A cancer associated with gay men? A gay plague?[2] The now infamous nonresponse by the United States government to the epidemic included the disregard by the Reagan administration of the spread and impact of the virus, a lack of investment in access to treatment, and the stigmatization of people living with HIV. The sexual politics of AIDS complicated the possibilities for research and public health interventions and contributed to a lack of clarity about the virus.

Experts disagreed about the likelihood that heterosexual sex was a key mode of HIV transmission. The idea that women were resistant to contracting HIV gained traction in the popular press. Take the 1985 *Discover Magazine* cover story "AIDS: The Latest Scientific Facts," which reported that women have "rugged vaginas."[3] According to text accompanying a cross-sectional image of a vagina, the organ's tough and resistant cells made women unlikely to contract HIV. This idea was repeated time and again. In a book published in 1990, reviewed by the *New York Times* and *New England Journal of Medicine*, *The Myth of the Heterosexual AIDS Epidemic: How a Tragedy Has Been Distorted by the Media and Politics*, journalist Michael Fumento reproduced the idea that differences in the tissue construction of the male urethra and rectum and the female vagina – the latter being constructed of tough cells that "resist rupture".[4]

In the broader struggle to understand who was at risk for HIV, the idea that women were biologically resistant to AIDS was repeated time and again by science journalists, in popular women's magazines including *Cosmopolitan*, on nightly news programs, and in national newspapers including the *New York Times*.

How did the world ultimately come to see women as "at risk" for HIV? How did a disease of men come to kill women? Against a linear narrative of scientific discovery and progress, as accounts of disease mitigation are often told, *Risk and Resistance* shows that it was the work of women's rights lawyers and activists, not only scientific experts, that fundamentally altered the legal and scientific response to the AIDS epidemic by changing core conceptions of who was at risk of contracting HIV. With this powerful example of the feminist struggle in AIDS, I argue that public health advocates not only fight to change legal rules, they may also destabilize scientific settlements and expert consensus for the sake of redistribution. In the context of AIDS, feminists not only changed the legal governance of AIDS, they altered the scientific trajectory of the epidemic. In doing so, feminists channeled money and services toward women in the AIDS response. Many of these feminists were women of color who centered race in their advocacy; they both raised critiques of the mainstream AIDS movement and joined forces with broad advocacy to demand services for people of color. Feminists advocated for women to be seen as a risk group for HIV in multiple locations: in US administrative agencies, courthouses across the country, as well as in global governance institutions.[5] This book excavates the impact feminism – with all of its ideological diversity – has had on scientific ideas and legal reform agendas in the AIDS response.

*Risk and Resistance* makes several contributions to existing scholarly literatures on law, feminist theory, science and technology studies, and public health.

Health law scholars and epidemiologists broadly define the social determinants of health as the conditions in which people live their lives that impact their health outcomes. Health law scholars understand law to be a social determinant of health in that the legal environment shapes health outcomes. While much attention has been paid to understanding legal frameworks, less attention has been dedicated to understanding how legal transformations occur with the specific goal altering epidemiology and medicine to bring about legal reforms.

*Risk and Resistance* bears down on the question of how social movements mobilize to transform laws and unsettle scientific consensus in order to alter the distribution of public health resources toward particular groups.[6] Most often, science in this book refers to epidemiology, the science of disease and its spread. At some points, however, as noted in the text, I discuss shifts in basic science.

The focus on social movements allows for a greater examination of how politics shapes public health law. The book argues against the idea that it is necessary to excise politics from health governance; instead I argue that a deep understanding of how law, science, and politics interact is necessary to understand and remedy deep inequalities that persist in healthcare.

Examining the role of social movements allows for a sustained examination of how legal and political activism can redistribute resources and legitimate its claims in the register of scientific neutrality. In the literature on law and social movements, legal advocacy plays an unsettled role in social change: Some social movement scholars argue that lawyers and litigation have the potential to deradicalize social movements and derail social change. In response, other scholars argue that while outcomes are indeterminate, advocates utilizing litigation strategies and seeking legal transformation are frequently propelled forward through the fight for reforms.[7] Rather than derail social change, the law offers a set of possible goals, a new vernacular for channeling movement desires, and the legitimation of advocacy claims.

Yet, while law and social movements scholars are interested in social change, and many have long recognized that legal mobilization has impact far beyond simply changing legal rules and their formal application, law and social movements scholarship might ignore the role of law, lawyers, and litigation for the sake of explicitly altering scientific consensus in order to redistribute material resources toward a particular group. In turn, this creates gaps in the legal scholarship about how social change related to a host of areas depending on science and technology occurs, including, as relevant here, in the realm of public health law.

The idea that law and science are made in isolation of one another is tied to the notion that law lags behind science. In other words, the legal regulation of science is doomed to perpetually lag behind scientific progress or, even worse, constrain scientific discovery.[8] Science and technology studies (STS) scholars call this the "law lag" thesis. More specifically, public health scholars similarly argue that the legal regulation of health should be based on medical and scientific evidence. In other words, science and expertise should lead the way. Each of these arguments suggests that while law and science interact, they are fundamentally distinct from one another.

Scholars, activists, and legal practitioners tend to reify the notion that science and law are distinct. This is done through the insistence that scientific and medical evidence should lead the way in crafting the regulatory environments on gender and health and through the flip of this, which is an insistence that good scientific and medical research and advancement not be tainted by an overly burdensome regulatory environment.[9] The feminist activist claim that women's decision-making on abortion be left to "a woman and her doctor" – a slogan found on buttons and bumper stickers – operationalizes (and exemplifies) the law/science distinction in its insistence that we preserve expert and evidence-driven medical practice without the taint of law. This analytic and activist move elides the way that evidence itself is the product of legal and social contestation.

Attempting to remedy this gap, STS scholars, largely drawing on the work of STS scholar Sheila Jasanoff, challenge the view that legal regulation and science can be kept distinct. Instead, these scholars use the idea of coproduction to examine the relationship between governance and the production of scientific and technical knowledge.[10] In the legal literature on social movements, very little attention is paid to the specific contours and pathways that legal rules, legal institutions, and court decisions – as well as litigation in court – alter the field of knowledge and can shape the distribution of material resources – including healthcare – between populations.[11]

As evidenced in the case of the feminist AIDS movement, this mode of inquiry – one in which the coproductive aspects of law and science are interrogated with an eye toward the distributive consequences – helps to identify the legal–scientific settlements that justify legal regulation.[12]

The story of women's activism in the AIDS response provides a powerful example of coproduction, as feminist lawyers go deep into the tangle of science and the distribution of welfare benefits to recraft who can be diagnosed with AIDS.[13] It is a clear example of how law does not always lag behind science. Instead, the law can play an important role in mediating, constraining, and creating possibilities at the intersection of science and rights.[14] And, in turn, how the ideologies of social movements, in this case the feminist critique of science, shape legal claims. By tracing one site of the constitutive relationship between law and science, the book draws out several lessons for law and social movements scholars thinking about how legal actors mobilize the law to alter science and vice versa: First, that social movement actors utilize litigation to unsettle scientific and medical consensus with the explicit goal of altering the distribution of rights and resources, and, second, that social movement frames – like the feminist critique of science – shape the form and substance of rights claims made by advocates.

The book proceeds as follows. Chapter 1, "'We Are Not Immune': A New Branch of the Feminist Women's Health Movement," begins by describing the emergence of a new coalition of feminists who turned their attention to the HIV epidemic in an attempt to understand how the virus would impact women. Together, they realize that an epidemic is brewing among women. The failure to recognize and respond to it is due, in part, to the Centers for Disease Control and Prevention (CDC) definition of AIDS that did not include gynecological infections. This definition resulted in the exclusion of women from AIDS data and in the Social Security Administration's determinations of who should receive benefits. Allying with lawyers and fellow activists, feminists set out to challenge the law and science of the epidemic.

Chapter 2, "Litigating Risk: The Law and Politics of Disease in the Administrative State," turns to the litigation and activism that resulted in the shift in the AIDS definition and turned attention to women's risk from HIV. The chapter tracks how litigation and advocacy changed settled ideas of who was at risk for contracting HIV. Feminists prevail – their success would result in many more women being diagnosed with HIV, resulting in a greater ability to access benefits. This life-changing shift would mark a major victory for the feminist women's health advocates focused on AIDS. Their story challenges the narrative of scientific progress and produces a new legal–scientific settlement on the question of women and AIDS.

Once women were diagnosed with AIDS in large numbers, and AIDS treatments were developed, more people with HIV began to survive longer. New AIDS drugs turned out to be toxic or intolerable for some people leading researchers to conduct new trials. A new problem emerged: Women were being excluded from clinical trials due to a 1977 Food and Drug Administration (FDA) guideline concerned about the impact on women's reproduction and the fetus. In practical terms, however, this meant that women could not access new drug trials and that what physicians knew about how to treat women was severely limited. Chapter 3, "Experiments in Risk: Clinical Trials and Women," follows feminist advocates as they set out to change the regulatory environment around clinical trials to mandate the inclusion of women. They did so by asserting – in keeping with the broader feminist women's movement at the time – that women have full autonomy over their bodies and may choose to take part in risky trials. Partly due to the shifting sensibility around ideas of women's choice and autonomy, the FDA produced new guidance in 1993 that took steps toward addressing the discrepancy between men and women in clinical trials.

The growing numbers of women living with HIV begged a question: Why and how were women at risk for HIV? Chapter 4, "Sex Bargains," tracks the emergence of a new logic that centers heterosexual sex as the site of women's vulnerability. Attributing vulnerability to HIV to heterosexual sex had a powerful effect: It minimized the emphasis on structural responses to the epidemic, from housing to harm reduction, and instead focused public health interventions on individual behavior. Feminist activists and scholars, as well as law and economics scholars, motivated by a desire to shape lawmaking on the epidemic in light of their own theories of sex debated one another on how to best respond. Partly due to the political and economic backdrop of the time, the two movements focused in on the sex bargain, the negotiation between two people before engaging in sex. Despite their different perspectives and goals, the convergence between these two scholarly and activist movements helped drive a response to HIV that would shift attention away from structural interventions and focus on individual behavior. This chapter tracks this debate and the impact it had on the legal response to HIV.

As heterosexual sex became a driving explanation, feminist debates about sex and power took center stage in the AIDS response. At the heart of this feminist struggle is the question of sex work. Some feminists, carceral antitrafficking feminists, saw sex work as the objectification and exploitation of women. Others saw it as a potential site of agency and power. Chapter 5, "The Sex Wars Come to AIDS: Risk and Consent," follows these debates as they moved into public health and the AIDS response. Sex workers were (and continue to be) among the hardest hit with HIV. They were also some of the most powerful advocates of a safe-sex approach. Empowering sex worker communities would turn out to be one of the most reliable ways to slow the spread of HIV. But for feminists who saw sex work as exploitation, these public health interventions were aiding in harming women. Buoyed by political conservatives and a larger movement to end human trafficking, carceral antitrafficking feminists successfully lobbied for restrictions on funding sex worker projects. The consequences were deadly.

In reflecting on the social movement activism documented in the book, and in thinking about contemporary public health crises, the Conclusion offers a new framework to describe the momentary stabilization of scientific facts in and through lawmaking: legal–scientific settlements. These legal–scientific settlements produce a range of distributional consequences that have material effects on people's lives and shape the ability of individuals to survive and thrive despite public health crises.

1

# "WE ARE NOT IMMUNE"

## A New Branch of the Feminist Women's Health Movement

> Somewhere behind a prison wall in Bedford Hills a movement or community was being built. It was a diverse group of women teaming together to meet the needs and fears that had developed with this new epidemic, AIDS ... they managed to build a community of women: black, white, Hispanic, learned, illiterate, robbers, murderers, forgers, rich poor, Christian, Muslim, Jewish, bisexual, gay, heterosexual – all putting aside their differences and egos for a collective cause ...
>
> — Katrina Haslip, 199[2][1]

In 1984, a New York court sentenced Kathy Boudin to twenty years to life in prison for being a passenger in a getaway van during a high-profile Brink's truck robbery that left two police officers and one guard dead.[2] Van driver David Gilbert, Kathy's partner and father of their young son, was given a seventy-five-year prison term, as was Kathy's friend Judy Clark, who drove a second getaway car. All three were members of the Weather Underground – a radical left-wing organization fighting alongside the Black Liberation Army for racial and economic equality. The botched robbery in 1981 was part of a plan to get cash to finance organizing efforts.[3] The shootout garnered international attention and became a flashpoint in a national conversation about the role of violence in the crusade for progressive social change.

Prison did not stifle the trio's activism. In 1986, Gilbert wrote to Boudin that AIDS was endemic at the Auburn Correctional Facility where he was being held.[4] Addressing AIDS felt especially urgent to both Gilbert and Boudin as Kuwasi Balagoon, a partner in the robbery, had died of AIDS while in prison with Gilbert. Gilbert created a peer-education program for inmates about human immunodeficiency virus (HIV) and acquired immune deficiency syndrome (AIDS) in 1987. The next year Boudin and Clark began organizing inmates at Bedford Women's Prison to press the warden to provide information on how women might be affected by the disease. Healthcare was a major issue at Bedford and they wondered if AIDS could be looming.

Although organizing was not permitted in the prison, Boudin and Clark began to gather signatures for a formal request that prison superintendent, Elaine Lord, create the space for women to learn about AIDS. The superintendent responded well. By all accounts Lord was a good woman who sought to make the prison as tolerable as possible. She too was worried about the prospect of women growing sick and dying in the prison infirmary. She supported efforts to bring women together to learn about AIDS. And, importantly, she supported their desire to help their ailing peers, to visit them in the infirmary, and to keep them company as they slowly died.[5]

A group of about thirty-five women came together for regular meetings to better understand the epidemic that seemed to be impacting their fellow prisoners. They named themselves AIDS Counseling and Education or ACE.[6] They sought to educate inmates about how to prevent the transmission of HIV, establish compassionate care standards for those who were HIV positive, provide support and information to women with fears, questions, and needs related to HIV/AIDS, and act as a liaison to community groups assisting HIV-positive women as they left the prison and reentered society. Their campaign was controversial at that time; inmates working together in a prison setting was often viewed as a potential act of insubordination. But the ACE model of peer education was so successful that within two years it was being funded by the New York State Department of Health's AIDS Institute.[7]

A young African American woman named Katrina Haslip was one of the approximately 900 inmates at Bedford Women's Prison. Katrina was a quiet woman. Prior to entering prison, she had converted to Islam and taught kindergarten at a religious school. But she'd resorted to using drugs to escape the frustration of growing up in poverty, which she believed was the outcome of racism. She had multiple arrests by the time she was eighteen, but it wasn't until her sister died of a drug overdose that she turned to sex work. In the early 1980s, Katrina took a man to a hotel room, where she picked his pocket. She was arrested, but later released. When she robbed another man not long after that, she was sentenced to prison for up to eleven years.

Katrina was diagnosed with the HIV virus in prison in 1987. At this time, there was no treatment for HIV. After learning her status, she cried for two weeks. She had received a blood transfusion, injected drugs, and sold sex – each posing a risk of HIV transmission. At the time she was diagnosed, Katrina was not a regular attendee of ACE. She wasn't open about her diagnosis.[8] But later that year, she took Boudin, her prison block mate aside, and revealed her AIDS diagnosis. She desperately needed a support system and found one at the prison's ACE meetings, where she disclosed her HIV status to the group. Over time she told others outside the ACE community about her status and the burden seemed to ease. Working in the prison library, she became a confidant to other women with HIV, providing them with advice and guidance and inspiring others to share their HIV status. Word of Katrina's work spread far and wide, as women departed Bedford and told others about the Muslim woman in prison who counseled them through their illness. Upon her release, Katrina became a leader in ACE OUT, a group for women released from prison with an HIV diagnosis. Her dedication to bringing attention to the plight of women living with HIV would make her the national face of a feminist movement that would alter the scientific definition of AIDS, fundamentally transforming the global AIDS response.

* * *

As knowledge about AIDS grew in the 1980s, so did fear of the virus. Many historians have documented the willful ignorance of the Reagan administration, the harsh words of blame and stigma surrounding the epidemic, and the chastising of certain communities that marked the early days of the epidemic. When AIDS activists began to mobilize to demand care and treatment in the early 1980s, their fight became part of a challenge to the broader social, political, economic order ascendant at the time: the retraction of the welfare state, cuts to social security and disability programs, and the uptake of personal responsibility narratives in the national debate about benefits. This political and economic dismantling of welfare compounded the struggles of people attempting to survive the AIDS epidemic.

While the heroic struggle of gay men and their allies in reworking key institutions and agencies in the 1980s and early 1990s has been well documented,[9] the story of how feminists engaged in the AIDS response remains largely untold. This is particularly true in legal scholarship where AIDS remains absent in scholarship on the feminist women's health movement (FWHM), resulting in an incomplete telling of how the healthcare system, and administrative state, was fundamentally reshaped by feminist activism. In the context of AIDS, this activism emerged from unexpected places: the feminists of the AIDS Coalition to Unleash Power (ACT UP), feminist welfare attorneys seeking benefits for their clients, and incarcerated women mobilizing inside and outside of prison. Including these accounts widens the lens and deepens our understanding of the scope of players and advocates that not only transformed law but the science and epidemiology of AIDS.

This chapter and the next document the beginnings of this new branch of the FWHM and offer a richer account of the genesis of the reproductive justice (RJ) movement. The latter, formally established in the early 1990s, would provide a key critique to the abstract legal formalism that was being centered in the broader reproductive rights movement. Reproductive justice advocates took what could be described as a legal critical approach to their law-oriented activism. Rather than focus on liberty and equality, which was encapsulated in the "pro-choice" reproductive rights rhetoric, RJ advocates sought to understand how legal rules were shaping the realities of people's lives on the ground. They saw coercive reproductive choices as an inherent part of the legal system. Choice was a mere rhetorical strategy that held no meaning. Reproductive justice advocates in the 1990s would look toward the background legal rules – taken-for-granted legal settlements – that shaped the distribution of goods in society (including food, housing, and healthcare). They questioned the political underpinnings of legal rules that led to deep inequality and an inability of women to live healthy lives.

In addition to describing how advocates sought to destabilize legal settlements, this chapter adds another dimension of history on the social movement organizing at the intersection of health and gender: the role of medical, epidemiological, and scientific evidence and expertise in mobilizing for the expansion of welfare for women living with HIV. In other words, it wasn't only the legal rules that required modification for redistribution – advocates interrogated how accepted scientific settlements, along with legal environments, became part of a set of background rules and practices that justified the unequal distribution of resources.[10] Feminist AIDS advocates took on the purported neutrality of not only the law, but of science. This chapter and the next dive deep into feminist organizing to disrupt the scientific and legal consensus – as they were instantiated deep in the administrative state – to rework our understanding of AIDS, to help people see that women were also "at risk" of HIV, and to demand resources necessary to their survival.

This chapter centers the redistributive goals of feminist organizing in the battle to change the administrative response to the epidemic. Their aims were clear: Feminists wanted healthcare, money to survive, and research dollars directed toward women impacted by HIV.

## THE FWHM BEFORE AIDS

The most recent iteration of the FWHM began in the 1960s and 1970s, before HIV, and was premised on second-wave feminist understandings of gender: most simplistically, that the political, economic, and scientific institutions of society are manifestations of a male worldview that subordinates women. Scientific knowledge was primarily by and about men and facts about medicine, disease, illness, and treatments were not inclusive of women.[11] Further, scientists, doctors, and epidemiologists conceptualized health solely through the "white male body".[12] The exclusion of women from research, feminists argued, had the narrow effect of being bad for women's health and the broader effect of preventing women from being equal members of society.[13] In making the claim that science excluded women, feminists contributed to the production of a frame that helped explain inequities experienced by women in the domain of health and medicine and beyond.[14]

The FWHM sought to rectify the male bias in science and medicine by generating knowledge of women's bodies and women's health through lived experience and demands that science be produced with the input of women. As described by sociologist Steven Epstein, feminist health activists promoted a politics of "inclusion and difference" – seeking to be included in medical research and knowledge while preserving the idea that women were biologically different than men.[15] Importantly, in arguing for the inclusion of women's bodies in scientific and medical research in order to get accurate information about women's health, feminist health activists implicitly reified the idea that scientific evidence can be produced in an objective, neutral manner. They did not seek to entirely undermine the institutions against which they fought. Instead, the activists sought to make medical and scientific knowledge more complete, more thorough, and more accurate to improve women's lives.[16] They sought to bring information to women to ensure that women could live without shame and stigma and access the care they needed. One of the most famous of the organizations that emerged during this time was the Boston Women's Health Collective, which published a mimeograph called *Our Bodies Our Selves* in 1970.[17] The book was distributed around the country and eventually around the world. *Our Bodies Our Selves* revolutionized women's health advocacy and access to information on women's bodies. Feminist ideas at the time, especially that inequalities in women's health contribute to sex inequalities, resonated with feminist lawyers who were engaging in formal critiques of sex inequality in the law.[18]

Similarly, advocates of color, and Black activists in particular, organized around the idea that racial exclusion created gaps in scientific knowledge about bodies. For racial justice advocates, the claim of exclusion was complicated by the fact that women's bodies, particularly the bodies of African American women, had often served as testing grounds for new procedures that were then broadly implemented.[19] In other words, Black women were included in research despite not always benefitting from the medical transformations following experimentation. Advocacy, however, focused in on the longstanding exclusion of minorities from medical research and activism.[20]

Feminists also made a deeper critique of evidence and expertise that drew on postmodernist strains of feminist analysis that were taking hold in law and the humanities. This critique complicated the engagement of feminists who sought to simply make the demand that science be more inclusive. The postmodern turn inside the women's rights movement questioned the objectivity and determinacy of science itself. Feminist philosopher of science Donna Haraway famously coined the term "the god trick" to identify the belief that there is a vantage point from which scientists could be fully objective.[21] She argued that knowledge is contingent upon the social construction of science and that we should see the producers of knowledge as "situated."[22] The postmodern turn impacted feminist legal thinking as well. In her well-known article, "A Post Modernist Feminist Legal Manifesto," feminist legal theorist Mary Jo Frug argued that there was a constructive function law played that was necessary to take on when thinking about feminist reforms: "legal discourse should be recognized as a site of political struggle over sex differences."[23] As has been noted by feminist epidemiologists, the tension between believing there are true biological sex differences that are deserving of attention and the belief that gender is socially constructed means that there is a disconnect, in that women are frequently taken to be a stable category in the literature on health inequalities despite a push to destabilize the category of gender in gender studies more broadly.[24] (It is worth noting here that there has been a similar debate taking place on issues of race and science in which legal scholars have been very active.[25])

Much of the feminist organizing for health in the 1960s and 1970s focused on service delivery and information sharing. As has been documented by historian Jennifer Nelson, the women's health movement saw community clinics as a key part of effectuating a broader set of progressive goals. And, drawing on the lessons learned from other advocates at the time – including New Left activist movements like the Student Nonviolent Coordinating Committee (SNCC) and Students for a Democratic Society (SDS) – feminists focused on community clinics, peer education, and self-empowerment as modes of addressing the health needs of women.[26] As time went on, community clinics increasingly integrated a women's liberation ideology into the service delivery. Abortion services, due to the key idea that they are deeply linked to women's liberation, became a central feature of women's health clinics.[27]

While service delivery drove much feminist engagement in the early days of the FWHM,[28] the larger liberal feminist move toward the state in the 1960s and 1970s shifted feminist activism on women's health issues toward law reform as a site of transformation. Legal strategies that built upon second-wave feminist ideas of sex equality, particularly with regard to the issues of contraception, pregnancy, and abortion, generated many constitutional and legislative battles.[29] In the early phase of feminist-inspired litigation for reproductive health, courts proved to be sympathetic to the demands of the women's movement, while legislative struggles had varied outcomes, exemplified by the failure of the Equal Rights Amendment and the passage of the Pregnancy Discrimination Act.

Key legal victories came to define the FWHM, most prominently *Roe v. Wade*, which decriminalized abortion in 1973.[30] Feminist activism was key to *Roe*'s success – although the decision foregrounded the importance of abortion as a medical issue,[31] rather than for sex equality.[32] For poor women, however, the gains of *Roe* remained limited despite the constitutional victory.[33] And the redistributive possibilities of *Roe* were dashed as feminists continued to push for access to abortion through the courts. Take the 1977 Supreme Court case *Maher v. Roe*. The plaintiff in the case challenged a Connecticut law that banned use of Medicaid funds for nonmedically necessary abortions. The Court held that a state is not obligated to pay for nonmedically necessary abortions simply because it paid for pregnancy-related services. In other words, Connecticut was under no obligation to pay for the abortions of poor women because the ban was rationally related to the "strong and legitimate interest in encouraging normal childbirth." The anti-redistribution element of this decision was further emphasized with the 1980 case *Harris v. McRae*, which relied on *Maher*. The plaintiffs in the case sought to challenge the application of the Hyde Amendment – the ban on federal funds to reimburse the cost of abortions under Medicaid. In finding that the Hyde Amendment served a rational governmental purpose – to preserve the life of the fetus – the Court held that states participating in the Medicaid program are not obligated to fund medically necessary abortions where federal monies are not permitted for reimbursement. In doing so, the Court explained that, as articulated in *Maher*:

> Although government may not place obstacles in the path of a woman's exercise of her freedom of choice, it need not remove those not of its own creation. Indigency falls in the latter category. The financial constraints that restrict an indigent woman's ability to enjoy the full range of constitutionally protected freedom of choice are the product not of governmental restrictions on access to abortions, but rather of her indigency.

In other words, the government does not cause poverty: Women are poor of their own making. And, when a woman is poor of her own making, she has the right to choose an abortion, but the government has no obligation to pay for her abortion. The cases foreshadowed what was to come in the broader political and economic landscape on healthcare.

As the 1980s arrived, so did the Ronald Reagan presidency and further attacks on the poor and the welfare system. The Reagan administration cultivated damaging new images of women on welfare. The idea that there were "welfare queens" – Black women living in luxury on the government's dime – proved to be a powerful narrative that galvanized right-wing support for dismantling welfare.[34] Black feminist advocates led the charge to respond to attacks on poor women, organizing to alleviate their inability to access reproductive healthcare. The gendered and racialized narratives of welfare, disease, poverty, and greed would cast a long shadow on the future of the AIDS epidemic and shape the response to it.

It was around this time that several important feminist organizations were founded, including the Black Women's Health Project led by Byllye Avery.[35] Focused on Black communities, Black feminist activists began to mobilize local, regional, and national organizations to begin the process of addressing the specific needs of Black women in the context of women's health. Some of the work replicated the broader FWHM, including encouraging women to learn about their own bodies, utilizing self-help techniques, and examining race and gender-based health disparities. The organizations took into account the specific cultural and racial contexts and settings that shaped the lives of Black women. The organizations and activists mobilized during this time would soon become key players of the movement to address women and AIDS.[36]

Alongside feminists focused on reproductive rights, many future feminist AIDS advocates also emerged from the broader queer and LGBT push for sexual liberation. These feminists were shaped by the intersections and tensions between second-wave feminism and lesbian activism, as well as by broader LGBT organizing for sexual liberation. As has been carefully documented by Alice Echols in her book *Daring To Be Bad: Radical Feminism in America 1965–1975*, the 1960s and 1970s saw a series of tensions and synergies within American feminism. Some of these split feminists along lines of sexuality – the notorious identification of a "Lavender Menace" resulted in a purge of lesbians from the National Organization of Women (NOW), which alienated lesbians.[37] As Echols notes, however, the rise of cultural feminism dampened some of the tensions between lesbians and heterosexual feminists. Cultural feminism emphasized the importance of female difference against male values, rather than against men. This allowed heterosexual women to find resonance in cultural feminism and appealed to lesbians who had been disaffected by feminism's uncomfortable relationship to sexuality.[38] As allies of gay men, many lesbian women identified with the LGBT movement alongside the broader feminist fight for equality and would go on to become intermediaries and key players in AIDS activism both for women and for men impacted by HIV.[39]

The connection between feminist lesbians and the AIDS struggle began to take shape by the 1980s. As noted by Deborah Gould in her book *Moving Politics: Emotion and ACT-UP's Fight against AIDS*, ACT UP began organizing in 1986 and 1987 with the first chapters of ACT

UP in San Francisco and Chicago, and then in New York.[40] While many in the FWHM were increasingly turning to courts and rights to effectuate change, ACT UP focused on acts of civil disobedience, street theatre, "zaps," and die-ins to demand, among other things, increased access to drugs and increased funding for AIDS.[41] Feminist advocates in the AIDS movement would effectively mobilize lessons learned from LGBT and queer political organizing as well as the broader FWHM and reproductive rights activism.

As the 1980s began, the FWHM, as it existed in queer organizing and in the broader women's health movement, deployed both radical and cultural feminist arguments in conjunction with a skepticism of the scientific and medical establishment. The core radical feminist idea that society is patriarchal, sexist, and structured by male values, provides a foundational critique of scientific and medical institutions. Yet, the idea, drawn from the feminist critique of science, that women's bodies are inherently different from men's bodies resonates with the cultural feminist claim that women have essential differences from men. Some of these distinctions, according to cultural feminists and feminists in the women's health movement, are rooted in the biological differences between men and women. For feminists focused on race, racial difference provided an extra layer of distinction for the manifestation of health issues. At times, feminists drew on racial difference to emphasize inequality of health outcomes. At other times, however, race became a way of biologically distinguishing groups to direct the attention of the medical and scientific community toward racial minorities.[42] It is important to note that these were not purely rhetorical arguments. The blend of radical and cultural feminist claims that animate the FWHM were deployed for the sake of redistribution in the context of a failing welfare state. The goal of advocates was to fight for health services and resources for women and people of color. They helped make women, and women of color, necessary recipients of AIDS care.

## AIDS IN THE FWHM: EARLY FORMATIONS

Beginning in the 1980s, a new disease was claiming the lives of women but was not receiving widespread national feminist attention: AIDS. A novel strand of the FWHM took form. This submovement, specific to HIV and AIDS, made up of HIV-positive women, feminist lawyers, and the broader women's health community sought to channel resources toward women by forcing recognition of the epidemic amongst women.

Activists effectively mobilized a key frame from the FWHM: that the science and research of the AIDS epidemic excluded women. This feminist insight challenged the idea that expertise came from the top and was owned by scientists. Instead, as has been described by sociology of science scholars, in resonance with law and social movements scholars,[43] this was science from below.[44] The transformation in perceptions of expertise and distrust in institutions, coupled with the feminist critique of science, proved to be a powerful and cogent collective action frame that allowed for mobilization.[45]

In the context of AIDS, as was the case in the reproductive rights movement, feminist activists felt they were up against the medical and scientific establishment as well as the public perception of AIDS as a disease largely impacting gay men. In many ways, they were correct. As described in the introduction, in public debate and discourse, the idea of women and AIDS was discounted. Some skeptics even offered biological rationales for the inability of women to contract HIV. Most famously, the women's magazine *Cosmopolitan* ran a cover article titled "Reassessing News about AIDS: A Doctor Tells You Why You Might Not Be at Risk of AIDS" arguing that women could not contract HIV through sexual intercourse.[46] Journalist and attorney Michael Fumento wrote in his book *The Myth of Heterosexual AIDS: How a Tragedy Has Been Distorted by Media and Partisan Politics*, that differences in the tissue construction of the male urethra and rectum and the female vagina – the latter being constructed of tough cells that "resist rupture".[47] Taken together, a message was being sent about communities at risk of contracting the virus: There was no need to fear a widespread heterosexual epidemic, and certainly not one amongst women, because biology would prevent this from happening.

Feminists took a different approach: They chose to believe the women coming forward saying that they had HIV. By the late 1980s new feminist formations began to push for recognition that women were contracting and dying of AIDS. Many of these feminists in this new formation drew not only from reproductive rights organizing but also came from LGBT movements.

### The Feminists of ACT UP

Within ACT UP, the ACT UP Women's Caucus and the COSTAS affinity group (a group named after an ACT UP member who had passed away) played a central and visible role in identifying issues and setting the tone for feminist engagement in the AIDS response. Several accounts of the early feminist formations within ACT UP exist. One, offered by Maxine Wolfe, a leader in ACT UP on women's issues, suggests that the origins of the ACT UP Women's Caucus date back to 1987.[48] This is when Wolfe and other women in ACT UP began to meet to discuss being women in an all-male organization (or, more specifically, lesbians in a gay male organization) and the necessity of combating sexism while dealing with death and dying. Wolfe and others began hosting "dyke dinners" to create a space to continue these conversations.[49] Alongside the dyke dinners, women in ACT UP began holding monthly meetings and social gatherings. Feminist AIDS advocates drew on the reproductive rights movement for inspiration. They claimed five specific principles from the feminist health movement as "radical and far reaching":

- Women's medical treatment was part of women's oppression: As a rule, all women received sexist treatment.
- Women needed to seize control of women's health and demystify common procedures.
- Collectivity, in both the operation and provision of health services, politicized healthcare and deprivatized women's common experiences, thus extending the tenet "the personal is political" to health.
- The feminist health movement and women's clinics needed to operate autonomously from the state.
- Service work done in a political context was political and women deserved to be paid for their work.[50]

Citing directly to the foundational work of the Boston Women's Health Collective, including the publication *Our Bodies, Our Selves*, the feminists of the AIDS movement credited prior work on reproductive rights with creating the space and laying the groundwork for the many ideas that would come to define AIDS activism as well.[51]

ACT UP feminists pushed the idea that women and AIDS was an important issue. The *Cosmopolitan* magazine article inspired one of their first actions on January 15, 1988. It began as a picket line outside of the offices of the magazine.[52] Then they demanded to be let into the building. The protest created a scene and quickly drew the attention of the police and the wider public. Police detained the women involved, eventually letting them go. Activists also called the editor of *Cosmopolitan* and asked the physician quoted in the article – a psychiatrist who had not worked on AIDS – to meet with them. The picketing and protests became a topic of conversation on prime-time television and helped initiate a discussion of women and AIDS on the national stage.

Interview by Sarah Suhlman with Maxine Wolfe, activist, ACT UP Oral History Project, in New York, NY (May 25, 2007); Interview by Liz Strong with Maxine Wolfe and Anne Strong, in New York, New York (November 5, 2017); Flyers from Protest, (on file with Lesbian Herstory Archive, Box 3, Folder 7).

By April of 1988, feminist advocacy on AIDS was beginning to consolidate into a coherent narrative comprised of several elements: Women were being ignored in the AIDS response due to the sexism of scientific and administrative institutions, men had more power than women in sexual relationships, and Black and Latina women were most impacted by the epidemic. The emerging accounts of women and AIDS were a clear product of the radical feminist frame that drove organizing in the broader FWHM. In a commentary in *On Our Backs*, a feminist publication, Linda Anderson and Samantha Winchester articulated the concerns of feminist AIDS activists regarding the power differentials between men and women in sexual relationships:

> The sexual politics between men and women, as feminists have pointed out, is affected by their differing economic situations. A low-income man's salary may only have to cover his costs while his long-term partner may only receive AFDC [Aid to Families with Dependent Children] which must pay for herself and her two children. She must weigh her access to his comparative wealth against her desire for safe sex and his unwillingness to use a condom. Further, having a man conveys a good deal of social status on a woman in many communities while single men continue to be viewed positively. And often there are far more women available for relationships than there are men. All these factors weigh into a [woman's] decision to "enforce" safe sex. Most women with little power in their relationships will not jeopardize the immediate well-being of themselves and their children for some mythical protection ten years hence.[53]

The idea that the structural inequality of women led to their vulnerability to HIV was foundational to the women's movement in AIDS activism and generative of further actions. Following the success of the *Cosmopolitan* action, in May of 1988, ACT UP partnered with AIDS organizations around the country and planned nine days of action on AIDS. One of the days was dedicated to the issue of women and AIDS. The plan was to go to Shea Stadium during a baseball game and display giant posters about women and AIDS.[54] Using Shea Stadium did more than provide a high-profile location; the women of ACT UP were targeting a spot that drew droves of heterosexual men.[55] News of the protest was leaked ahead of time by the *Village*

*Voice* leading to fears of potential arrest since Shea Stadium was private property. But the ACT UP Women's Caucus convinced the Shea Stadium management to introduce them on LED screens that lit up the stadium with the words "Welcome to the National Women and AIDS Day Committee." Hundreds of ACT UP members attended the protest, and thousands of flyers were handed out, along with condoms provided by the Gay Men's Health Crisis. Instead of being afraid of the activists, the public relations person at Shea Stadium helped distribute the ACT UP flyers.

Unknown to the staff of Shea Stadium, however, members of the ACT UP Women's Caucus booked seats in three different sections of the stadium, with the goal of attracting public attention to the issue of women and AIDS. As the game went on, activists strategically unfurled banners in the first half of the 3rd, 5th, 7th and 8th innings. The messages on the banners read "Don't Balk At Safer Sex," "AIDS Kills Women," "Men: Use Condoms," "No Glove, No Love," "Strike Out AIDS," and "Silence Equals Death." In the 8th inning the activists unfurled a giant ACT UP banner. The protest received national attention and became one of ACT UP's most high-profile protests.

### The Lawyers, Plaintiffs and the Legal Case

In New York in the mid 1980s, Terry McGovern, a poverty lawyer and organizer working with MFY (Mobilization for Youth) Legal Services, a long-time poverty law center in New York, was seeing a new client base. Men and women were walking into her office dying of HIV and in desperate need of legal services. Many lawyers didn't want to take their cases; at times lawyers in her office succumbed to fears that HIV could be spread by casual contact and sprayed the chairs and table with Lysol after clients left.[56] McGovern's expertise was housing, and her new client base included sick women who were being evicted due to illness. Many of McGovern's clients, primarily African American and Latina women, told her that they believed that their recurrent illnesses were due to HIV infection. She believed them. As one of the few lawyers who was willing to work with people living with HIV McGovern was inundated with people needing assistance. She knew she needed help, so she began to fundraise. With a 30,000-dollar grant from the New York Community Trust to do work specific to HIV and AIDS, she founded the HIV Law Project.

Many of McGovern's clients were coming out of the Bedford Hills Correctional Facility for Women – a women's maximum-security prison founded in 1892 as a women's reformatory.[57] They were being referred to her by the Women's Prison Association.[58] McGovern began to hear stories of Katrina Haslip, a Muslim African American woman who had worked in the library at Bedford and counseled women living with HIV. Many of her clients had also interacted with AIDS Counseling and Education (ACE), the prison peer-counseling program. McGovern saw the impact of the program firsthand: Her clients arrived at her door with their medical records and knowledge about how to navigate the system, emboldened by Katrina Haslip's support.

Among other issues, McGovern's clients came to her seeking social security benefits. She noticed that women who stated that they had AIDS were having difficulty getting benefits, despite presumptive disability funds earmarked for people who were diagnosed with AIDS. She sought answers among activists; one of her first stops was an ACT UP meeting.

The night McGovern attended the ACT UP meeting would become a turning point in feminist AIDS activism. At the meeting, members of ACT UP discussed how the CDC definition excluded women.

Led by Terry McGovern, healthcare providers and advocates, including women from Bedford, pieced together a complicated interaction between the CDC and Social Security Administration (SSA) regulations on disability systematically excluded women from diagnosis and benefits. Here is how it played out: The widespread belief that women were not a risk group for HIV was resulting in women not being diagnosed with HIV or AIDS. It is important to remember that during this period, AIDS was being diagnosed symptomatically – without an HIV test. (HIV testing was not available in an affordable, reliable form until the mid 1980s,[59] and it was not in widespread usage until the early 1990s. The CDC did not require an HIV test for diagnosis of HIV or AIDS until 1993.)[60] How did physicians know what symptoms to use? Most clinicians were diagnosing people utilizing the CDC definition of AIDS developed for surveillance purposes.[61] As Cathy Cohen describes in her book *The Boundaries of Blackness: AIDS and the Breakdown of Black Politics*, despite its claim to develop disease definition largely for disease surveillance, the CDC became a primary "signaling institution" for the delivery of AIDS-related medical care.[62]

The CDC definition did not list gynecological issues, specifically invasive cervical cancer and pelvic inflammatory disease, that frequently manifested in HIV-positive women as symptoms of AIDS. In turn, even when women had manifestations of AIDS on the CDC surveillance list they were not being diagnosed with HIV or AIDS.[63] The absence of gynecological conditions in the CDC definition appeared to validate the widespread belief that women were not at risk of HIV. The challenge of getting a diagnosis was further complicated by actual service delivery. Because many people being diagnosed with HIV were seeing internal medicine physicians, and these doctors were diagnosing people based on the CDC definition, women were not being diagnosed. Nor were they receiving diagnosis at the gynecologists' offices, where they were presenting with severe gynecological issues. Gynecologists were not in the business of diagnosing AIDS. Women were falling through the cracks.

The lack of gynecological illnesses in the CDC definition, and its impact on AIDS diagnoses, can be best understood in terms of the longer institutional history of the agency. From the foundation of the CDC in 1946, the agency's focus was on the science of disease control. Epidemiology became a central way that the CDC tracked disease and produced "facts" about the way disease was spread.[64] As more diseases were identified as a concern for surveillance and tracking, the CDC expanded, and that increased the influence of epidemiologists. The CDC's mandate to define and surveil disease was one that allowed the institution to make the claim that it was governed by science, not politics.

The AIDS epidemic made the contradictions of this institutional position clear. In 1981, the CDC began to construct its medical definition of AIDS. The first definition was telling. In noting the presence of pneumocystis carinii pneumonia (PCP) among young men, the official CDC report concluded that "the fact that these patients were all homosexuals suggests an association between some aspect of a homosexual lifestyle or a disease acquired through sexual contact and pneumocystis pneumonia in this population."[65] And, as Cohen describes, the focus on gay men sent a strong message, intentionally or not, that this was a disease of gay men. The production of this information from the CDC had the effect of presenting the illness as a gay disease on objective terms. To be clear, this is not to say that gay men were not severely impacted by HIV. Of course, history tells us that these predictions were correct; the devastating impact of the virus was felt by hundreds of thousands of gay men and their families. What is relevant to notice, however, is that while the CDC is hypothesizing about the "homosexual lifestyle," it metastasizes into fact that lands in fertile ground for stigma and homophobia. This had circular effects and produced blind spots: The identification of AIDS as a gay disease justified ongoing study of gay men and AIDS to the exclusion of other groups (including women who were largely from racial minority groups – Black and Latina).[66]

For feminist AIDS activists, the failure to diagnose women had a second important consequence. As activists figured out, the exclusion of women had a direct impact on who was able to get benefits and healthcare. The SSA, housed in Health and Human Services in the 1980s and early 1990s, was (and continues to be) an administrative agency statutorily responsible for administering and enforcing the Social Security Act. The SSA has two programs that administer monthly cash benefits to people who are unable to work due to disability: supplemental security income (SSI) or social security disability insurance (SSDI).[67] Qualifying for SSI or SSDI also allows access to health coverage through Medicaid or Medicare. SSI or SSDI, therefore, became a source of both income and healthcare for people diagnosed with HIV. At this time, the SSA was using the CDC definition of AIDS, and people who fit this definition were being presumptively[68] categorized as disabled and, in turn, they were able to receive SSI or SSDI.[69] This was important because time was of the essence: People were dying and needed healthcare services and financial assistance. Because the SSA was utilizing the CDC definition of AIDS to determine eligibility, women were being denied disability benefits. This was driven by two forces. The first was that women could not meet the presumptive disability definition because they were not being diagnosed with AIDS, and that was because their symptoms were not on the official CDC list of AIDS-defining illnesses. An emerging political dynamic also contributed: Because of a push to cut back on disability benefits by the Republican administration, even women with an official AIDS diagnosis were often denied benefits on the premise that their manifestation of AIDS was not an actual or debilitating manifestation of the illness.

When women did not qualify for the presumptive disability benefit, they had to go through the arduous five-step assessment required by the SSA to be categorized as disabled.[70] The process – which is still used today – is designed to test whether or not someone can work and earn money. Its ideological underpinning is clear: A person should take responsibility for themselves. Each step seeks to eliminate any individuals capable of working from qualifying for benefits. The first step considers whether the person is involved in a substantial gainful activity (SGA). "Substantial" is a dollar amount set by the SSA. If the individual is engaged in a SGA they are not disabled. If they are not engaged in a SGA, then the SSA moves onto step two: assessing whether the person has a severe impairment. A severe impairment is a condition which will prevent the claimant from engaging in SGA for twelve months, or one that will result in death. If the impairment is enumerated by the SSA in step three, then the individual is disabled. If an illness is not on the enumerated list, then the individual must have a functional capacity test that assesses the individual's ability to do sustained work. With the data generated from the functional capacity test, the SSA determines in step four if the individual can do any past relevant work that they may have engaged in. If the individual is found to be able to do past relevant work, then the person is not considered disabled. If the individual cannot do past relevant work, then the person moves onto step five, which considers whether the individual can make an adjustment to do another type of work. If not, the person is declared officially disabled. If so, the person is not found to be disabled.[71]

The disability assessment, including the functional capacity test itself, took so long that women often died prior to being designated as disabled. In turn, many women with AIDS were locked out by the process, dying without any state support and little capacity to support themselves.[72] Women's rights activists took note of this: HIV-positive women, they said, were apparently "dead but not disabled." For feminists, this stood in stark contrast to the many men who were being diagnosed and given benefits immediately.[73]

The decision of the SSA to use the CDC definition to determine who would or would not qualify for presumptive benefits was in and of itself controversial. According to welfare attorneys and activists, the CDC definition, written for the sake of surveillance, was narrow. The SSA, responsible for benefits including medical care, could have written an expanded definition delinked from the CDC definition, but it failed to do so.[74]

Another dynamic also frustrated activists: accountability in the rulemaking process. The SSA typically allows for a notice and comment period before it issues final rules. This period of time is considered an essential part of ensuring public participation in administrative rulemaking. During this time, experts and community members are able to provide comments for the agency to consider. Yet, in the case of the rules on disability and AIDS, the SSA published its interim regulations on presumptive disability under an exception which allowed them to become applicable immediately, circumventing the notice and comment period.[75] Advocates lost their opportunity to have their voices heard and understood this to be a denial of accountability – the loss of a way to participate in broadening the scope of the disability benefits.

The exception granted to the SSA mandated, however, that it hold a notice and comment period after the implementation of the rule, given the failure to do so in advance. And although many advocates felt that it was too little, too late they still registered their concerns. Advocates filed comments pointing out that the SSA was not bound to the CDC definition of AIDS, because the definitions of AIDs utilized by the SSA and CDC were developed for unique purposes: the CDC's definition for surveillance, the SSA's definition for the delivery of disability benefits and medical care. Commentators aimed to draw attention to the idea that the surveillance definition might be far too narrow, given the number of people being disabled by AIDS who were not appearing on the official AIDS counts.[76]

By 1989 feminists were ready to launch their first protest against the CDC definition of AIDS outside of the CDC headquarters in Atlanta, GA. The protest took place on January 8th and 9th. The 8th was dedicated to repealing Georgia's sodomy law and the 9th focused on changing the CDC's definition of AIDS and, as it was also known at the time, AIDS Related Complex (ARC). Planning for the protest had begun months earlier with teach-ins and logistical meetings at the Lesbian and Gay Community Center in New York.[77] To prepare for the teach-ins, members of ACT UP, including Linda Meredith,[78] and Risa Denenberg, a nurse practitioner, consulted physicians in New York who were seeing AIDS patients. Advocates would go through anonymized physician records of women with AIDS to see what they were dying from. This helped to build an evidence base, despite the lack of epidemiological data.[79] This solidified their belief that the CDC definition had ignored the health issues being faced by women with HIV.[80] As advocates prepared for and executed the protest, they developed a series of background briefings to educate the advocacy community about the deep administrative entanglements that were leading to the disenfranchisement of poor women who had received an AIDS diagnosis or who simply believed that they might have AIDS. The documents noted that AIDS was not a singular disease, but a complication of symptoms; the management of the disease must include new symptoms as they arose.[81]

But what would constitute a new definition of AIDS? Even among advocates this was a controversial question. Should it be a range of symptoms, as it had been, that would lead to an AIDS diagnosis? For feminists, this was the answer, though it was clear that the list of AIDS-defining illnesses produced by the CDC had to be expanded to include the range of gynecological issues impacting women living with HIV. Within ACT UP though there was disagreement as members of the Treatment and Data Group (T&D) had concluded that a better way forward would be to rely on CD4 (or T-Cell) counts which reveal the level of white blood cells a person has. The T&D settled on 200 T-Cells as the cutoff for an AIDS diagnosis. Anyone with a CD4 count of 200 or less should be diagnosed with AIDS. Its position had the appeal of an objective number, unlike the symptomatic diagnosis. It also reflected the growing availability of blood testing. For the feminist activists, however, the objective cutoff wasn't good enough. It wouldn't reflect that many people who were sick from AIDS actually had CD4 counts higher than 200. They believed this was particularly true for the gynecological manifestations of women.

This split in perspective would follow the activist struggle going forward. Yet, despite disagreement, the ACT UP community banded together to push forward. Many people were arrested at the protest including HIV attorney Terry McGovern.[82] ACT UP paid the bail for forty-eight people; the money was provided by the ACT UP bail fund and from the ACT UP coffers.[83]

The fight to change the CDC definition of AIDS, and the SSA's dependency on that definition was just beginning.[84] In July 1990, women in ACT UP met with Anthony Fauci, the head of the National Institute of Allergy and Infectious Diseases (NIAID), an institute of the National Institutes of Health (NIH). According to the ACT UP transcript, the meeting was tense.[85] Fauci began by making clear that he was not meeting with ACT UP Women's Caucus members due to their threats, but rather due to their shared concerns. Feminist advocates presented Fauci with the most updated information that they had about women and AIDS and argued that women were dying more quickly than men due to AIDS because of a lack of diagnosis. They made several specific demands. First, they wanted to ensure that Fauci and the NIH acknowledged that existing information about women and AIDS justified the greater inclusion of women in research. In other words, the NIH, NIAID, and the NIH Division of AIDS (focused on biomedical research) should rectify the absence of women from research. The women then spoke directly to the CDC definition of AIDS, contending that women's "opportunistic infections are not acknowledged by the CDC." They demanded a conference on women and AIDS that would include not just medical researchers, but women impacted by HIV/AIDS and clinical workers. They asked that the outcome of the conference be a detailing of symptoms in HIV's manifestation in women and the development of protocols for women impacted by HIV.[86] They also made a series of demands that included prioritizing research sites with women and HIV, and not excluding women from drug treatment programs.[87] Fauci agreed to sponsor and fund a conference for women and AIDS.

In a letter shortly afterward reminding Fauci of his commitments, Linda Meredith, founder of ACT UP DC, wrote a letter on behalf of ACT UP reiterating that they felt that the NIH, NIAID, and the Division of AIDS were lacking information on women and AIDS: "We know that there is currently a lot of information about women and HIV/AIDS: what they die from, what they get, what they need. You obviously do not have this information, and the conference will provide it for you. Then the pressure will be on you to put out that information to save women's lives."[88] A few weeks later, Fauci replied to Meredith's letter outlining steps to explore the AIDS response pertaining to women. Thanking ACT UP for expressing its concerns about women with HIV he asked to plan a follow-up meeting including a conference on women and AIDS. He already had the cooperation of CDC and the public health services in planning the agenda for the conference and stated that he hoped to have community participation in the planning, naming "women of color, and health care workers who are women who deal with women with HIV."[89] Although members of the ACT UP Women's Caucus were some of the most vocal voices on women and AIDS at the time, Fauci added this line, an attempt to critique the feminists of ACT UP for their inability to speak for all women: "It is clearly our impression from discussions with other groups, and I am sure you will agree, that ACT UP does not represent all women with HIV disease."[90] For feminists in the AIDS movement, this type of critique was symptomatic of a larger problem. Maxine Wolfe would later note:

> A little bit about the difference in the way women AIDS activists are treated at these meetings compared to male AIDS activists, from my point of view. And, this specifically applies to women AIDS activists who "raise women's issues." Researchers seem to assume that any male AIDS activist attending these meetings is gay and HIV+. On the other hand, when it comes to women AIDS activists the sexism, racism, and lesbophobia of the researchers becomes apparent. They assume that any white woman AIDS activist is a lesbian, HIV-, and has no children. On the other hand, they assume that any Latina or Black woman AIDS activist is heterosexual, HIV+, and has been pregnant and does have children .... The researchers don't even talk about Native Americans or Pacific Islanders.[91]

Women's Caucus activism clearly paid off. That month, the issue of *NIAID AIDS Agenda* announced the upcoming conference on women and AIDS.[92]

Although the feminists of ACT UP had been long active, they officially launched the ACT UP Women's Caucus that same month. Their announcement declared that they sought to challenge the "inherent sexism, racism, heterosexism, and classism that exists in all aspects of different women's lives, including social services, treatment, research, etc."[93] The Women's Caucus fought to highlight the differences between men and women in the epidemic. In a background report written by ACT UP, the organization argued that the

> CDC definition ignores the anatomical differences between men and women, and the fact that a woman's first HIV-related symptoms are often gynecological. Women have vaginas, uteruses, fallopian tubes, and ovaries. Men do not have these organs .... Because the CDC definition continues to be centered in how AIDS is manifested in gay men, many related illnesses that occur in women and IV-drug users are excluded, thereby excluding them from a number of treatments, services, benefits, and from clinical trials.[94]

While not necessarily focused on the CDC definition of AIDS or the SSA disbursement of benefits, similar women's movements around the country began to coalesce and join the effort to support women living with HIV. In 1989, activist Dazon Dixon-Diallo had founded the Atlanta-based organization, SisterLove, dedicated to addressing the AIDS epidemic in the African American community. SisterLove, born "on the porch" of the Black Women's Health Initiative, specifically engaged the issue in the Black community.[95] Dixon-Diallo helped organize women of color to join the fight against the CDC definition. She worked alongside other groups, including the Brooklyn AIDS Task Force (BATF) and Life Force, also known as "Women Fighting AIDS, Inc." BATF, also founded by African American women, drew attention to issues arising in the epidemic at the intersection of HIV and poverty: homelessness, access to benefits, and substance abuse. Life Force was a program for women with HIV in Brooklyn established in 1989 by women living with HIV. Life Force sought to reduce the incidence of AIDS by focusing on women and their families, utilizing the peer-education model. At the organization's weekly meetings, it distributed information about HIV, family planning, healthcare, and stress reduction.[96] Haslip was an active participant in Life Force, after her release from prison, and in 1990, Patricia Nalls, a Caribbean-American woman, started a hotline for HIV-positive women after receiving her own HIV diagnosis. Five years later, it had grown into The Women's Collective, an organization for HIV-positive women in Washington, DC.

Many of these smaller feminist organizations served African American and Latina women, who were frequently dealing with issues of poverty, housing, and homelessness alongside their HIV diagnosis.[97] The groups responded to the needs of women who sought their own spaces to discuss their realities of living with HIV, distinct from those for HIV-positive men. Many of these organizations looked and acted differently from ACT UP. They were primarily women of color, seeking to address needs holistically and transform the epidemic within the social and cultural boundaries of the community. This meant that they were not only up against their own marginalization in the AIDS response as women, but also up against social and religious conservatism in their own communities.[98]

## CONCLUSION

Feminists understood the lack of awareness and interest in women's vulnerability to HIV and the related denial of care as the product of women's ongoing subordination in the context of the medical establishment.[99] The disconnect between women's realities and what was being documented scientifically had material consequences: Women were dying as a result of not being diagnosed with HIV, there were no gynecological providers in HIV centers,[100] and women were falling through cracks in the AIDS response. Some feminists understood gay men to be implicated in what Linda Singer called the "gay male hegemony":

> ... the conditions of sexual epidemic have been exploited as an occasion for recirculating homophobic discourse, which, in this case, especially targets gay men. But the centrality that the AIDS crisis now occupies in the public consciousness is an indication that gay men are no longer exclusively positioned as victims or pariahs, but have also come to occupy a central role in determining how the AIDS crisis is being represented, and what strategies are being used to cope with it. Safe sex techniques began as a local discourse within the gay community. Their current level of cultural circulation is testimony to the gay community's success in promoting a local product to the status of national prominence. The effect of this gay male hegemony has been a figuration of the dimensions and issues considered under the rubric of epidemic ... one effect of this hegemony is that although increasing numbers of women are suffering from the disease, most of the literature tends to ignore this fact.[101]

Animated by the sense of exclusion captured by Singer, and frustrated by the state response, activists sought to broaden the CDC's AIDS-defining illness list with the hope that it would influence the SSA, and in turn allow women to qualify for SSI and SSDI benefits. The many formal and informal organizations addressing the needs would come together in a fight against both the purported neutrality of the CDC and the explicit politics of disenfranchisement of the SSA.[102]

2

# LITIGATING RISK

## The Law and Politics of Disease in the Administrative State

In October 1990, lawyer and activist Terry McGovern filed suit against Health and Human Services (HHS) in an effort to broaden the Social Security Administration's (SSA's) definition of AIDS. *S.P. v. Sullivan*, and the activism surrounding it, would become a key milestone in the feminist fight to demand recognition in the struggle against AIDS.[1] The case challenged the denial of Supplemental Security Income (SSI) and Social Security Disability Insurance (SSDI) for women suffering from AIDS-defining illnesses, whose symptoms were excluded from the US Centers for Disease Control and Prevention (CDC) definition of AIDS.[2] McGovern, the plaintiffs, and advocates had three goals emanating from the litigation and advocacy surrounding it. First, to force the SSA to delink its disbursement of benefits and medical care from the narrow definition of AIDS being utilized by the CDC. Second, to mandate that the SSA broaden its understanding of what constituted a disabling illness in the context of AIDS (to include female-specific illnesses). And third, to utilize the litigation as another opportunity to pressure the CDC to change the medical definition of AIDS.

McGovern was a new lawyer. As she was preparing for litigation, she often wondered if she was in over her head.[3] But after witnessing other lawyers spray their office chairs with disinfectant when an AIDS patient would depart, dying and desperate, she knew there were few attorneys willing to take cases for people living with HIV.

For her clients and the many advocates supporting the lawsuit, litigation provided a key opportunity to force the government to respond *in court* to the inadequacies of the SSA's process for providing financial support and medical care to people living with AIDS.

While the lawsuit travelled through the courts, the ACT UP Women's Caucus and advocates from a range of organizations, including Life Force: Women Fighting AIDS and SisterLove, sought to hold government leadership accountable. They did this by mobilizing large-scale grassroots efforts alongside state-centered advocacy: writing letters, protesting outside of government offices, participating in notice and comment periods, and introducing bills to the legislature.

This chapter follows the litigation and advocacy of ACT UP, lawyers, and of women living with HIV from 1990 to 1994, as they slowly turned the heads of CDC experts toward women's issues in the epidemic, resulting in a new medical definition of AIDS. In documenting this story, the chapter challenges a core idea in new literature on law, health, science, and technology, which often describes law as lagging behind scientific progress. The story of women and AIDS argues that this oft-repeated thesis mischaracterizes the relationship between law, social movements, and science. Rather, this chapter argues that law and advocacy can alter a scientific and medical landscape. For feminists organizing in the context of AIDS, the belief that law and advocacy can alter science (rather than simply rely on it) is central to the success of redistributional efforts in the context of public health activism.

For feminists, making the connection between law, science, and redistribution was especially important in the time period in which this feminist fight was playing out. As documented by historian of medicine Keith Wailoo, the Reagan administration was explicit about the distributional relationship between medical expertise and disability benefits. In mandating that physicians validate disability claims, the Reagan administration ensured that the denial of benefits was the product of purportedly objective expertise. This move divested power from potentially sympathetic administrative judges.[4] And, for those paying close attention, it made medical objectivity part of the target of activism.

This political environment – in which purported medical objectivity could be the foundation for contracting the welfare state and cutting people off of disability services – provides the backdrop against which *S.P. v. Sullivan* takes place. Advocates realized that to change the distribution of resources, they had to change the science itself. Importantly, taking on purportedly objective ideas generated through scientific and medical means was not foreign to the specific group of advocates in this story: that had been a project of the feminist movement since at least the 1960s. With AIDS, the feminist critique of science and medicine had a new home and a new group of advocates carrying the project forward: welfare lawyers and AIDS activists. This chapter argues that litigation and advocacy can alter scientific understandings of disease, and, in turn, change the core distribution of goods and services related to healthcare.

## FEMINISTS LITIGATE AIDS

The *S.P. v. Sullivan* plaintiffs exemplified the types of issues faced by women in the epidemic, from the gynecological manifestations of the virus, the repeat denials of SSA benefits, and the consequences for their children. Sandra[5] was a twenty-three-year-old Latina living in Manhattan. Her two children were in foster care. She tested HIV positive in 1989 and applied for SSI because of increasingly worsening pelvic inflammatory disease, weight loss, headaches, vomiting, shortness of breath, and dizziness. Her application was denied twice, despite her hospitalization. In August of 1990 Sandra had a hearing. She submitted medical reports documenting the ongoing issues of pelvic inflammatory disease, anemia, weight loss, and vomiting. She also had a T-Cell count of 200–300 indicating that her immune system was depressed. She was denied SSA benefits again. At the time the litigation began she was waiting to get a rehearing. Sandra's two children had been taken to foster care due to her "inability to afford better living conditions."[6]

The plaintiff Barbara,[7] a thirty-nine-year-old African American woman, applied for disability benefits in April 1989, providing evidence from a physician that she was unable to work. Barbara lived with her three minor children, one of whom was a three year old who also had HIV. She suffered from numerous gynecological illnesses. Barbara required a home healthcare worker to assist in caring for her and her children. She was denied SSI and SSDI. Barbara reapplied but upon reconsideration her applications were also denied.[8]

Monica was thirty-one years old and Latina. She applied for disability insurance benefits on July 20, 1988 because she had been disabled since May 2, 1984 by a combination of impairments including chronic, intractable gynecological complaints.[9] Her treating physicians had informed her in 1987 that she was infected with HIV. Monica struggled with a wide range of gynecological issues including a ruptured ovarian cyst, tubal infection, ovarian cancer, and undiagnosed vaginal bleeding. The SSA denied Monica's initial application and denied her again at reconsideration. She was unable to attend her last hearing because she was hospitalized for attempted suicide. The adjudicators found Monica disabled but said that her disability only began with her HIV diagnosis. She appealed the decision and was waiting for another hearing at the time the lawsuit was filed. In the meantime, she used her initial benefits to rent an apartment. She'd been sleeping on her parents' floor until then. She hoped that the additional benefits would aid her living situation as well as her family's.[10]

Feminist ideas, shaped by the broader feminist AIDS struggle, drove the litigation and the claims for relief. The first claim was that the policies, standards, practices and procedures of the SSA were arbitrary, capricious, and contrary to the Social Security Act because plaintiffs were being denied disability benefits without meaningful assessment of relevant medical evidence and in turn were experiencing harmful delays, considering the likelihood of death, in receiving disability benefits and medical care. The second claim was rooted in the Due Process Clause of the Fifth Amendment. Plaintiffs argued that there was no meaningful assessment of the determinations made regarding the plaintiffs' ability to work creating a harmful delay in the award of disability benefits. Third, plaintiffs argued that the policies, standards, and procedures violated the Equal Protection Clause of the Fifth Amendment because they had created and maintained two classification systems for people with HIV-related impairments – those included in the CDC definition and those not included in the CDC definition. In turn, the plaintiffs argued that the designation of people as disabled was arbitrary and irrational. Fourth, and related, the plaintiffs argued an equal protection violation of the subclass of women, because "on information and belief the Secretary, acting with a discriminatory purpose, has maintained a definition of disability which excludes a class of women by excluding the most common manifestations of disabling HIV-infection in women."[11] Women, they also argued, were being disparately impacted due to the secretary's failure to recognize as disabling any of the most common manifestations of disabling HIV infection in women. The plaintiffs claimed that the policies, standards, and procedures of the SSA also disparately impacted members of racial minority groups because many of the common manifestations of disabling conditions found in

African American and Latinx persons were not on the enumerated list of illnesses.[12] As articulated in filings:

> Since it [the CDC] began its epidemiological surveillance of the epidemic, the CDC has focused its research on the segment of the United States population in which the HIV epidemic was first manifested: a predominantly affluent, predominantly white group of male homosexuals. Thus, most of the epidemiological data collected by the CDC reflects the opportunistic infections which were typical of that particular population subgroup.
>
> The CDC has been publicly criticized for its failure to study or fund studies of HIV infection in women, children, and intravenous drug users, and poor people, and for its consequent exclusion from its definition many of the most common manifestations of HIV-related disease in these populations.[13]

The fifth claim for relief harkened back to the failure of the SSA to provide an opportunity for the public – through notice and comment – to respond to the proposed rules in violation of the Administrative Procedures Act.[14]

These claims accompanied demands for relief that included benefits for women while they waited for decisions, and a directive to disability adjudicators highlighting the failures of the SSA list of impairments. In order to provide fair process to the plaintiffs, they demanded that instructions be issued to adjudicators of disability claims acknowledging that HIV may manifest in ways other than those described on the CDC list. They sought that the adjudicators of disability hire medical experts who were informed about clinical manifestations of HIV-related impairments, and train others to evaluate HIV-related disability claims.[15] The plaintiffs also asked that presumptive disability be paid to any and all claimants with proof of infection with HIV "and a treating physician report reflecting that the claimant is disabled or unable to work."

The day the lawsuit was filed, the ACT UP Women's Caucus, ACT UP COSTAS, and ACT UP DC planned a protest in Washington, DC.[16] The organizers were thorough in their planning: organizing childcare for women participating in the protest and ensuring lawyers were on standby in the event that individuals were arrested. Information was distributed to protestors clarifying that those people who were arrested for civil disobedience could be taken to custody by Federal Protective Services or DC Metropolitan Police. As a best-case scenario, they hoped to only receive citations.[17] A few weeks before the protest, a press release announced that "hundreds of AIDS activists from around the country will besiege the Department of Health and Human Services in Washington, D.C. on Tuesday October 2nd, to demand that women with HIV/AIDS be given the same immediate (presumptive) disability benefits now given to men."[18]

Members of ACT UP New York came down from the city to Washington, DC in buses and stayed at the Carlyle Suites Hotel. Linda Meredith, member of the ACT UP Women's Caucus and ACT UP COSTAS, served as point person for the protest.[19] She had been active on AIDS issues after hosting several AIDS activists at the Democratic National Convention while living in Georgia.[20]

As was often the case at ACT UP protests, a background sheet was provided to all participants which explained why the protest was happening and what people should be angry about. For this protest, the backgrounder explained that the definition of AIDS excluded women and that women should also receive presumptive benefits from the SSA. It noted that the time between diagnosis and death was approximately twenty-seven weeks for women, a timeline that made the SSA responsible for "killing women" by forcing them to undergo an unnecessarily long process to receive a disability diagnosis.[21] Advocates met at 9 AM at the First Congregational Church in Washington DC and departed for the protest at HHS a few hours later.

Hundreds of activists arrived on the doorstep of HHS on October 2, 1990. The demands at the protest matched those of the lawsuit. Feminist activists and ACT UP members arrived at the building holding signs that read "Women Don't Get AIDS. They Just Die From It" and "Women and AIDS: Dead But Not Disabled." Flyers produced by ACT UP DC stated "SSA operates with a 60 billion surplus, a surplus that has been raided by the Reagan and Bush administrations to decrease the Federal deficit. These policies send a clear message that women's lives are expendable."[22] The flyers emphasized the gender and racial differences between HIV in men and in women in the epidemic: "The CDC definition of AIDS is based on symptoms seen in white males, and ignores the fact that women with HIV/AIDS get chronic vaginal candidiasis, pelvic inflammatory disease, cervical cancer, liver disease, endocarditis, tuberculosis and septicemia. Using their definition, 65% of women with HIV/AIDS die without a CDC diagnosis of AIDS."[23]

A chant sheet was distributed to each of the activists. The chants targeted Louis Sullivan, head of the HHS at the time. The slogans spoke directly to changing the CDC definition: "SSA has got to pay, we need benefits today!"; "Women with AIDS need disability, change the rules for eligibility!"; "Killing by omission, change the definition!"; "Racist, sexist, anti-dyke, Louis Sullivan, take a hike!"; and "Presumptive disability for women who have HIV!"[24]

By this time, Katrina Haslip, who had been organizing women with HIV in prison, was now on probation. Despite her risk of violating probation by traveling to Washington, DC, she showed up to the protest.[25] There she and Terry McGovern, despite having communicated for years, met for the first time. Haslip gave testimony at the protest. She described how the SSA had only given her eighteen dollars in cash and thirty-three dollars in food stamps. At the time she was thirty-one years old and her T-Cell count was very low: forty-seven. By all counts this would qualify her as having crossed the threshold from HIV to AIDS. She told the crowd:

> The reality is that women have real disabling symptoms of HIV that aren't the same as gay white men. Our symptoms can be early signs of the progression of AIDS. I want this to be acknowledged before I develop more severe symptoms and before death. The definition has to be expanded so that the opportunistic infections women get are included, and so that women can be entitled to the same disability benefits.[26]

Iris Delacruz also spoke. Like Haslip, Delacruz had been in Bedford Women's Prison. She was a white thirty-seven-year-old woman who was also living with HIV. She spoke about being an intravenous drug user with a repeated history of pelvic inflammatory disease. She was not a likely candidate for pelvic inflammatory disease as she had no prior sexually transmitted infections (STIs) or gynecological problems. Despite being an active drug user and having pelvic inflammatory disease, she was never given an HIV test. She had been organizing women with HIV to demand better from medical and public health agencies.[27]

Eighteen people at the protest were arrested. As the protestors were chanting, and the lawsuit was filed, Congressman Ted Weiss of New York made a statement in the House of Representatives. Like the advocates, plaintiffs, and lawyers, he called for the SSA to remedy the inequalities faced by women in the epidemic. Weiss spoke to the need for a more accurate definition of AIDS to ensure that women are not being excluded from the response to the epidemic.[28]

Together the litigation and activism were paying off. As described by McGovern:

> I think the combination of having the litigation and the demonstration and all this ACT UP work that had gone on finally started to scare the government a bit. Because they had to respond in court. And they could see that … all this ACT UP work that had gone on had really, really kind of big allies were developing at this point. I mean, the American Medical Association came in on the lawsuit, which was crazy, unbelievable. ACT UP had gotten a lot of very prominent groups to sign on to this stuff. So, I think they really started to get very nervous. And I think in terms of positive women, suddenly people were seeing positive women as leaders, also. Who were saying I've been denied disability. This is, so it wasn't just generalized complaints. There were specific things that needed to be changed. So I think it was an extremely powerful moment in this whole struggle.[29]

There was a gender dynamic to the activism itself. The men involved in ACT UP had education, access, and skills. For McGovern, working with poor women of color meant that her clients were struggling. They understood the hurdles they faced but they did not have the political savvy, nor did they look like the men they were negotiating with. But, despite the vast differences in life experience, many of the men in ACT UP supported the women's advocates as they staged protests and fought for the definitional change.

As the multipronged effort continued, the case and activism garnered national attention, shifting the public conversation about AIDS away from the perspectives of skeptics and toward the advocates arguing that women had long been contracting HIV and constituted a risk group. The *Baltimore Sun* ran an article the day after the lawsuit was filed with the headline "U.S. said to ignore women with AIDS." Phyllis Sharpe, a mother of six who was living with HIV, and a plaintiff in the litigation, was quoted in the article: "You have to be half dead to be declared disabled."[30] *USA Today* ran a short article with an image of two ACT UP activists, David Falcone and Kathy Chou, in which he held her head as she enacted sickness.[31]

## CONFRONTING THE CDC

Momentum was building. On November 17, 1990, the ACT UP Network (the coordinating body of ACT UP chapters from throughout the United States) called for a week of outrage from November 26 to December 4. To mark it ACT UP planned a series of protests and actions around the country related to women and girls.

Two days later, on November 19, members of ACT UP met with CDC representatives in Atlanta. The conversation was transcribed by ACT UP. The ACT UP members present included Katrina Haslip, Tracy Morgan, Chip Rowan (from ACT UP Atlanta), and Maxine Wolfe.[32] Haslip was also there in her capacity as a representative of Life Force. CDC representatives included Gary Noble, Deputy Director of the HIV Unit at the National Institutes of Health (NIH), and Ruth Berkelman, Chief of the Reporting and Analysis Section of the CDC.

Advocates began the meeting by stressing the need for more attention on issues related to women. Haslip delivered a presentation describing the opportunistic infections women were experiencing. Morgan presented available research on the symptoms of HIV as they manifested in women. Wolfe then raised the issue of the CDC's definition and the exclusion of women from AIDS diagnoses.

Following the ACT UP presentations, CDC staff responded. The activist transcript reflected both tensions and convergence in the issues that were raised by advocates. ACT UP members argued that sexism and homophobia were precluding the CDC from taking up women's issues. Gary Noble responded to this claim. He denied that these were problems of the CDC staff working on HIV, but acknowledged that "culture" makes it impossible to escape the possibility that sexism and homophobia are present. All of the advocates and experts present agreed that women were not being appropriately captured in the current surveillance system.[33] For the ACT UP activists, there was a simple answer to structural bias against women and racial minorities: Expand the AIDS definition to include gynecological issues. This would increase the number of diagnoses among women and have the corollary effect of allowing women to get presumptive benefits from the SSA. The CDC was concerned that expanding the definition might have complicated repercussions. First, because this was a surveillance definition it hoped to have the definition as tight as possible: no false positives, no false negatives. Expanding the definition could produce numerous false positives. And, some of the failures of surveillance weren't due to the CDC definition but to medical practice, which itself introduced many errors into the AIDS diagnosis.[34] The CDC had opted for the most cautious strategy: to only count the most severe manifestations of AIDS. Advocates recognized the cost of this: While a narrow definition would create few false positives, it could create many false negatives, leaving people who had

AIDS without a diagnosis. It was a cost–benefit analysis justified by the goal of the CDC's efforts: to surveil disease correctly.[35] By erring on the side of producing false negatives instead of false positives the CDC could more accurately claim that it was taking a cautious approach to counting AIDS cases. There was pressure on the CDC by the federal government to get the numbers exactly right. Importantly, a broader definition would produce confusion among scientists and medical professionals attempting to track trends in the spread of the virus.[36] Ultimately, the CDC had to retain its integrity as an institution grounded in evidence and science – one resistant to political pressure. While the CDC admitted that the evidence base on HIV was thin, it held that it was even more so for women. It made the choice to restrict the definition to only what appeared to be the clearest symptoms associated with immunocompromised people, leaving women out.[37] The CDC argued that to add on illnesses without an evidence base, including those like pelvic inflammatory disease or candida vulvovaginitis, had the potential of leading to an upward swing in AIDS diagnosis. Because these conditions were not only manifesting in women with HIV, this could result in many false positives. Retaining control over surveillance was key to preserving the integrity of the CDC.[38]

For activists at the meeting, the reticence of the CDC staff to consider altering the definition to include women at the cost of institutional legitimacy was a symptom of the very problem they had diagnosed: sexism. They argued in response that the CDC did not wait to gather necessary evidence about AIDS in gay men or children.[39] Nor did the CDC hesitate to craft early definitions of AIDS based on little evidence. Advocates argued: "Nobody waited for years to do those studies for gay men; nobody did it for children …. This is very very typical – white men do not have to wait[40] to be included, everyone else needs proof, beyond a shadow of a doubt."

Activists demanded that the CDC explain how it was that early definitions of AIDS, based on little data, were pulled together quickly, while now further into the epidemic women were not benefitting from an aggressive response to AIDS.[41] As one advocate argued,

> All I keep hearing and I still hear the same thing, that because these things appear in women, and because they just get worse when women are immunosuppressed, they shouldn't be in the definition of AIDS. And, that you are going to scare a lot of "nice" women who get these infections anyway but I know that the "not nice women" are going to

> die …. Let's be real. We don't know any more about the male opportunistic infections that are in there. But the criteria you are setting for putting in indicator and opportunistic infections is a double standard. You have not required that from other indicator diseases or opportunistic infections and it's just for women that you are requiring it.

CDC staff held their ground. They argued again that the illnesses associated with HIV in men were all a result of immune system suppression. Thus, there was reason to believe, given the appearance of the illness, that it was being caused by HIV especially when taking into account context.[42] The CDC staff felt this was distinct from the claims being made by women's rights advocates because the conditions they sought to add to the CDC definition of AIDs were not necessarily linked to immunosuppression but instead to cancers and illnesses that could appear in any woman regardless of her HIV status. To this, advocates pressed that women who had HIV were not experiencing regular manifestations of pelvic inflammatory disease or other illnesses. Instead, women with HIV were experiencing more severe forms and repeated illness which could largely be accounted for due to HIV suppression of the immune system.

Finally, while CDC experts were sympathetic to the fact that the SSA was using the CDC definition for disbursing benefits, including access to medical care, it insisted that the CDC was not responsible for care – only for surveillance. The SSA was responsible for ensuring that people were receiving care, and the CDC punted all issues of care to the SSA – even though the CDC had repeatedly asked the SSA to stop using its narrow AIDS surveillance definition to disburse benefits.

The meeting ended with little resolution. Angry at the lack of progress, an unidentified activist living with HIV told the CDC staff, "You would save yourself an awful lot of trouble if you just got together all of these clinicians and just asked them what they were seeing. I hold each of you personally responsible for the death of every woman with HIV I know, including myself."[43]

Continuing pressure on the CDC a few weeks later, on December 1st through 3rd, activists including ACT UP COSTAS, Terry McGovern, members of Life Force, and women living with HIV went back to Atlanta to protest at the CDC. By this time advocates had recruited many HIV-positive women to join the movement. They were among hundreds of women attending the protest. On Saturday, December 1st, SisterLove Women's AIDS Project, which was based in Atlanta, hosted a Community AIDS Resource and Education Fair at Morehouse College, a historically Black college. In keeping with the tradition of ACT UP actions, that night there was a party for the advocates and activists participating in the protest. On December 2nd, advocates gathered to prepare posters for the protest. On December 3rd at 11 AM they gathered to go to the CDC.[44]

The demonstrators' demands were clear: altering the AIDS surveillance definition to include chronic pelvic inflammatory disease, chronic refractory vaginal candidiasis, and cervical cancer. They also wanted the CDC to augment the definition to ensure that anyone with a CD4 count under 200 be counted as having AIDS. They demanded that the CDC improve its data collection process on the causes of deaths of people with HIV, and establish a mechanism for regular reviews and revision of its surveillance definition. Importantly, ACT UP demanded that members of affected communities be included in the process of review and revision.[45] As the protest received national attention, the pressure on the CDC mounted.

## THE FIRST BOOK AND CONFERENCE ON WOMEN AND AIDS

Given the lack of information about women and AIDS, ACT UP and the ACT UP New York Women and AIDS Book Group decided to take matters into their own hands by publishing their own book: *Women, AIDS, and Activism*. Released in 1990, the book was the product of an ACT UP Women's Caucus teach-in conducted at the Lesbian and Gay Community Services Center in New York City in March 1989.[46] The book pulled together what little information was known about women and AIDS at the time and sought to stake a place for women and AIDS in the national conversation about the epidemic. The book lays out the ideological foundations for ACT UP and laid the groundwork for what would become the dominant narrative about women and AIDS: that patriarchy and sexism were the cause of women's infections and the neglect of women in the AIDS response.[47] A chapter titled "Sexism and Women's Position in the AIDS Crisis," by Kim Christensen, provides text that animates the overall project:

> Sexist attitudes have had an enormous impact on the treatment of women in the AIDS crisis in the medical profession, public policy officials, and even some AIDS activists. Even more than sexism – a set of

> bigoted attitudes about gender – has been the institution of patriarchy which perpetuates male control of women's labor time, sexuality, and reproductive capacities. This male-control may be exercised by an individual man, as in the case of a battering husband, or by a male dominated institution, such as the Supreme Court, Congress, the New York Stock Exchange, the governing bodies of any of the major religions, or the medical profession.
>
> Violence against women, including the legal/societal toleration of this violence, is one of the most blatant aspects of patriarchal oppression.[48]

There was also mention of the role of race in AIDS-related inequalities.[49] At several points in the volume, authors raise the difference in infection rates between women of color and white women.[50] Women of color authored chapters documenting their own experiences in the epidemic.

While social factors played an important role, several chapters raised the biological dimensions of women and AIDS. This was central to the newly established narrative about women and AIDS given the deep belief that female bodies were intrinsically different from male bodies. Some of this difference was attributed to organ-specific disease (pelvic inflammatory disease), some due to pregnancy and reproductive organs (gynecological cancers), and some to unique manifestations of STIs in women.[51] In the context of HIV, feminists had also begun to speculate that many of the issues that impacted women's vulnerability to other STIs might also increase women's risk of contracting HIV.[52]

The book was reviewed in feminist publications, including *On Our Backs* and *Sojourner: The Women's Forum*, and that helped carry the book from the health activism space to the larger feminist community.[53] The dialogue it engendered picked up on the growing concern about sexual violence in the larger feminist movement. The reviewer in *On Our Backs*, for example, took issue with the assertion in *Women, AIDS, and Activism* that sex offenders should be able to voluntarily and not mandatorily test for HIV. "What ramifications does this statement hold for women, who are disproportionately the victims of male sex offenders," she asked.[54] The review in *Sojourner* connected the issue to reproductive rights, highlighting data that suggested that clinics were turning away women living with HIV who wanted abortions.[55] Papers produced for the LGBT community, including the *Village Voice*, also covered the release of the book. Acknowledging that the editors of the book were primarily white, mostly lesbian women – a contradiction when it came to who was contracting HIV – the review praised the editors for expanding the contributions to include nonACT UP members, which broadened the voices and highlighted the plight of lesbians in the AIDS struggle alongside the destructive role of gender.[56]

AIDS activists also carried the ideas from their book into the first conference on Women and HIV/AIDS. The event took place at the Sheraton Hotel in Washington, DC.[57] Fifteen hundred people were in attendance for panels spanning a range of issues impacting women in the epidemic.[58] The conference included representatives from the National Institute of Allergy and Infectious Diseases (NIAID), and several subgroups from the NIH, including the Office of Research on Women's Health, the National Institute of Child Health and Human Development, and the National Center for Nursing Research.[59] A range of government agencies cosponsored the event including the Office of the Surgeon General, the Office of Minority Health, the National AIDS Program Office, the Alcohol, Drug Abuse and Mental Health Administration, the Food and Drug Administration, and the Health Resources and Services Administration.

Although the meeting was a demand of women's organizations, advocates felt that they were largely excluded from the planning.[60] Linda Meredith, a leader of the ACT UP Women's Caucus in DC, who had been appointed to the Steering Committee for the National Conference, resigned citing exclusion from the planning process as well as the appointment of a staff person who was not using inclusive planning methods for the conference.[61] Despite her resignation she spoke on a panel entitled Status of Women's Research.[62]

Their outrage at being excluded from the planning of a conference their advocacy helped create primed the advocates to protest. Their high-profile targets were Anthony Fauci, Director of NIAID, who had promised inclusion of women's rights advocates when communicating with Linda Meredith, and James Curran, the head of the CDC task force on AIDS. In the campaign to change the CDC definition of AIDS, Curran was an important figure. Part of his mandate was to define the disease itself. He had already been targeted by advocates. In one action, ACT UP members sent 20,000 postcards to his home. On them was a picture of his face with a target on it. While his family was upset by the barrage of postcards, Curran was unfazed. He felt that he was the target due to his position at the CDC and not due to his personal work, which had been long dedicated to issues regarding women's health. He hung the postcard on his wall at the CDC, next to awards he had received from the LGBT community, to remind himself of the range of reactions emerging from the demanding work of responding to the epidemic. Together, the flyer and award were a sign of the difficult work.[63]

During Curran's talk at the conference, he argued that the CDC definition could not be expanded because of the lack of an evidence base. He was interrupted by ACT UP Women's Caucus members who hung a banner and gave out leaflets criticizing the slow response to the issue of women and AIDS. Dr. Fauci also spoke at the conference, presenting general information about the epidemic. During the question-and-answer session he was challenged by women in Life Force, who pointed out that they already knew all he'd explained about the broad dimensions of the epidemic – they wanted specific information about women. When Daniel Hoth, head of the NIH Division on HIV, tried to speak, twenty-five HIV-positive women stopped him midway and read a statement together articulating three specific demands: change the CDC definition, give women disability benefits, let women into clinical trials.[64]

Alongside pressuring senior government officials, advocates used the opportunity to organize. They distributed copies of the *Treatment and Research Agenda for Women with HIV Infection*. It was a photocopied and bound manuscript describing the many issues related to women and AIDS.[65] The book was a call for research and action on the issue of women and HIV, and characterized women as the "most misdiagnosed, underdiagnosed, and underserved" population in the AIDS epidemic.[66] It detailed the variety of conditions that women with AIDS tend to get, echoing the demands for more attention to pelvic inflammatory disease, cervical cancer, and Human Papilloma Virus (HPV).[67]

The conference produced recommendations on women and AIDS that were to be distributed to Public Health Service agencies. While the recommendations were wide-ranging, they all advocated increased attention to women and AIDS: for an exploration of how HIV manifests in women, for more studies about HIV transmission and the existence of co-infections and cofactors of transmission, for a study of precancerous reproductive organ and genital tract lesions among HIV-infected women, and for investigation into the psychosocial needs of HIV-positive women.[68] The call for greater understanding of the biological workings of AIDS came with calls for specific modes of preventative care, including the need for gender-specific (gynecological) evaluations.[69]

## 1991–1992: THE TIDE BEGINS TO TURN

The conference, litigation, and advocacy were creating a stir and government officials were aware of it.[70] The national conversation on women and AIDS was also beginning to shift. Mainstream papers reconsidered the epidemic amongst women: In 1991, a *New York Times* headline read that "80,000 Women May Carry HIV." In 1992, *Time* magazine ran a story "Losing the Battle, Highlighting the Shifting Epidemic to Women," and *The Atlantic* magazine wrote that heterosexuals with AIDS were the second epidemic. The coverage had impact: The federal judge overseeing *S.P. v. Sullivan* read a *New York Times* article about a demonstration on women and AIDS. Despite the government's best efforts, she refused to dismiss the case.[71]

With the litigation ongoing, AIDS activists continued to carry feminist ideas forward. A key event came in 1991 when Democratic Representative Robert Matsui of California introduced H.R. 2299, calling for an AIDS Disability Advisory Panel to assist Congress and the secretary of health and human services to more effectively meet the needs of people living with HIV. The panel was to consider the special concerns of women, among other populations, and comprise nine members, including at least one person who was living with HIV. Reflecting feminist demands, the panel was tasked with considering the specific course of HIV infection amongst women and "the symptomatic manifestation of HIV infection in women as it differs from men."[72] The bill listed interim standards for impairments that would result in a person being deemed disabled; they included cervical dysplasia and cancer, chronic vaginal candidiasis, and pelvic inflammatory disease that was unresponsive to standard medical therapy.

These gynecological illnesses reflected the feminist demand that women-specific identifiers be included in the determination of AIDS-related disability. In driving this point home, Republican Congresswoman Constance Morella, a cosponsor of H.R. 2299, stated that she was "deeply concerned" by the SSA's use of a CDC definition that "continues to rely mainly on AIDS-indicator conditions in men."[73] In January of 1991, she wrote to Linda Meredith that she planned to cosponsor Matsui's bill,[74] indicating that her support for the bill may have partly been in response to advocacy by the ACT UP Women's Caucus.

Under pressure in June 1991, the SSA released revised regulations acknowledging that challenges had arisen in its use of the CDC definition to provide SSI and SSDI. Although the new regulations acknowledged that women and men experienced HIV differently, they did not meet the demands of activists and women living with HIV who called for a determination of disability based on identified illnesses specific to women. Instead, the new draft regulations of the SSA still required a determination of functional impairment, even if gynecological conditions associated with AIDS were present.[75] In response, and as evidence of the high-profile nature of the debate, over 3,000 comments were received by the SSA. The feminists of ACT UP critiqued the AIDS definition for not going far enough. Terry McGovern also sent a letter to Lorraine Novinski at the Department of Justice. The letter requested that a series of illnesses be added to the list, including chronic pelvic inflammatory disease, chronic anemia, recurrent herpes, and chronic genital ulcers.[76]

In April 1992, as the litigation was ongoing and the new SSA rule was still under consideration, the Subcommittee on Social Security and the Subcommittee on Human Resources held a hearing to identify the obstacles faced by women, children, and individuals with HIV-related disabilities from qualifying for SSI and SSDI. The official rationale of the hearing echoed feminist ideas about why women had not been detected with having HIV and had been denied benefits: "SSA's medical criteria for HIV-related disabilities are based largely on studies of adult males, they exclude many symptoms experienced by women and children." The feminist influence in the context of AIDS was on display as ideas of biological differences in the manifestation of HIV and AIDS appeared in testimonies by politicians, medical experts, and activists alike.

Testimony from lawyers representing AIDS clients criticized the SSA for slow assessments of disability and failure to be responsive to the needs of women. In her testimony, in which she described her increasingly worsening health, Phyllis Sharpe, a beneficiary of social security, mobilized ideas of inclusion and difference to argue that the SSA was failing to address the needs of women: "The old definition was bad enough. All the medical conditions which were listed were from studies of gay white men. How does that apply to me? I have a different body chemistry than a gay white man. Now the new definition has problems."[77] Sharpe and other advocates had support from leading medical organizations, including the American Medical Association (AMA), the American Academy of Pediatrics, and the Physicians Association for AIDS Care (PAAC). Each of these institutions carried the weight of an association of physician-experts whose primary allegiance was to scientific evidence rather than politics. Yet their testimonies read as similar to those of feminists, and often appealed not to science but to the morality of not addressing the issue of women and AIDS. Each organization argued that its primary constituents would benefit from a broadening of the SSA definition by allowing a greater number of individuals to receive benefits. The AMA and PAAC made strong statements in favor of expanding the AIDS-defining illnesses list.[78] Referencing the litigation before the courts, the AMA statement made clear that the SSA needed to better respond to people living with HIV, highlighting the fact that the challenges of qualifying for disability benefits are "compounded for women, children, and others who are not typical of the earliest and most thoroughly studied individuals infected with HIV."[79] The PAAC made a passionate appeal:

> HIV disease is a disease of the disenfranchised of our society. It is a disease of the medically indigent, of the poor, of the homeless, of gays, of injection drug users, of people of color and of women – groups who at best have been relegated to some secondary status as citizens, and at worst have been targets of discrimination and sexism.
>
> Women may have suffered disproportionate [sic] from this epidemic than other groups. First, they have suffered because their initial symptoms of HIV disease often have not been diagnosed due in part to the perception by many physicians that HIV disease is a disease of gays and injection drug users. Over and over, from every major city in this country I have met women who have told me horror stories of the failure of their physician to diagnose their HIV disease ... Next, when women are finally diagnosed with HIV, many of these women are unable to find a physician who can diagnose and appropriately treat the many manifestations of this disease unique to women. Many of these unique manifestations are gynecological disorders – conditions with which many primary care physicians and many HIV specialists are unfamiliar. However, gynecologists are generally not familiar with HIV disease, which leaves women in a classic Catch 22.[80]

Despite the testimony of physicians at the hearing, the SSA resisted the passage of H.R. 2299, stating that its current guidelines for determining disability relied on "documented scientific information" and that this was foundational to the crafting of SSA regulations.[81] In doing so, it pushed back with another powerful frame: the objectivity and neutrality of science.[82] Building from this counterframe it argued that it could not and should not take guidance on how to define an

AIDS-defining illness from legislators or other nonscientists. The SSA argued that it was working with the NIH to ensure that the newest medical listings for determinations of disability included issues facing women to ensure science-based regulations on AIDS.[83]

By this point in time, the SSA was under pressure to do better. The hearings were overwhelmingly critical of the SSA's resistance to being more inclusive of women with HIV in its disability determinations. To drive home the general dissatisfaction with the SSA, Senator Thomas Downy quoted the MFY Legal Services and HIV Law Project brief before the court in *S.P. v. Sullivan*:

> We filed the lawsuit because our clients experienced terrible delays and were subject to incredible hardship in their attempts to qualify for benefits. We watched clients die before they ever qualified. We watched them grow sicker and sicker while we fought a system which recognized none of their impairments as severe and disabling HIV-related disease and almost every single plaintiff in the lawsuit was eventually found disabled at their application date, 1, 2, 3, or 5 years before they actually won benefits.[84]

In response to this criticism, the SSA implied that it would revisit its proposed rule, which would now benefit from the several thousand comments it had received. In keeping with its emphasis on an expert-driven process, it argued that in considering the comments its rule would reflect the experience of physicians and service providers to improve the experience of filing for disability benefits. By this time, the CDC had repeatedly communicated to the SSA that the SSA should not use the CDC case definition to assess disability.[85] Yet, the SSA continued to do so.

Although the CDC definition was not the central focus of the hearings, because the SSA relied on the CDC definition to make its disability determinations in the context of HIV, the CDC definition was also being called into question.[86] The CDC felt bound: It wanted a careful list of symptomatic illnesses that were an accurate representation of the virus. This produced pressure to ensure that illnesses not associated with HIV were not on the symptomatic list used for diagnosis. The CDC also felt that it had a more effective strategy in the pipeline; with the increasing use of blood tests it could utilize CD4 counts to determine if a person has AIDS. The CDC landed on 200 cells/ul as a cutoff. In other words, having a CD4 count below 200 cells/ul would result in a diagnosis of AIDS. The idea was that 200 cells/ul would capture many people living with HIV but still be slightly above a CD4 count that would necessarily render someone ill.[87] From Curran's perspective the 200 cells/ul was an inclusive definition because it would allow for an AIDS diagnosis for many people who were not yet experiencing the symptoms of AIDS.

Congress had also begun to seek answers to the question of the AIDS definition. In 1992, the Subcommittee on Human Resources and Intergovernmental Relations for the House Committee on Government Operations, the Office of Technology Assessment (OTA) issued a report exploring the implications of the alterations in the AIDS case definitions. The report noted that the CDC was resisting any modifications to the AIDS case definition for three primary reasons. First, the CDC argued that doing so would increase the complexity of the definition and thus complicate state-level reporting of AIDS. Second, and related, the CDC did not want to add in any infections or cancers that did not have an already established relationship to HIV; the list as it existed only had infections and cancers that appeared in immunocompromised individuals. The CDC argued that broadening that could result in an artificial inflation of the AIDS count. Finally, the CDC preferred to rely on CD4 counts rather than the existence of nonopportunistic illnesses in making determinations on the progression of HIV to AIDS.[88] This decision would allow the CDC to determine AIDS status through a number rather than through illnesses like pelvic inflammatory disease. This appealed to epidemiologists who felt a numerical measure would allow for a standardized approach rather than one reliant on diseases not always associated with immunocompromised individuals. The CDC predicted that the expansion of the AIDS case definition would result in a 52 percent increase in the total number of living AIDS cases in the United States, with an increase in reporting amongst women. According to the OTA, the federal agency responsible for advising Congress on scientific and technological issues, states reported that with a change in case definition to include gynecological health issues the number of AIDS cases would increase between 36 percent and 135 percent. In turn, there would be financial costs: The more people diagnosed with HIV and AIDS the greater the burden on state and local governments to provide services.[89]

In the face of ongoing resistance from the CDC, a coalition of organizations, including the HIV Law Project, ACT UP, New Jersey Women AIDS Network, and the American Civil Liberties Union (ACLU), developed a proposal that demanded the addition of gynecological conditions including invasive cervical cancer and pelvic inflammatory disease. The proposal had over 300 signatories including individuals and organizations.[90] It was delivered to CDC officials in June of 1992 at the International AIDS Conference. Activists also engaged in a carefully planned national campaign. They arrived at the CDC in Atlanta and at the Health and Human Services Agency in Washington, DC carrying signs that read "The CDC Definition Is Sexist, They Are Killing Women" and "Women and AIDS: Dead but Not Disabled!" Key leaders in the AIDS response, including Fauci, were targeted by activists at conferences. In Atlanta, feminists were arrested at the CDC demanding that women be included in the AIDS definition. They encouraged people on the ACT UP list to call senators and demand the inclusion of women-specific illnesses in the AIDS definition and question the CDC's lack of commitment to women. As described by activist, Maxine Wolfe:

> They [the CDC] were so afraid of us by that time. We had done all these demonstrations. We had gotten groups that were so diverse, to support this campaign, from all over the country. We showed that we could get Congress people who would start to investigate the CDC. We used every single tactic that you could possibly use. It was really like community organizing and political organizing at its best. It went from the grass roots up, and we had this committed group of people. We would send out a letter and say, write a letter to your Congressman, and all these people would do it, because they wanted to change it.[91]

With discussions ongoing, the CDC decided it would move to a definition of AIDS that emphasized CD4 counts and defined AIDS as anyone with a CD4 count under 200. Some segments of ACT UP agreed with this strategy and felt that 200 cells/ul represented a good compromise. This solved part of the problem in that the new AIDS case definition would be inclusive by default. Feminists considered the consequences of this. On one hand, the new definition would allow more women to be detected with HIV and AIDS. On the other hand, it did not get to the core concern that female-specific manifestations of AIDS would be left off of the list of illnesses. At the urging of physicians in their movement, feminist activists felt that they should push ahead with naming gynecological conditions, with one important modification. McGovern was concerned that they would only be able to move forward for symptomatic conditions that had a robust evidence base, given the CDC's emphasis on evidence-driven guidelines. Feminists knew they would have to modify their claims to fit the CDC's perception of itself as a value-neutral institution. From this perspective, cervical cancer was the only gynecological condition that had an evidence base.[92] So activists narrowed their broader set of symptomatic illnesses to the more limited demand that invasive cervical cancer be included in the list of AIDS-defining illnesses.

In September 1992, the CDC held an open meeting about the transformation of the definition of AIDS. An official transcript of the meeting reveals that the CDC had begun to warm to the idea of broadening the definition of AIDS, and that epidemiologists had begun to question the reliability of the CDC's data. This created yet another opening for feminists to demand that gynecological issues be included in the CDC definition. These shifts meant that the CDC had to rethink its boundary between science and advocacy. That was evident in the opening remarks by CDC representative James Curran, who acknowledged that the AIDS surveillance definition should be revised soon because of the "serious morbidity due to HIV infection that is undercounted." "Many people," he acknowledged, "are hospitalized and some die with HIV infection without being counted as a case of AIDS."[93] Importantly, Curran stated that while the CDC did not address healthcare and social services for people living with HIV, it clarified the ongoing need for services. For Curran, the "AIDS surveillance has served and will continue to serve as the conscience of the HIV epidemic in our country." The statement appears to be a clear reference to the denial of benefits from the SSA – with the CDC acknowledging that whether or not it sought to have this role, it would hold the key to understanding and responding to the epidemic.[94] The expanded definition sat in the most "simple, direct, and objective" way to assess advanced immunosuppression: CD4 counts.[95]

Supporters of the expansion of the AIDS-defining illness list spoke at the meeting. Marion Banzhaf of the New Jersey Health Department presented a consensus statement signed by over 250 organizations calling for an expansion of the AIDS definition, and demanding that the surveillance definition include cervical cancer, cervical dysplasia, pulmonary tuberculosis, and recurrent bacterial pneumonia.[96] Women's advocates also pushed against the use of CD4 tests as the exclusive way to determine HIV or AIDS status because the request for a CD4 test normally only occurs because of the assumption that a person has HIV. This would continue to leave women with HIV without a diagnosis.[97] Terry McGovern drove home the point in emphasizing that CD4 counts alone are not enough to determine whether a person had progressed to AIDS, arguing that many gay men with Kaposi's sarcoma or pneumocystis pneumonia had CD4 counts above 300 or 250 respectively.[98] Women living with HIV also spoke, advocating that invasive cervical cancer, chronic vaginal yeast infections, and pelvic inflammatory disease be added to the list of symptomatic illnesses which could trigger an AIDS diagnosis.[99] They argued that the evidence base had changed – mandating a new definition of AIDS for the 1990s. They demanded to be recognized, and as one activist remarked:

> I leave you these words so that every time you hear my voice or see my face you'll know I'm holding you accountable and responsible for the unnecessary suffering of women the world over. Because I will not distort my voice! I will not cover my face! And I certainly will not live the remainder of my life hiding in the shadows! My name is Wendy Alexis Modeste and I'm a proud African-American woman who, despite the CDC, is living with AIDS in Syracuse, New York![100]

Despite strong advocacy for expanding the definition, many participants argued against adding illnesses.[101] From their perspective, the CD4 count of 200 represented the most objective and consistent way to determine whether someone's HIV infection had progressed to AIDS. Despite the differences in position on the expansion of the CDC definition (between those supporting only the shift to 200 CD4 count and those who wanted the inclusion of symptomatic illnesses) speakers tended to agree that people of color and poor individuals would not receive the CD4 count blood tests due to an inability to pay for them. In a panel on cervical cancer, tensions about whether or not to include invasive cervical cancer reemerged. Advocates called for the inclusion of invasive cervical cancer and epidemiologists presented growing evidence that women with HIV do experience forms of cervical cancer that rapidly progress. Yet, despite this, one epidemiologist concluded: "I'm going to look at this only from the epidemiological point of view. I think disability should be awarded on the basis of disability and that the rationing of health care in the U.S. by income is inexcusable, but the definition is not the way to change that."[102]

Although the speaker was not from the CDC, the position reflected the concerns that epidemiological and scientific surveillance should remain distinct from the distributional implications of the AIDS definition. Other medical experts leaned into broadening the definition, evidenced by the statement from a professor at the University of Puerto Rico School of Medicine who "hoped to see an inclusion of premalignant cervical conditions as well as advanced cervical cancer in the AIDS case definition" because that "would improve the chances of such women and will give a better perspective of the condition as it relates to women."[103] Similarly, a representative of the American College of Obstetrics and Gynecology emphasized the need to integrate gynecological care into the AIDS response because gynecologists were not tuned into the AIDS epidemic and cases were being missed. Inclusion of invasive cervical cancer would bring the field of gynecology directly into the diagnosis of AIDS.[104]

Numerous ACT UP members from cities around the country (including New York, DC, and Los Angeles) joined other activists and members of Life Force in continuing to pressure those resisting the inclusion of cervical cancer during conference discussion periods.[105] Advocates were frustrated with what they saw as a blatant double standard: the obvious denial of the inclusion of women's issues, while symptomatic illnesses associated with men were included from the beginning of the epidemic, despite little evidence of the connection to HIV. One after another, they stepped up.

Linda Meredith, representing ACT UP, argued that although the CDC was not responsible for helping people access healthcare, it was in fact responsible for tracking the epidemic accurately.[106] The National Minority AIDS Council representative Anita Taylor told the group that the expansion of the definition to include gynecological conditions would sensitize health practitioners to the possibility of HIV infection in women and help with early diagnosis and treatment of women.[107] Getting the definition right in order to help people access Medicaid and social security benefits was especially necessary for indigent people and people of color living with undiagnosed HIV, she said.[108] And journalist Susan Shaw, from the People With AIDS Coalition, argued that understanding the relationship between science and politics was crucial to formulating an equitable AIDS response: "We would like science to be apolitical," she said. "But the fact is science is political, and people with AIDS are trying to use it to their best interests."[109]

Their interventions seemed to strike a chord. During the question-and-answer period, epidemiologists and physicians began to reveal their own ambivalence about the accuracy of epidemiology. In striking terms, one epidemiologist noted the shortcomings of the field:

> [E]pidemiology is not a pure science. Epidemiology is a fairly clean science. But we never have the luxury of being an absolutely pure science,

> and there are always compromises both in specificity and sensitivity that we have to make [in] our case definition. So we don't hold ourselves out as being in any way even nearly an ivory-tower type of science.[110]

The idea that there was an attainable, pure science by which to understand the AIDS epidemic – and that epidemiology did not meet that standard – produced an opening for legitimate activist claims that in fact the evidence that had been driving the CDC definition thus far was incomplete.

James Curran's comments at the end of the meeting reflected the transformation underway at the CDC. The goal of the meeting was to understand how to expand the definition, he said. He acknowledged that HIV creates unique issues due to the underlying discrimination faced by people living with HIV, which is compounded by fear in the epidemic: "Health care workers are afraid. People in schools are afraid. Other people are afraid. And that's on top of racism, sexism, and something that we didn't hear much about today, and that's homophobia,"[111] he said. He also offered up a practical reason for settling on the number 200 as *the* number for using a blood cell count to determine if someone had AIDS:

> So why did we pick less than 200 CD4 cells? The reason we picked less than 200 CD4 cells as one approach to expanding the AIDs surveillance definition is that every doctor that does any good and knows how to take care of an HIV-infected patient does approximate CD4 counts. And the CD4 count is one measure that is based upon the adequacy of medical care. And, in general, people who have less than 200 CD4 counts need a lot more intensive preventive medical care and curative medical care … so we want to reflect what we think is the ideal medical care.[112]

For Curran, adding the CD4 count cutoff also mattered because it would further incentivize doing the CD4 tests to begin with. He described how public health officials sought out diagnoses of HIV so that they could approach the legislature to demand increased funding for HIV. Curran also suggested there was a structural issue with the diagnosis of HIV through gynecological conditions – that many internal medicine physicians did not feel comfortable conducting pelvic exams. To him, this was "crazy." Adding gynecological conditions, like cervical cancer, to the case definition would send "an important message to doctors, to women, as well as to society … that gynecological problems are an important part of the spectrum of disease in women, and that getting pap smears because of concerns about cervical cancer is an important concern and issue."[113] Curran's position reflected a shift away from maintaining a narrow definition of AIDS that would exclude cases from being detected and toward a broader definition of AIDS that would ensure delivery of care and better surveillance.

## FEMINIST VICTORY

In December 1992, the CDC issued revised guidelines inclusive of invasive cervical cancer.[114] Advocates credit their own activism for the shifting definition. And, even while the OTA acknowledged that it was lawyers who brought the issue of invasive cervical cancer to its attention as an AIDS-defining illness,[115] the CDC credited the change to new data in the way HIV manifests in women.[116] By positioning the change as one based on evidence, the CDC was able to sustain its image as an institution driven by scientific evidence and resistant to politics.

A few days before the official release of the CDC's announcement, McGovern went to the bedside of Katrina Haslip to share the good news. Haslip whispered a statement to McGovern, her eyes closed in exhaustion. The statement was read out loud at a press conference held by advocates:

> I don't want for one moment, the CDC or the FDA or any of our state and city entities to smile today and act like they have done me a grave justice. In fact, it was activists like the women's caucus of ACT UP, Black AIDS Mobilization, and community based organizations that are grass roots and peer-oriented that pressed the CDC into changing this definition.
>
> They probably still don't think our vaginas are important or women's healthcare is important. This is their form of pacifying us and trying to silence us. I do not want them to come smiling today or tomorrow at a press conference like they have discovered something new or that they have added these conditions because there is new statistical data.
>
> Women's health groups like the Women's Prisoner's Association, the Division of Substance Abuse, the Borough President's Offices, Women and AIDS group and community based organizations like Manhattan Task Force on AIDs have lost blood, sweat and tears, have suffered pain, aches, frustrations, lost loved ones and they themselves have died [and] while we waited and watched the CDC did nothing.

> So, okay, you gave us a few things but we will not carry on a farce. We will not be silent. We will continue to scream and advocate for ourselves on women's health issues and CDC you will stop killing women by the omission of certain gynecological illnesses and you will learn to record data about women and study and research the natural history of this disease in our bodies. Shame on you CDC, we will never be silent again.[117]

The news of the definitional change received national attention. And despite her immense frustration, in a story about women and AIDS in the *New York Times*, Haslip declared victory:

> I am, and have been, a woman with AIDS, despite the C.D.C. not wishing to count me. We have compelled them to.[118]

Soon after, at the age of thirty-three, Haslip died. The guidelines went into effect one month later.[119] Hers was not counted as an AIDS death.[120] Her framed photo sits on McGovern's desk still today.

Following the shift in the CDC definition, and in consultation with experts, lawyers, and people living with HIV, the SSA revised its rule in 1993. The SSA, however, went even further than the CDC, including both invasive cervical cancer and pelvic inflammatory disease on the listing of illnesses that, when paired with an HIV diagnosis, would allow for a greater possibility of receiving benefits. Taking on the feminist position, the agency acknowledged that "HIV infection manifests differently in women than in men."

This was a feminist victory. Now embedded in the scientific institutions that defined AIDS – and in regulations that managed the flow of resources – was a feminist idea that would fundamentally alter the response to the epidemic.

In September 1994, the World Health Organization (WHO), in its *Weekly Epidemiological Record* – a publication that serves as a means for rapid dissemination of information on disease outbreaks and progression – updated its definition of AIDS.[121] In keeping with the shift in the CDC definition, the WHO also added invasive cervical cancer to its case definition for AIDS surveillance, which meant a positive HIV test coupled with one of a list of illnesses would result in a diagnosis of AIDS. The expanded list of illnesses reflected feminist demands: Invasive cervical cancer was now included.[122]

The change in the surveillance definition meant that more women living with HIV around the world were counted among those infected by the virus or having a diagnosis of AIDS.

The onslaught of diagnoses among women would transform the face of AIDS. Acknowledging the uptick in heterosexual transmission and the fast-growing number of women suffering from AIDS, the United Nations (UN) agencies declared that the global epidemic had feminized.

Women and girls were now one of the fastest-growing groups contracting HIV. But a question still remained on the table: How should experts explain the fast-growing epidemic among women? As Chapter 4 reveals, feminists had an answer.

3

# EXPERIMENTS IN RISK

## Clinical Trials and Women

In 1988, the Food and Drug Administration approved zidovudine (AZT) for the treatment of AIDS.[1] It was momentous. Around the world, activists, researchers, and people living with HIV celebrated the possibility of life amid the carnage of AIDS.

Reality, however, soon set in. AZT was a powerful drug with harsh side effects, and not everyone could tolerate the medication. As researchers began experimenting with these new drugs, it wasn't long before feminists identified a troubling aspect of drug development on HIV: Women were being excluded from clinical trials that could help them survive out of concerns that the drugs could harm a potential fetus.

Take the case of Irene. In 1991, Irene fell deeply ill with AIDS. Her CD4 count had dropped below 100, indicating severe HIV infection allowing for an AIDS diagnosis.[2] Like many others living with HIV, the side effects of AZT were unbearable to her. Sick and in need of intervention, Irene's physician advised her to enroll in a clinical trial to access some of the potentially lifesaving medications being tested on people living with HIV. But when Irene went to enroll in a new drug trial being conducted by Johns Hopkins University and Hoffmann-La Roche Company, she was told she could not enroll unless she was surgically sterilized. Irene was willing to take regular pregnancy tests and contraception but was unwilling to get surgical sterilization. She was excluded from the trial.[3]

As more women were diagnosed with HIV, cases like Irene's multiplied. The root cause of these exclusions was 1977 Food and Drug

Administration (FDA) guidance that specifically recommended excluding women of childbearing age from clinical trials. Denying women participation in clinical trials had immediate downstream consequences. Not only could women not access the possible experimental drugs for HIV, but the lack of women's participation in clinical trials produced uncertainty for researchers and physicians who were treating women and wanted to know how sex or pregnancy might impact the use of the medication before they were willing to prescribe it. Together, these dynamics meant that women could not access experimental or approved medications.

Recognizing that progress would come from working in the knotty interactions between legal institutions and science, feminists fought to help women access AIDS clinical trials and drugs. This chapter highlights how feminist AIDS activists contributed to a larger push to force the FDA to transform how the agency regulates sex and gender in scientific research. Their efforts would lead to a profound shift in the study of women in drug development, both in and outside the context of AIDS.

While prior chapters focused on the coproduction of law and epidemiology, this chapter examines how feminists demanded more clinical trial research on women to alter the knowledge environment about women, HIV, and treatment. Feminists asserted at every step that it was women who should decide whether or not to bear the risk of harm through the drug development and rollout process – pregnant or not. These feminist arguments were successful, at least in part, due to the broader shifting legal sensibility that women ought to have more autonomy over their bodily choices developed in a series of constitutional US Supreme Court decisions which drove forward the idea that women ought to have privacy and autonomy over aspects of their reproductive decision-making. AIDS activists built on the momentum of the moment to help move the FDA to lift guidance that undermined a woman of childbearing years from participating in clinical trials.

The feminist struggle around AIDS was central to the change in the FDA rules. Though the feminist women's health movement had long identified the FDA rules on clinical trials as an issue, it was the fight for AIDS drug treatment that helped propel forward the movement's goal of altering FDA guidance. This chapter focuses in on several crucial dynamics of this fight. First, it looks at how AIDS activists sought to disrupt the regulatory frames around scientific research to force the production of better information about women. They did this in service of redistributive goals: to get women medical care and treatment. Second, the chapter highlights the role of pregnancy. Much to the chagrin of feminist AIDS activists, the hesitancy to enroll women in clinical trials vanished when it came to experimentation for the benefit of the fetus. This was a key concern in the ACTG 076 trial that set out to prove that AZT could stop mother-to-child transmission of HIV. While the success of the trial, and the new ability to prevent mother-to-child transmission, ended political controversy around ACTG 076, feminist concerns about autonomy and consent raised in the context of the trial continued to be salient over the coming decades. Finally, this chapter tracks how the legal ideas of choice and autonomy, pushed by feminists and increasingly a part of constitutional jurisprudence, becomes integral to achieving women's participation in clinical trials.

## EXCLUSIONS FROM CLINICAL TRIALS

Long before AIDS, the feminist women's health movement raised concerns about how women were receiving care and treatment for a host of health issues. The largely male medical establishment discounted women's health concerns and denied them research to substantiate their claims. The reticence about including women in clinical trials and a lack of funding for research extended to women's health issues, including menstruation, menopause, pregnancy, and breast cancer.[4] As has been widely documented by feminist historians, legal scholars, and sociologists of medicine, feminist advocates took up the cause of increasing and improving knowledge about women's health by working to get this guidance altered. They began a long struggle to fight for what medical sociologist Steven Epstein has called, in his foundational work on AIDS and clinical trials, "inclusion", a struggle for representation in clinical trials based on one's sex, gender, and racial identity.[5] They claimed that the white male body at the center of all research needed to be unseated, and a more diverse range of individuals should be included in clinical trials.[6] As Epstein showed, advocacy by community groups would bring questions of identity directly into the realm of knowledge production.

Chapters 1 and 2 document how feminist women's health and AIDS activism converged to change the Centers for Disease Control and Prevention (CDC) definition of AIDS. Building on the work of scholars and advocates, this chapter shows how these two movements, with many shared actors, mobilized legal tools to demand more inclusive research.[7]

From the start of the AIDS epidemic, AIDS activists were interested in treatment. Patients longed for a cure. Treatment activism, "drugs into bodies," became a core and central feature of AIDS activism.[8] People were dying, and advocates were pushing forward.[9] Scientists, too, were searching for a solution.

AIDS activists felt that AIDS treatments should be developed and approved faster to ensure that people could receive lifesaving treatments quickly. To understand the history of this period and the activism directed at the FDA, it is necessary to first understand the drug approval process, which became a central target of AIDS activists and feminist advocates.

The FDA, situated within the Department of Health and Human Services, was and continues to be the agency responsible for protecting the health of the public by regulating the "safety, efficacy, and security" of "human and veterinary drugs, biological products, and medical devices."[10] The agency plays a powerful role in the governance of medicine and healthcare: It approves all drugs before they can be marketed and sold in the United States. The process for drug manufacturers begins by filing a new drug application (NDA).

To get an NDA, the FDA requires that data be presented for drug approval. Based on proof of efficaciousness, the FDA will approve the medication. Each drug requires a three-phase trial before a sponsor submits a NDA for FDA approval. The NDA is required for marketing approval. In Phase I, the sponsor studies the drug in humans. Generally, small numbers of healthy volunteers or patients are treated over a short period of time. Phase I is designed to look into individual tolerance for a drug and dosing. It also allows for an exploration of pharmacokinetics, the way the drug is processed in the body.[11] Phase II studies are early-stage control trials often involving small population samples. They demonstrate effectiveness and relative safety. Phase III trials are large trials in which the drug developer will study several thousand people. This is the last step before approval. Sometimes, before a Phase I trial, an animal trial will be rolled out. These animal trials might be able to show the risks of the drugs before humans are involved.

In 1977, the FDA created a guidance document titled *General Considerations for the Clinical Evaluation of Drugs*.[12] In this guidance, the FDA stated that women of childbearing potential should be excluded from Phase I trials and only be included in clinical trials if enough information had been amassed in Phase I and II trials (as well as animal reproduction studies) on efficacy and relative safety of the drug being tested for women of reproductive age. The 1977 guidance defined "women of childbearing potential" as "premenopausal females capable of becoming pregnant." The definition included women who are single, actively trying not to get pregnant, and using "oral, injectable, or mechanical contraception; women whose husbands have been vasectomized or whose husbands have received or are using medical contraceptive devices."

The guidance was developed in response to what is now known as the thalidomide tragedy. Thalidomide was prescribed to pregnant women in Germany to help address morning sickness. Due to the use of the drug, thousands of children were born with physical disabilities. The drug was not widely used in the United States, but it led to the 1962 drug amendments, which increased the FDA's authority to approve drugs.[13] It also precipitated concerns for pregnant women as research subjects. The result was the 1977 FDA guidance.[14]

The thalidomide tragedy also fed fears in the pharmaceutical industry that drug trials on pregnant women could lead to tort claims.[15] Lawsuits following the use of thalidomide, costing companies millions, were invoked by both the FDA and pharmaceutical companies to caution against enrolling women in trials, feminist scholars feminist scholars were skeptical about this claim. After all, an untested and harmful drug could also result in lawsuits.

These factors – the thalidomide scandal, the 1970s guidance which followed, and fear of tort liability – justified the exclusion of women from trials and produced downstream effects.[16] Pharmaceutical companies could not say with certainty that a drug would not be dangerous for a woman of childbearing potential or in pregnancy. The lack of inclusion meant very little was known about how drugs might impact women differently than men.

## EXPERIMENTAL TREATMENTS FOR WOMEN

By the late 1980s, scientists sought to find treatments for AIDS. With death rates soaring among those infected with the virus, time was of the essence. But for activists, scientists were not moving fast enough. The AIDS Coalition to Unleash Power (ACT UP) began a series of demonstrations that would make it famous: "die-ins," protests, and arrests at administrative agencies. Activists disrupted conferences and demanded meetings with leading agency heads and scientists.[17]

Partly in response to this pressure, the National Institute of Allergy and Infectious Diseases (NIAID) created the AIDS Clinical Trials Group (ACTG) in 1986.[18] Located within the NIAID headed by Anthony Fauci, the ACTG would focus its attention on AIDS research and treatment. Despite this major step, the new group did not escape the scrutiny and critique of AIDS activists. They felt drug trials being conducted by the ACTG were too slow. Even worse, the trials contained placebo groups. This meant that some portion of the trial participants living with AIDS were receiving "sugar pills" with no possibility of benefiting from participating in the drug trial. AIDS activists felt that this turned desperate patients into guinea pigs. AIDS activists demanded that there be no placebos in AIDS-related clinical trials. Including people in AIDS clinical trials was a way to give some treatment, any treatment, even experimentally, to people who were dying.

By 1987, the FDA approved AZT to treat HIV. Despite the celebration of AZT, new problems emerged: The drug was hard to tolerate. And for feminists, another issue arose: It was necessary to get women enrolled in clinical trials so that they could access experimental medications. Women were being excluded because of the 1977 guidance, despite the exception that allowed for enrolling women in clinical trials if they faced life-threatening illnesses.[19]

The broader feminist women's health movement and feminist AIDS activists knew that to get women access to treatment they also had to demand their inclusion in clinical trials.[20] Shifts in the law laid new groundwork for this feminist fight for reforming clinical trials. Though 1973 marked a major shift in the idea of bodily autonomy for women with *Roe v. Wade* decriminalizing abortion, cases in the following decades challenged, and often won, a right to continued access to abortion and birth control. Implicitly and explicitly, these cases reinforced the idea that women ought to be able to make their own reproductive choices.

Law was not the only field experiencing a shift in understanding and thinking about the role of women in society. Sex and gender had an increasingly centered role in the field of public health.[21] At least since the 1980s, critical strands of epidemiology gave rise to the new field of feminist epidemiology. Leading epidemiologist Nancy Krieger and public health expert and activist Glen Margo, for example, pushed for the need to focus on women in the AIDS response.[22] Feminists were not alone in raising questions about identity in clinical trials.

Racial justice advocates and public health scholars (many of whom were also feminists) were raising questions about the use and role of race and racial categories in scientific and public health research. This debate was contested and complicated: Biomedical research often (though not always) cemented ideas of sex and racial difference. At the same time, social scientists and public health practitioners often leaned into the idea that race is socially constructed and that racial disparities in health ought not to be conflated with biological race differences.

The FDA was paying attention to the new debates on identity in scientific research.[23] By the mid 1980s, the presence of AIDS and the activists outside its doors motivated the FDA to understand if and how women were excluded from clinical trials and the impact this was having on health outcomes. The FDA began to investigate the impact of its 1977 guidance. In 1983 and 1988, the FDA conducted investigations into clinical trial practice. Its research reinforced what feminists had been arguing. There were significant disparities in the enrollment of women in some categories of disease studies, making it hard to unpack the thorny relationship between sex and pharmaceuticals.

A broad coalition of ACT UP members joined feminists in decrying the lack of inclusion of women in clinical trials.[24] A 1988 ACT UP booklet titled *FDA Action Handbook* illustrates the issues activists were concerned about. Prominent ACT UP advocates Jim Eigo, Mark Harrington, Stephen Spinella, and Margaret McCarthy criticized the FDA for its exclusion of women:

> For years, women have been systematically excluded from almost all drug trials … The reason given for excluding women from drug trials is usually that the studies on the effects of the drug on a fetus have not been done. Researchers will argue that you can't trust women not to get pregnant. Researchers sometimes only allow women into trials, including AIDS trials, only if they agree to be sterilized. Some researchers may allow women into trials if they show them that they are using birth control and have repeated negative pregnancy tests.
>
> Researchers have a "moral" problem with allowing women into studies if a fetus may be harmed. But they do not have a problem with any birth defects that may be caused if a man in a study is sexually active, causing the birth of a child with birth defects.[25]

The booklet calls out the FDA for its lack of inclusion of women and others who were being excluded, such as people of color and intravenous drug users.

> The FDA has exacerbated this by discouraging researchers from including women in trials and by approving drugs that have only been tried in white, middle-class, educated urban men for years and years. The FDA has the power to make regulations to require that trials include women, people of color, IV drug users, etc. If the FDA stated that they would no longer accept data that was not representative of the population with the disease, then drug manufacturers would have to do what they said.[26]

According to advocates, the need for clinical trial access was partly driven by lack of ability to pay for access to AZT.

> Even if they had a private doctor, the one drug which has been approved for treatment through prescription is AZT, which costs $8000–10,000 per year, more money than 50% of the women in the United States earn per year if they are in the paid labor force. For these reasons, for women in particular, participating in a clinical drug trial will be their only access to traditional medical treatment for AIDS. Yet women are hardly represented in government-sponsored drug trials which are being conducted.[27]

Informal barriers also blocked access to clinical trials, according to advocates. Women, for example, often had to pay for any preliminary exams to qualify for the trial, or a lack of support services, including childcare, made it so that women couldn't attend the trial.[28] Women did not know about trials as activists noted that most were not advertised in low-income neighborhoods.

To AIDS activists, these exclusions were murderous: "By not making participation in drug trials an option for women, either through intended exclusion or de-facto exclusion, the FDA, government-sponsored ACTGs, local governments and health care institutions and officials, are actively responsible for women's deaths."[29]

Agitation on the question of clinical trials and AIDs had also reached the national stage. In January of 1988, the *New York Times* Science Section declared in a headline that "AIDS Research on New Drugs Bypasses Addicts and Women." The article describes how "findings on homosexual men may not apply to other groups" leaving open questions as to whether these life-extending drugs will benefit "drug users, nonwhite, and women."[30]

In response to its internal research and increasing public pressure, the FDA issued a new guideline in July 1988 that called for researchers to provide drug safety and efficacy data by gender, age, and race.[31] Together, the FDA and the General Accountability Office focused inwards on the agency called for taking up the issue of sex and gender in drug trials.[32]

As the agency evaluation continued, advocates pressed for further action. Feminist activists of the ACT UP Women's Issues Committee wanted a Women's Health Committee of the ACTG and made these demands in letters to Dan Hoth, Director of the Division of AIDS at the National Institutes of Health (NIH), and Anthony Fauci, Director of the NIAID. In keeping with the ACT UP activist model, they also disrupted scientific conferences with banners that said: "NIAID: Form a Women's Committee Now."

Activists also targeted researchers directly. For one action, organizers attended a meeting for a drug called foscarnet, a new antiviral being developed for the treatment of HIV. During the meeting, advocates managed to insert a slide into the projector to broadcast a message: "This drug is not for IDUs [injecting drug users], women, people of color, or poor people."[33] At another event, ACT UP advocates made fortune cookies and placed them on the tables for the coffee break. Upon opening them, researchers were met with ACT UP slogans: "Congratulations, your research has not saved the life of one PWA [person with AIDS]"; "It's 1991. Is there a gynecologist on your team?"; and "Can you say Vagina?" The fortunes even reminded researchers that "large randomized trials will never tell us anything about women."[34]

In a book published by activists on women and AIDS, leaders in ACT UP Maxine Wolfe and Iris Long, key players in the fight to change the CDC definition described in Chapters 1 and 2, wrote an essay, "Through the Eye of a Needle: Women's Access to Drug Treatments through Clinical Trials." Their chapter describes an epidemic among women who are Black and Latina, often use drugs, are often likely to be poor, have no medical coverage, and must rely on public services for health. Their inability to access medications through the formal or underground market grounded their argument: "For these reasons, women's participation in a clinical drug trial will be their only access to traditional medical treatment for AIDS."[35]

Though this chapter focuses on the FDA, AIDS advocates also frequently targeted the NIH, the agency responsible for funding research on public health issues. For feminists, actions at the NIH and FDA were deeply related. They both were meant to push scientists to understand that the epidemic was not only impacting women but that the lack of knowledge about women's bodies and the lack of inclusion in clinical trials were leading women to be excluded from the AIDS treatment response.[36] During one of the most famous ACT UP protests in 1990, ACT UP NY/ACT UP DC lesbian and gay affinity group stormed the NIH and Dan Hoth's office. Activists raised signs that said "NIH, You Can't Hide, We Charge You With Genocide." Speaking at the protest, Phyllis Sharpe, a prominent Black feminist AIDS activist told the *Los Angeles Times* that the NIH does not "want to save me or my child." The protest resulted in the arrest of sixty people.

As activists pushed outside the agencies, within government change was also afoot. There was a growing concern that "a failure to include sufficiently diverse populations could erroneously lead to treatment protocols skewed toward a norm of middle-aged, white males."[37] Leadership in Congress and in the agencies mobilized to push for better research and funding on women's health. With the George W. Bush administration, David Kessler became head of the FDA in 1990. And Bernadine Healy became the first woman to head the NIH in 1991. Both Kessler and Healy were interested in raising awareness about issues of women's health. The NIH had joined the call to improve women's involvement in clinical trial research and Healy would launch the first NIH Women's Health Initiative. Kessler hired Ruth Merkatz to become the first director of the FDA's Office of Women's Health. Others, like Congresswoman Barbara Mikulski, a Democrat from Maryland, led the charge from within Congress proposing laws to ensure clinical trial inclusion and launching congressional and public debate and discussion on the topic.[38] Merkatz would later credit AIDS activists who she attributed as pushing forward the agenda to include women in clinical trials noting that the push came from feminist advocates.[39]

In 1992, the Government Accountability Office (GAO) released its report on women's health. Focusing on new drug approvals between 1988 and 1991, the GAO report found that – despite the change in the guidelines – only 50 percent of these trials were pursuing an analysis of the drug based on sex.[40] The report highlights the low enrollment of women in many clinical trials and the rationale being the FDA's own policy precluding women of childbearing potential from participating in Phase I and early Phase II trials. The report also provides evidence that gender differences impact drug usage and effects, with several examples, including drugs for hypertension and anesthesia.[41] These differences are attributed to differences in women's size and body fat, and the presence of naturally occurring and ingested hormones.[42] The report was an important step forward in the agency's acknowledgment of the importance of studying sex and gender in the context of drug trials.

## EXPERIMENTING WITH PREGNANCY: ACTG 076

As advocacy and internal investigations continued at the FDA, by the early 1990s, a new set of concerns had emerged around the issue of pregnant women who would give birth to children with HIV. The issue of infants and children with AIDS had become one that could engender public attention and sympathy in a way in which prior rhetorical strategies on AIDS could not. Headlines featured the faces of infants dying of AIDS around the world. Infants known as Boarder Babies were often left to the care of hospitals, some living for years among patients in unstable housing. Compelling accounts appeared in national newspapers about the uncertain future for children with HIV and their parents.[43]

At the time, an infant born to a woman with HIV had a 30 percent chance of having HIV and a very high chance of dying within a few years of being born. Several pathways for HIV transmission from mother to child had been identified. HIV might travel through the placenta; it could be transmitted during birth via exposure from blood and vaginal secretions or through breast milk and breastfeeding. Transmission from mother to infant could occur during pregnancy and early in childbirth.[44] The infants who contracted HIV before treatment was available most often succumbed to the virus.

By 1991, scientists were beginning to consider the possibility that providing antiretroviral drugs to pregnant women could help stop transmission to the child. However, understanding how to save infants required enrolling pregnant women in clinical trials.

This frustrated feminists who had been fighting to include HIV-positive women in clinical trials: Were women not worth studying for the sake of studying women? Why were women only a point of intervention when it came to pregnancy? Even while feminists had held onto the idea of choice and autonomy as the cornerstone of women's participation in clinical trials, they were suspicious of the government's sudden interest in pregnant women.

Researchers charged ahead: Could there be a drug that prevented mother-to-child transmission? In 1991, a new study was launched: the AIDS Clinical Trial Group 076 (ACTG 076). The name represented its status as the 76th trial performed by the ACTG. The trial enrolled 180 women who were given AZT and 183 who were given a placebo.

The women who participated met several criteria: They had low T-Cell counts, were only experiencing mild symptoms, and had never taken AZT before.[45] The medication was given to women during pregnancy and then again during labor.[46]

Advocates were concerned about several dimensions of ACTG 076. Drawing on interviews with advocates from the time period, scholar and activist Sarah Schulman outlined some of the primary concerns of feminist AIDS advocates. First was the idea that the trial design itself was flawed. If the only available medication to potentially treat mother-to-child transmission of HIV was being tested, was there a need for a control group? Feminist advocates did not think so – all women in the study should have the opportunity to potentially benefit from the drug.[47] Second, because these trials, unlike many of the others, were being conducted in hospitals with a greater representation of poor women and women of color, the denial of a life-saving treatment raised questions of unethical testing on racial minorities. This idea was echoed in the media. A *Newsday* article from this period quotes Dr. Carol Levine, Executive Director of the New York City Commission on AIDS: "People ought to be very clear about what they are doing here … I think it's very troubling since the majority of these women and children are members of poor minorities." Levine goes on to note that there are consent issues in a trial that is "unprecedented" given that AZT, known for its inability to be tolerated due to high toxicity, could be given to "healthy fetuses and newborns."[48] In other words, pressure to take the experimental medication to save one's child would undermine the ability of a woman to meaningfully consent.

Finally, and perhaps above all else, was the idea that women were being used for the sake of the potential life of the child,[49] but they were not being given adequate attention in clinical trials as patients themselves.

Complicating things further, the ACTG trial generated tensions within ACT UP and between activists and scientists.[50] Feminists who raised concerns, perceived to be HIV-negative and white, sought to stop the trial and distrusted community engagement mechanisms that had been set up by NIAID that would allow experimentation on pregnant women to continue when the experiments were only for the sake of the fetus.[51]

While some in ACT UP wanted to stop the trial, others felt that the trial should continue forward.[52] Activist and scholarly accounts suggest that these tensions came to a head at a meeting of the ACTG in which community members were able to ask questions.[53] Here, women in ACT UP, primarily white women, protested the research study. This seemed to upset one physician in particular, a member of the ACTG, who felt that this was an opportunity for Black women to get access to medication.[54] Some of the men of ACT UP also felt that the protest stepped on the feet of the activists in ACT UP who had developed expertise in clinical trials.[55] Despite protest and internal activist debate the ACTG 076 trial continued.[56]

## THE CITIZEN'S PETITION AND A NEW RULE: LET WOMEN CHOOSE

Like in previous moments, legal advocacy comprised a core piece of the advocacy around altering the study and acknowledgment of women and AIDS by scientists. In 1992, the year the GAO released its report, three lawyers, Terry McGovern from the HIV Law Project, Martha Davis from the National Organization of Women (NOW) Legal Defense Fund, and Alma Gomez from the American Civil Liberties Union's AIDS project, utilized a mechanism at the FDA that allows citizens to petition the agency. As noted in Chapters 1 and 2, McGovern's legal advocacy was central to the CDC changing the AIDS definition to be more inclusive of gynecological conditions associated with AIDS with the result of more diagnoses for women (at this time, most AIDS diagnoses were based on symptoms due to a lack of availability of tests). Her advocacy had now taken her in a new direction. Identifying women as having HIV meant that they needed treatment. The three lawyers wrote a citizen's petition critiquing the FDA for not having gone far enough to ensure women were participating in clinical trials. They wrote it not only as representatives of their organizations but also for the ACT UP Women's FDA Working Group and for AIDS Counseling and Education for Women in Transition from Correctional Facilities (ACE OUT). The citizen's petition sought to ensure that women would be enrolled in clinical trials.

Their target was the 1977 guidance excluding women of childbearing potential from clinical trials. The 1977 guidance was having a negative impact on AIDS care. The petition noted that as of January 1992, "women's enrollment in the ACTG studies reached 1,151, including 154 pregnant women. Men's enrollment for the same period numbered 13,628."

Now self-made experts in clinical trials,[57] the lawyers and advocates made a range of arguments and recommendations regarding how and why women should be included in drug research. The petition reflects a set of legal arguments that were gaining momentum at the time in a range of cases on abortion and pregnancy: that women ought to have full bodily autonomy and choice. Here, the petition reflects the idea that women should be able to choose their own risks as they navigate life-and-death situations. It made a strong and clear appeal to the FDA: that women ought to be included in clinical trials – even at the earliest stages.

The authors of the citizen's petition sought to allow women to use experimental drugs. This would require allowing women to determine their own risk-tolerance while ensuring oversight. They offered possibilities on how to ensure that decision-making both protected choice and autonomy while ensuring safety. They argued, for example, for the need for animal reproduction studies to be completed alongside Phase I testing of a drug. Animal reproduction studies could help establish whether there was a threat of reproductive harm caused by the drug. Based on the outcomes of animal reproduction studies and Phase I trials, women could be best informed about the possible risks of participating in a clinical trial. Where reproduction studies demonstrate significant harm to the fetus, and there is no life-threatening illness at stake, drug sponsors and investigators can require that pregnant women be included with full and informed consent. Feminists advocated for a more robust informed consent that would include the long- and short-term and/or potential risks but would ultimately leave the decision on whether or how to participate to women.[58]

Equality arguments also feature prominently in the citizen's petition. Men were able to participate in clinical trials regardless of the possibility of intergenerational harm while women were excluded. Feminists sought that male and female participants be treated identically with regard to access to trials. In addition to including women in the trials, this would mean assuming that men, too, could play a role in transmitting potential issues – dislodging the focus on women.

Drawing on legal frameworks, the citizen's petition states that the 1977 guidance fails to meet the two-part test for equal protection. It discriminates against women and, therefore, can only be sustained if the party seeking to uphold the policy shows by "exceedingly persuasive justification" that the classification serves "important governmental objectives and that the discriminatory means employed are substantially related to the achievement of those objectives."[59] The authors note that even if one assumed that fetal protection is an important governmental objective, the exclusion of women is not substantially related to that objective because it is overbroad and underinclusive. It supports the exclusion of all women of childbearing potential, and there is no comparable guideline for men.

The petition tapped into the line of constitutional changes that enabled this argument, including two cases decided by the Supreme Court the year prior: *United Automobile Workers v. Johnson Controls* and *Casey v. Planned Parenthood.* In *United Auto Workers*, an employer had barred women from working in an area of a plant where their lead exposure would have caused possible fetal harm. To work in this location, women would have to show proof of sterilization. The Supreme Court held that this proof of sterilization was facially discriminatory because it did not apply to men as well as women.

Despite the contextual differences – *United Auto Workers* is about work, not clinical trials – the case was important in emphasizing the evolving set of ideas around the risks women ought to be able to take with their reproductive choices. This idea of bodily autonomy was bolstered by a decision that came out only months before the petition was filed: *Casey v. Planned Parenthood.* The decision, known for its reworking of legal standards in the abortion context, was deployed by the authors of the citizen's petition to make the point that the court had spoken about the idea of privacy and autonomy. Taken together, these cases helped the feminist authors make a controversial point: that women ought to be able to choose their own risks, even when pregnancy and a potential fetus are at stake. Pushing back against the paternalism of the state, the petition authors argued that privacy and autonomy outweigh "any generalized governmental interest in avoiding fetal toxicity." The petition argued that the "exclusion which extends to women with life-threatening diseases or who are seeking treatment places an undue burden on these women's exercise of reproductive choice." (Though there were exceptions to life-threatening illnesses when it came to women's participation in clinical trials, advocates pointed out that this was being ignored in the context of AIDS clinical trials.)

These themes also resonated broadly with a shift brought about at the FDA through ACT UP activism. Looking back on this moment,

Lewis Grossman, in his book *Choose Your Medicine*, notes that this period would come to fundamentally shift the inner workings of the FDA – allowing drugs to be used by patients earlier in the clinical trials process – a shift that aligned with the deregulatory tendencies of the Reagan administration.[60] It was a convergence of interests between progressive advocates for HIV treatment and the conservatives concerned with deregulation. Feminists, too, found a place inside this logic. Their fight for autonomy and choice was a part of the bigger movement that was changing how we should understand women's risk-taking during pregnancy in law and in the regulation of clinical trials.[61]

## NEW GUIDANCE FROM THE FDA

Ruth Merkatz came under specific pressure. In one instance, she heard a noise outside of her office and women's AIDS activists were marching for women's inclusion in clinical trials. They chanted "Get the facts, Ruth Merkatz." At another event, feminist activists threw toilet paper at Merkatz while she spoke at a podium.[62] She was sympathetic to their concerns seeking to root the agency shifts in the register of science while aware of the shifting sensibility that women ought to be able to choose to take risks, evidenced by the Supreme Court.[63] She was working within the agency to transform the guidelines on clinical trials.

Growing pressure on the agency, alongside the FDA's own internal investigations and support for transformation, resulted in new guidance. In July 1993, the agency published the Guideline for the Study and Evaluation of Gender Differences in the Clinical Evaluation of Drugs.

The new guidance acknowledged that it had been difficult to get early accumulation of research on women in the context of drug use because women were largely excluded from Phase I trials.[64] Mirroring feminist claims, the language contextualizing the new guidance states that "the early exclusion may have perpetuated, in a subtle way, a view of the male as the primary focus of medicine and drug development, with women considered secondarily."

The new 1993 (draft) guideline reflected the arguments in the citizen's petition and the broader cultural shifts toward women's autonomy and decision-making. As proof of this cultural shift, the 1993 guidance cited the Supreme Court's contemporaneous opinion in *United Automobile Workers v. Johnson Controls*, raised initially in the citizen's petition. Speaking directly to the issue of pregnant women in drug trials and comparing it to that of decision-making around employment, the supplementary material to the FDA guidance notes that:

> While the purposes of clinical trials to develop safe and effective drugs are manifestly different from the purposes of private employment, FDA takes serious note of the Court's position on the women's right to participate in decisions about fetal risk and believes it is appropriate to consider the Court's opinion in development policy on the inclusion of women in clinical trials.[65]

For the FDA, updating the guidance would mean modernizing the clinical trial guidelines to match the idea that women ought to be able to take risks during pregnancy.

The guidance, however, stops short of requiring drug companies to include women of childbearing potential. Instead, it articulates that the FDA expects a "careful characterization of drug effects by gender." By this, the agency wants gender-disaggregated data on the pharmacokinetic differences (differences in the way a drug is "absorbed, excreted, metabolized, or distributed) as well as pharmacodynamic differences ("differences in the pharmacologic or clinical response to a given concentration of the drug in blood or other tissue") by sex.

At the same time that the proposed guideline was released, Ruth Merkatz published an article in the *New England Journal of Medicine* arguing that gender matters in research. Clearly supporting the feminist arguments surrounding the expansion of the FDA effort to include women, Merkatz noted that "responses to drugs are influenced by many factors, including age, sex, ethnic background, metabolic phenotype, body-fat content and distribution, and body size."[66] She states that if these differences are recognized and adjusted for "in the dose or dose interval, choice of drug, monitoring procedures, or other aspects of drug administration [this] can improve outcomes for patients."[67] According to Merkatz, because of the GAO report, the FDA would now review all new drug applications to make sure they appropriately analyze for sex. "If such analyses are lacking, the FDA will call for their submission and may consider refusing to initiate review of the application if sex-specific analyses are not provided within a reasonable period."[68] Like the rule, she stops short of asserting that women should always be required in relevant clinical trials.[69]

Merkatz also acknowledged the alchemy between law and science that produced the new guidance. The Supreme Court's decision *United Automobile Workers v. Johnson Controls* was "very much a factor in convincing everyone that … the restriction at FDA needed to be reconsidered." Merkatz stated that "Although the purposes of clinical trials are manifestly different from the purposes of employment, the court's emphasis on the woman's right to participate in decisions about fetal risk underscored the principles of autonomy and informed consent."[70]

Activists did not believe the FDA had gone far enough in its new guidance. On October 18, 1993, Terry McGovern and Martha Jones of the HIV Law Project and Martha Davis of the NOW wrote a memo critiquing the draft guidance. In their critique, McGovern, Jones, and Davis argued that the guidance should mandate the inclusion of women in clinical trials and noted that the guidance does not eliminate gender-based restrictions on accessing clinical trials (or require analysis of drug responses in light of potential gender differences). They stated their complaint:[71]

> The closest the FDA comes to requiring that women be included in clinical trials is in a vague passage which states that "in some cases, there may be a basis for requiring participation of women in early studies." The disease under study must be "serious and affect women," and "especially when a promised drug for the disease is being developed and made rapidly under the FDA's accelerated approval or early access procedures, a case can be made for requiring that women participate in clinical trials at the early stages." The 1993 Guideline does not define these provisions and it does not commit the FDA to monitoring the IND [Investigational New Drug Application] process to ensure that trials meeting the vague criteria enumerated will include women.[72]

Alongside their frustration with what they felt was weak language in the guidance document, feminist advocates were also concerned that some of their points were simply ignored by the FDA. In their response to the revised guidance, they once again noted that animal reproduction studies were key to showing whether a drug could cause fetal abnormalities or had potential long-term reproductive effects. They argued that if the FDA mandated the animal reproduction studies, it would enable the agency to determine whether persons of "child-producing" potential who wish to participate in a clinical trial were at risk of experiencing reproductive effects.[73] But, as the advocates point out, the FDA does not require these animal studies often due to worries of delaying the actual clinical trials from the beginning. For feminist advocates, a delay, which they estimated to be between 41 and 136 weeks, was worth it for the possibility of safely enrolling women.

Second, feminist advocates were frustrated that any generational male-mediated effects of drugs were ignored. They argued that women are either excluded from the study or asked to use contraception and be tested for pregnancy, but the FDA "does not recommend restricting men of child-producing capacity in the same manner" even though men included in studies lack the knowledge about risks to childbearing.[74]

For feminists, the draft 1993 guidance was not an adequate response to the citizen's petition.[75] The clear message from advocates was that the agency can force drug companies to include women and ensure women's autonomy through informed consent.[76] Where uncertainty persists in drug development, it should be up to the woman to decide whether or not to participate.

As they awaited a response, a National Task Force on AIDS Drug Development convened in November 1993 to expedite the search for new therapies against AIDS and HIV. One goal was identifying and removing any barriers or obstacles to developing effective treatments. Terry McGovern, now a member of the National Task Force on AIDS Drug Development given her advocacy in this space, was tasked with making recommendations to Donna Shalala, the secretary of health and human services. In keeping with her prior advocacy, McGovern advocated that the Department of Health and Human Services remove specific barriers to the participation of women of childbearing potential in clinical trials.[77]

As McGovern pushed the agency from within for greater inclusion, activism outside of the agency also continued. In September 1994, for example the national ACT UP Women's Caucus met with Merkatz and Theresa Toigo, the deputy director of the Office of AIDS and Special Health Issues. In the meeting, members of the ACT UP Women's Caucus, including Mary Lucey, expressed concerns about the lack of inclusion of women living with HIV in administrative processes at the FDA and in clinical trials.

In response to the concerns raised at the meeting, the FDA sent a letter to Mary Lucey on October 12, 1994. The letter defended the 1993 guidance, stating that it makes clear that "a gender analysis is expected in new drug applications and identifies specific pharmacokinetic issues in women that should be addressed, including effects of the menstrual cycle, effects of exogenous hormonal therapy including oral contraceptives, and the effects of the drug on the pharmacokinetics of oral contraceptives."

Yet, even as the FDA restated its commitment to the inclusion of women in clinical trial research, the agency washed its hands of responsibility when it came to the lack of inclusion of women living with HIV in relevant drug trials – arguing that it wasn't the FDA's fault there was always an exception for life-threatening illnesses.[78]

Two weeks later, on October 27, 1994, McGovern, Davis, and Gomez received a formal response from the FDA to their citizen's petition filed in December 1992. The 1992 petition predated the interim 1993 guidance, and the FDA treated the guidance as a partial response to the complaints lodged by McGovern, Davis, and Gomez.

In the formal FDA response to the citizen's petition, authored by Interim Deputy Commissioner for Operations Linda Suydam, the agency recognized that the 1977 guidance looks "outdated"; ideas in it appear "rigid and paternalistic."[79] This is particularly true, the response notes, given the transformations in Supreme Court jurisprudence. Noting that it is not a case about clinical trials, Suydam acknowledges that the FDA still "took particular note of the Supreme Court's position as articulated in *United Automobile v. Johnson Controls* on a woman's right to participate in decisions about fetal risk."

Though Suydam stated in her response that the FDA granted the petition in part by publishing a new guideline,[80] in reality, the updated guidance failed to address many of the concerns raised by the team of feminist lawyers.

Keeping with prior assertions by the agency, Suydam, for example, disclaimed FDA responsibility for the lack of enrollment of women in clinical trials, stating that the agency never "recommended gender-based restrictions in clinical trials of drugs intended to treat life-threatening illnesses."[81] Second, she stated that where the studies do have barriers to participation, this is because study populations must be clearly delineated: "Thus, the desire to eliminate gender-based restrictions needs to be balanced against the need to answer specific scientific questions." But, again, she noted that the agency had never said there should be an exclusion on the basis of gender from any trial in patients with immediate life-threatening diseases.[82]

Suydam pointed to the fact that researchers may be worried about tort liability. Sponsors, she said, may be "unwilling to administer the drug to women of childbearing potential without multiple protections against potential fetal exposure." She asserted that the FDA would scrutinize any exclusions. The FDA would not, however, interfere in questions of contraception, she wrote. Decisions about contraception should be made on an individual basis by the woman and the study physician or other counselors.[83]

But what about during pregnancy? McGovern, Davis, and Gomez had argued that the FDA should prohibit the exclusion of pregnant women if the pregnant women if the pregnant women have given full informed consent to participate in drug trials. The FDA resisted this proposal. Suydam noted that early trials often do not offer any therapeutic benefit and that the "deliberate exposure of a fetus to an experimental drug raises serious ethical questions." The FDA further argued that animal toxicity studies would reveal potential harms.[84] But, again, the FDA noted that it does not recommend against access to clinical trials in the context of life-threatening emergencies.[85]

Feminist advocates inside ACT UP also resisted the new guidelines. A document produced by the ACT UP Women's Caucus criticized the agency for stopping short of requiring inclusion. Under the banner "Say It: Women Get AIDS," it criticized the guidelines for falling short of the goal of including women and demanded "guidelines that require inclusion of women on all levels of clinical AIDS drug trials." The flyer considers various actions including an encampment and street theatre in front of the federal agency.

In September 1994, advocates made good on their promise, issuing flyers produced by members of ACT UP. The flyers, some printed on pink and blue paper, demanded a "public trial" and a "public spanking" and called to "convict the FDA." The goal was to "demand the inclusion of women in all clinical trials." Organizers also met with David Kessler, head of the FDA, to make presentations about the issue of women and clinical trials and ensure that there be increased meetings with women living with HIV.[86]

A year after the guidance was issued, the ACTG 076 trial showed that AZT could virtually stop the transmission of HIV from mother to child.[87] The study was so successful that researchers ended the trial so that there would no longer be a control group and all enrolled could access the medications. There was a new standard of care that would decrease the number of infants born with HIV.

Feminists stopped their protests of ACTG 076, ceding to the reality that the drug was having a positive impact. But their suspicions of the potential harms of drugs developed for the fetus weren't misplaced nor were their fears that pregnant women might bear the brunt of potentially coercive public health policies to better infant outcomes. These critiques would shape the discourse of feminist activism around pregnancy and AIDS in the decades to come.

## THE STRUGGLE CONTINUES: STILL NO FDA MANDATE TO INCLUDE WOMEN IN CLINICAL TRIALS

At the heart of the feminist fight to remake knowledge about women is a redistributive goal: better healthcare. The deaths of women living with HIV made this fight urgent. Feminists sought to alter the regulatory environment around clinical trial research with the specific goal of allowing women to access to drug trials and medications that would serve women better. Their fight embodied the feminist ideals of the 1990s – autonomy and choice – in this case, enabling women to take risks necessary to best treat their own health conditions.[88] The 1993 guidance produced a shift in the inclusion of women in clinical trials, but the lack of a mandate, and the ongoing exclusion of women from trials, motivates activism still today.[89]

4

# SEX BARGAINS

By 1994, cases of HIV among women were skyrocketing. In the United States HIV was now the second leading cause of death among Black women and the fourth leading cause of death among women between the ages of twenty-five and forty-four. Globally, women and girls were declared the fastest-growing group with HIV.

This recognition was a feminist victory. The campaigns waged against public health institutions, described in Chapters 1 and 2, had successfully forced epidemiologists and legal actors to acknowledge that women, too, were at risk for HIV. But questions remained: *Why* were women contracting HIV? And now that the data included women, why was it the case that in some regions, particularly sub-Saharan Africa, women had HIV in *greater* numbers than men? This latter question raised a new concern that fundamentally challenged the dated belief that there would be no epidemic amongst women: Were heterosexual women *more* vulnerable to contracting HIV than other risk groups?

As these questions circulated, many experts, including public health experts and advocates, attempted to explain how the disease was spreading and, in turn, regulate the epidemic.[1] This required asking: What role should the law play in managing the risk of contracting HIV?

The answers to these two sets of questions – why were women vulnerable and what is the role of law – would ultimately have enormous consequences for how public health institutions would design and implement interventions to stop the spread of HIV.

In this chapter, I document the rise of a new logic about law, risk, and transmission in heterosexual relationships that I call the sex bargain. The sex bargain stems from the idea that sex results from a negotiation between two people. I will show how the sex bargain became the primary explanation for thinking about a heterosexual individual's risk of contracting HIV. Two ideological camps, law and economics, and feminist theory, intellectually tussled and, eventually, converged on the idea of the sex bargain.

This convergence had enormous consequences for responding to the epidemic: It narrowed the vision of addressing AIDS away from the social and structural determinants of health toward a focus on individuals. The idea that the sex bargain offered the primary way to intervene in the AIDS epidemic was reinforced through the interaction of advocacy, law, and science. As advocates relied on law to identify rights claims, lawyers inspired epidemiologists to begin asking questions. In turn, the results of these epidemiological findings strengthened the legal and advocacy claims.

One particularly influential strand of thinking about sex bargains came from law and economics. Richard Posner and Tomas Philipson, for example, wrote in 1992 that we should treat "risky sexual behavior as a market in which trading takes place under condition of uncertainty about quality."[2] This core concept would go on to provide the foundation for their book published in 1993, *Private Choices and Public Health: The AIDS Epidemic in an Economic Perspective*. Their work inspired epidemiological studies that offered financial incentives to reduce the demand for risky sex and seeded new ways of imagining how to regulate AIDS.

While some, like Posner and Philipson, focused on promoting a law and economics approach to AIDS, a competing set of actors focused on recalibrating rules and risk to benefit women. Feminists, who had long been fighting for a place in the AIDS response, were now necessary. Unlike the epidemiologists, feminists had long been theorizing how and why women were at risk of HIV. Feminist expertise on AIDS not only filled a gap created by the oversight of epidemiologists, but some feminists were now epidemiologists themselves.[3]

A mutual view united many feminists: The subordination of women by men was a constant and unchanging universal issue in women's lives.[4] While sexual domination may shift in its presentation, it was universal, consistent, cognizable, and recognizable at the time of the sex bargain. Contrary to the law and economics view of sex, according to feminists, given the power imbalance between women and men, and reality of physical and emotional abuse, women are often unable to protect themselves from contracting HIV. Even as feminist rejected the idea of a fair bargain, they largely accepted the idea that it was important to focus on the moment of negotiation around sex. It was at this juncture that feminists had begun to make key interventions on ideas of consent and male accountability. In other words, they converged with law and economics scholars on the idea that the moment of the sex bargain was an important site of intervention.

Why does the centering of a sex bargain model by feminists and law and economics scholars matter? I argue that the focus on the sex bargain had the powerful effect of individualizing responsibility for contracting HIV. In doing so, it served as a distraction from the broader legal, economic, social, and political dimensions of why people were actually at risk for contracting HIV. The idea of the sex bargain helped silence discussions about the social determinants of health and the upstream structural issues like poor housing and education that rendered people unable to address health concerns. Instead, it focused expert attention, including that of lawyers and epidemiologists, on individual behavior. As the idea of the sex bargain took hold in competing theories of law's response to AIDS, it reworked how scholars and advocates conceptualized the response to the epidemic. Advocates carried their ideas into national and international forums. The sex bargain fit neatly into the political moment of the time, which featured a growing discourse on personal responsibility, an increased reliance on crime control, and the continued retraction of the welfare state. It helped further an individualized response to public health crises and silenced feminist ideas that challenged this new common sense of about women and AIDS.

This chapter begins by following the feminist idea percolating outside of the AIDS context that had growing salience in the fight for women's equality: that the crux of women's subordination to men was sexual violence. The chapter traces this idea as it enters the world of HIV, just as legal scholars, including prominent voices in law and economics, and advocates, were debating how to think about the legal architecture of the AIDS response. As the sex bargain idea takes center stage in thinking through heterosexual risk, feminists fight for the notion that sexual subordination makes it impossible for women to bargain equally for sex. And, as epidemiologists begin to study heterosexual transmission, feminist and nonfeminist ideas, especially those of law and economics scholars about sex bargains, are validated through public health inquiry.

## VIOLENCE AND ACCOUNTABILITY

Long before AIDS, feminists began to theorize women's subordination as rooted in sex. Understanding how the idea of sex subordination and an inability to bargain for safer sex became the primary explanatory factor for feminists when it came to HIV transmission requires rewinding the clock to see how sexual violence against women (VAW) became one of the primary concerns of the women's movement by the 1980s and 1990s. While this section does not aim to give a complete history, it lays the groundwork for the later feminist encounter with AIDS and the law and economics movement.

Amid competing strands of feminist thinking, radical feminism began in the 1960s to shape the tenets of feminist organizing in ways that would hold sway for decades to come. Since at least this period, radical feminists argued that gender structures society as much as – or more than – class and race.[5] Feminists argued that a patriarchal worldview structured every aspect of life from care work and employment to reproduction. In some instances, radical feminists argued that to engage with any of these institutions, including the state, was to only further women's oppression.[6]

Of the many issues tackled by radical feminists, one stood out among the rest as the most powerful mobilizing cause: VAW, especially sexual violence.[7] Feminists believed that VAW was the product of patriarchal gender socialization, which results in men being powerful and women being weak. As they set their eyes on a new world with greater equality and less violence, feminists began to promote their worldview in law and society. In her book *In an Abusive State: How Neoliberalism Appropriated the Feminist Movement against Sexual Violence*, Kristin Bumiller describes how feminists developed a series of rhetorical moves to help the issue of VAW gain traction. The most powerful among these rhetorical strategies was the "gender war." In the gender war, men used sexual VAW to retain power in various dimensions of life.[8] Sexual objectification and violence was *the* connective tissue between women beaten and abused in the home and women assaulted on the street.[9] This line of thinking inspired the anti-rape movement, which pushed this metaphor further, arguing that "women and children exist in constant fear of encounters with perpetrators and are subjected to the ubiquitous sadism of sexuality under this regime of domination."[10] As the issue of VAW became institutionalized as a key feminist concern, including by the National Organization of Women in the 1970s, addressing violence rose on the feminist agenda.[11] The powerful image of the battered woman laid the groundwork, according to Bumiller, for the "potential for all women to become victims" and, in turn, the need for the state to intervene. Feminists also sought to make it appear that sexual violence was at the root of social disorder.[12] A huge question began to drive feminist politics on violence: What was the right way to cure this social problem?

As the 1970s progressed, the more radical feminist view – that the state itself was patriarchal and would always reproduce patriarchy – was largely abandoned for a new project: making the state work for women. Central to this project was dismantling what was understood as the public/private divide. The public/private divide was an ideological frame that helped further the notion that the home and violence in the home were outside of the domain of state intervention. For feminists, the public/private divide was an ideological tool that justified refusing to intervene on the issue of domestic violence. Dismantling the public/private divide would require demanding that the state intervene in women's lives, particularly with regard to VAW. While engaging government in the response to VAW took many forms, lawmaking became central to the feminist agenda in the hope that altering the legal landscape on women and gender would revolutionize women's life experiences.[13]

By the 1980s, the anti-domestic-violence movement was in full swing, and with the rise of carceral approaches to addressing social problems, criminal law was centered as a site of feminist engagement on issues of sexual violence and sexual objectification.[14] Their focus was not entirely unjustified; at the time, police did not arrest abusive men, and prosecutors did not take them to court. The widespread push for feminist consciousness-raising on violence issues had primed feminists to be ready to move and take concrete action, and altering policing and prosecutorial practices offered this opportunity. Feminists began a "carceral dance"[15] with police departments, embedding themselves into state governance to ensure that police would no longer ignore domestic violence. With the election of Bill Clinton in 1992, feminists sought to further institutionalize federal funding for efforts to end VAW. In 1994, feminists had a significant win with the Violence Against Women Act (VAWA) as part of the

Violent Crime Control and Law Enforcement Act of 1994.[16] In its location as part of a larger crime control bill, VAWA reflected the turn to punitive law reform in the context of gender-based violence. Most controversially, VAWA encouraged state governments take on certain criminal legal reforms when receiving federal funding. These laws sought to remedy the issue of police officers and prosecutors dropping domestic violence cases. Criminal law now took a central role in ending VAW. Crime control measures could remedy women's victimhood.[17]

The feminist ideas that would come to shape domestic advocacy had an increasing uptake in the global arena as well. By the mid 1980s, VAW had become an issue of international concern. The United States had an oversized influence on how issues of VAW would be understood globally. The US government was already the largest funder on issues of gender, including family planning services, and as time went on, funding began to go explicitly to ending violence. While the US government funding for ending VAW was subject to political pressures based on the party in office, the broad project of ending gender-based violence remained a priority because feminists had successfully aligned themselves with the larger political trends. Importantly, this meant that American feminists – albeit with differing visions of how to end VAW – influenced the design and administration of programs to address the issue of violence. Although AIDS was not on the minds of these early scholars and activists, the idea of *sexual* oppression of women would come to play an essential role in AIDS activism, given that the virus was sexually transmitted.

The pathways that feminists and feminist ideas took as they traveled through global institutions varied. Still, the dominant feminist framing – that women's lives were being structured by violence against them by men – remained intact.[18] Feminist ideas about patriarchy and violence traveled through networks of national women's rights movements, often hand in hand with the broader human rights struggles that connected them. As documented by Sally Engle Merry in her book *Human Rights and Gender Violence: Translating International Law into Local Justice*, while ideas about gender violence took hold and were situated locally – drawing on cultural norms and local vernacular – human rights organizing on women's rights often generalized experiences of VAW.[19] The United Nations Decade on Women began with the First World Conference on Women held in

Mexico City in 1975. The event inspired a global movement of women's rights activists who sought to engage UN mechanisms and galvanized feminist organizing locally and internationally.[20] In the years leading up to the First World Conference on Women feminist organizations came together to share ideas and redesign the laws pertaining to women. The women's rights network Isis International, founded in 1974, and WIN news founded in 1975, each served as a conduit for national women's rights organizing globally. Through this activism, the issue of VAW became increasingly central to the global human rights agenda. The core idea that male subordination of women was a powerful determinant in how women could live their lives became a near-total explanation for the many human rights issues identified by feminists.

As tracked by several scholars,[21] the criminalization of VAW also began to appear in international law and advocacy in the 1980s. This followed the uptick of criminal-law-oriented responses to domestic violence in American feminist organizing. In her book *Agenda Setting, the UN, and NGOs: Gender Violence and Reproductive Rights*, Jutta Joachim argues that criminal law began to take priority internationally when experts became more integral to designing an international law response to the issue of VAW. Social scientists began to demonstrate that VAW was a structural concern, prompting the call to criminalization.[22] Defining the problem as a criminal concern helped to launch a standardized international response to VAW.

## SEX BARGAINING, RISKY SEX, AND VAW IN THE AIDS RESPONSE

By the mid 1990s, a surge in diagnoses of women following the definitional shift described in Chapters 1 and 2 brought AIDS not only into the viewfinder of feminists but also legal scholars who were thinking about how to best use the law to address the HIV epidemic.[23]

Law and economics scholars were prolific on the issue of AIDS. Troubled by the emergent orthodoxy about the response to the epidemic – that the public sector should play a prominent role in the AIDS response – law and economics scholars set out to ensure that economics, or what Richard Posner would call "economic epidemiology," became a part of the larger debate and discussion on how to think through an AIDS response.[24] The view of law and economics scholars suggested that too much public sector intervention (i.e., government intervention) into the AIDS response could be counterproductive. "Articulate, organized high-risk populations (in particular male homosexuals) … and medical and public health professionals … confronting a competing interest group of moral conservatives" result in a non-efficient response to the epidemic, not effective in stopping the spread of HIV, and redistributes resources incorrectly.[25]

In his 1992 book *Sex and Reason*, Richard Posner outlined a way to imagine sex as a rational behavior that economists should study. Posner argues that it is false to think of sex as irrational. Like the desire to curtail hunger – an embodied feeling out of our control that has a rational response – the decision to appease our sexual desires, too, is rational.[26] With the AIDS epidemic taking hold, Posner and his co-author Tomas Philipson, in a later book *Private Choices and Public Health: The AIDS Epidemic in an Economic Perspective*, brought the idea of rational sex to the AIDS response. The book's stated goal was to understand how governments should ideally intervene in the AIDS response. They argued that there is a way to arrive at the optimal regulation of AIDS that allows for the correct number of infections and amount of disease. They acknowledge that people might find the idea of regulating a disease, rather than eliminating it, "repulsive." Yet Posner and Philipson argue that their exploration demonstrates how attempts to reduce HIV transmission to zero may cause more harm than good or expose flaws in legal interventions.

In setting out to accomplish the goal of calibrating the public response to AIDS, Posner and Philipson focus on heterosexual transmission. In law and economics terms, rational, risky sex occurs in a "market in which trading takes place under condition of uncertainty about quality."[27] In turn, "risky sexual trades … are analytically similar to conventional market transactions that take place under uncertainty."[28] Posner and Philipson flatten the playing field between sexual partners: Risky sex is the outcome of a utility calculation, with rational actors making decisions based on the particular supply and demand of risky sex (different supply and demand calculations may come into play if you are gay, or Black, or a prisoner, for example).[29]

The idea of a "voluntary" transaction is important for law and economics scholars. By viewing sexual interactions as voluntary, the epidemic could be managed by ensuring that transmission is curbed by incentivizing people to act differently.[30] In turn, as the title of Posner and Philipson's book suggests, individual choice is emphasized (as well as the related idea of personal responsibility, which flows from the choices one makes).[31] Focusing on the individual and their behavior allows Posner and Philipson to conclude that almost all government interventions, from sex education to voluntary HIV testing, may, at worst, increase transmission of AIDS or, at best, have no effect on spread of the disease.

This is best illustrated with an example. According to Posner and Philipson, a government may choose to increase access to HIV testing.[32] Posner and Philipson set up two scenarios: First, where a person's test results are given to their sexual partner before the next sexual intercourse through partner-observed testing (where the potential sexual partner observes the test being administered), and second, where the person being tested can keep the test results confidential. They predict that in both cases, the governmental intervention will not necessarily decrease rates of HIV infection and may potentially increase them. Why? They argue that HIV testing increases "potentially infective behavior" regardless of whether the person is negative or positive.

According to Posner and Philipson, partner-observed testing could "increase the demand for risky sex and hence the likelihood that the disease will spread," even if one accepts the assumption that a positive person is eliminated from the pool of potentially infective people. This is because if a person who seeks risky sex tests negative, they will continue to seek risky sexual encounters. They will continue to put themself at risk, potentially contracting HIV. If they test positive and stop engaging in risky sex, there is no increase in risky sex, "but there may not be a decrease given that only one person – the potential partner – received the test results." The intervention, therefore, does not necessarily yield the desirable result of decreasing HIV transmission.[33]

In the case of partner unobserved testing (i.e., confidential testing), Posner and Philipson make an additional assumption: People either act as egoists or altruists. This assumption is necessary because it helps us understand why someone would be tested to begin with. The logic proceeds as follows: An egoist thinks little about the consequences of their action on others and is motivated by accessing "the sexual trade."[34] The altruist gets an HIV test to ensure they are not spreading the virus. After testing negative, an altruist will feel free to have risky sex, but the person they are having sex with might be positive, transmitting HIV to the altruist. An altruist will not have sex if they find out they are positive, and this, Posner and Philipson argue, is a disincentive to getting tested to begin with. The altruist will continue to have sex with a larger group of individuals, some negative, thereby transmitting HIV to them. If an egoist were to test positive, it likely would not change their efforts to engage in risky sexual behavior. When asked, an egoist might conceal their own status leading to more transmission of HIV.[35] Following from this, governmental interventions around sex were not making things better and may even increase the transmission of HIV.

The ideas pushed by law and economics scholars – that we should think about sex as the outcome of a voluntary bargain here, and that it is possible to have sex as equals – would become a powerful set of ideas in the AIDS response. It comported with the political moment in which the law and economics scholarship would find its stride and purpose: one in which government intervention into issues of health, education, and welfare was de-emphasized and personal responsibility celebrated.

The notion of an equal trade in sex rubbed feminists the wrong way. That sexual partners could freely negotiate sex contradicted feminist claims that women are often coerced into sex due to their structural subordination related to economic and gender inequality. For dominance feminists, sexual domination, which underpinned the logic of the VAW movement, was a key reason that women were contracting HIV, not personal poor choices. They engaged the language of the sex bargain, but reframed the question of choice as coercion. Lawyers and activists writing on the epidemic were quick to point to the gender and power dynamics that may influence women's vulnerability to contracting HIV. A volume published in 1992 by the American Civil Liberties Union (ACLU), for example, highlighted the way gender was understood to play a role in why women contracted HIV:

> Heterosexually active women approach the issue of negotiating sex practices with a partner in a context that is fundamentally different in two critical ways from the situation of gay men. First, two male partners more often bring equal social power to what is essentially a bargaining situation. By contrast, women as a group lack the same social power as men. Many heterosexual women, for financial or cultural reasons, do not have equal power to negotiate behavior changes in a partner. Second, two male partners who alternate positions in anal or oral intercourse stand at equal risk of becoming infected unless they use condoms. In heterosexual vaginal intercourse, however, women are more likely than men to become infected. Thus, men engaging in heterosexual intercourse are at less risk than their female partners of becoming infected, and have less of a selfish motivation to use condoms.[36]

This characterization of heterosexual sex as often unequal mapped onto the sex-subordination idea of feminism that was gaining ground through the VAW movement, and was central to how feminists would begin to characterize sex between men and women.[37] Notice, also, that in this description of sex offered by the ACLU, while women do not have agency, men have the full capacity to negotiate their sexual interactions with each other and with women. In this feminist frame, women are the only ones who are constrained by financial and cultural circumstances.

Posner, and later Posner and Philipson, were aware of and directly engaged in this feminist critique of sex as an outcome of a fair and equal bargain. Take, for example, how, in *Sex and Reason*, Posner acknowledges the deep influence of feminism in the academy and beyond. In the book, he offers a typology of the field of legal "sexology," writing that, on the one hand, there are legal philosophers who think about how the law "ought to regulate sexual and other morals" and are "overwhelmingly polemical, and highly repetitious," and focused on the right to privacy, speech, and the First Amendment.[38] He notes that these legal sexologists are actually not so interested in sex.

On the other hand, there are the feminists. Posner turns to Catharine MacKinnon and Andrea Dworkin, who he notes are two of the leading feminist voices on sexual violence at the time. By the time Posner wrote *Sex and Reason*, MacKinnon had already achieved national fame as a leading voice in the anti-sexual-violence movement. Pornography was one of her chief targets. MacKinnon and Dworkin declared that pornography promoted the eroticization of domination and worked to have it banned. (In the next chapter, we will see how their specific ideas about pornography ballooned in the AIDS response.) Although Posner dismisses much of what MacKinnon and Dworkin say on sexual violence as "hyperbole," he suggests that MacKinnon and Dworkin might indeed have contributed "nuggets of truth" to the broader debate about the sexual objectification and understanding of the devaluation of women.[39]

What he did not acknowledge in *Sex and Reason* – but what Posner and Philipson later take on explicitly in *Private Choices and Public Health* – was the feminist theory that sexual subordination and gender inequality lead women to be coerced into sexual encounters. In response to this, Posner and Philipson argue that if one takes feminists seriously and views society (or patriarchy in the case of feminism) as shaping the capacity to bargain, the entire logic of a rational bargain comes tumbling down. Rather than coercion, we should see the challenges faced by women as a supply and demand issue.

To make the case that what could be perceived through a feminist lens as coercion in bargaining is an issue of supply and demand, Posner and Philipson use the example of heterosexual relationships and HIV transmission in the Black community. Posner and Philipson argue that Black women are at high risk of contracting HIV because of a supply problem: There are not enough Black men. According to Posner and Philipson, because Black women have fewer options, Black men can demand more risky sex for less compensation to Black women. Or, according to Posner and Philipson, "just by being willing to have a relationship with her."[40]

> Feminists will want to go further and argue that many ostensibly "voluntary" transactions in the sexual market are products of subtle forms of coercion. Our suggestion ... that gender inequality in the black community may be a cause of the greater prevalence of AIDS among black than among white women could be taken as support for the feminist position. However, to argue that the low effective sex ratio among blacks "coerces" women to engage in unprotected sex would be tantamount to regarding all market transactions as coerced, since their terms are determined by (among other things) the relative numbers of suppliers and demanders. In any event it would be a mistake to place too much weight on gender inequality as a fact in the AIDS epidemic; women who contracted the AIDS virus in sexual intercourse account for only 5 percent of new AIDS cases and 4 percent of the cumulative number.[41]

By arguing that gender equality is a supply and demand issue and not a power issue, Posner and Philipson evade the subject of a preexisting distribution of power, money, and resources that alters women's bargaining capacity.

Their quote also highlights that Posner and Philipson were working with data on women and AIDS from before the transformation that occurred following feminist activism to change the AIDS definition. As the passage concludes, they suggest that few women are contracting HIV due to heterosexual sex. Yet, as the numbers did begin to change – mainly because feminists had successfully shifted the focus of scientific institutions toward the epidemic among women, and the understanding of heterosexual risk grew – they argued that this did not undercut their argument that women's bargaining position was the result of a supply and demand problem.

By 1995, in East Africa, for example, heterosexual women comprised a significant portion of detected cases of HIV. In writing about the region in their article "The Microeconomics of the AIDS Epidemic in Africa," they dug in further, stating,

> We argue here that the differences between the course of the disease in the United States and in Africa can be explained by the same mode that we used to explain the behavior of the disease in the United States. Indeed, one part of our analysis – that of the different incidence of the disease in black compared with white women – seems … directly transferable to the African situation.[42]

Again, they argue that the bargaining position of Black women vis-à-vis Black men in the United States is decreased due to the ratio of marriageable Black men to women, suggesting that women have to make a "net transfer" to a Black man to "induce marriage or any other form of long-term sexual relationship." While, in the African context, Philipson and Posner are more willing to acknowledge that "legal disabilities and pervasive discrimination" play a role in bargaining position – a nod toward feminist critiques of women's inequality – they stop short of making the feminist claim that these factors result in coercion.[43]

At odds with their own skepticism about coercion, they prescribe efforts that suggest that they acknowledge that structural issues may play a role in bargaining and suggest that governments ought to make efforts to "lessen the economic inequality between men and women in Africa by reducing the incidence of prostitution and strengthening the ability of women generally to bargain for safe sex."[44]

Scholars and technocrats carried these ideas into institutions. Both feminists and law and economics scholars would see their ideas flourish in the response to AIDS. And in turn, these competing ideas would underpin often conflicting legal and policy positions toward the role of government intervention in the epidemic.

The paths each set of ideas took differed. Posner and Philipson helped launch the field of economic epidemiology. It shifted policy discussions from studying behavior to using incentives to alter people's behavior. Although there are many examples of the domestic and global reach of Posner and Philipson's book on policy, one stands out: the 1994 World Bank report on AIDS titled *Confronting AIDS: Public Priorities in a Global Epidemic*. The World Bank report is pivotal because the lending institution's proposals on the rule of law and legal intervention are taken seriously by countries that have received loans from the bank. In this report, the bank describes how governments might intervene in the AIDS epidemic to overcome the health crisis. The report draws an enormous amount of inspiration from Posner and Philipson. Quoting almost directly from the book jacket of *Private Choices and Public Health*, the World Bank report begins:

> Most things in life entail some risk, yet people willingly take risks when they perceive that the benefits of an action outweigh the costs. For example, drivers speed and pedestrians dart across busy streets, despite the increased risk of injury or death. People start smoking although they know it might lead to lung cancer and heart disease. Sometimes risk enhances pleasure. Mountain climbers scale the Himalayas, their thrill perhaps intensified by the danger they face. All of these decisions reflect individual preferences and an assessment of costs, benefits, and risks. Sex and injected drugs offer very intense if short-lived pleasure. *Do individuals also weigh costs, benefits, and risks when deciding whether and how to engage in these activities? Fortunately for efforts to slow the epidemic, the answer is yes.* A substantial body of economic research, much of it in developing countries, has shown that actual and perceived costs and benefits, some of which can be affected by government policies, significantly influence private decisions about marriage, childbearing, and contraceptive use. It is therefore reasonable to assume that sexual behavior that spreads HIV can also be influenced by public policy. Similarly, studies have shown that under the right conditions drug users change their injecting behavior to reduce the likelihood of being infected with HIV.[45]

Notice the emphasis on individuals who make voluntary and willing choices to protect themselves in an epidemic. This theme, recurrent in the work of law and economics scholars, fits within the broader ideological leaning of the World Bank and the growing perspective that personal responsibility should underpin the way the government intervenes in social programs, from health to housing and beyond.

The core idea taken up by law and economics and transported into public health was that of incentives. Treating sex and other decisions that could impact public health as a rational outcome of a cost–benefit analysis (as described by the World Bank above) meant that behavior change could be incentivized. In other words, with the idea of "economic epidemiology," Posner and Philipson changed the way one could look at public health by not simply focusing on the spread of illness but on the incentives to alter the course of an individual's choice. Applied to AIDS, if Posner and Philipson were correct, incentives should change the cost–benefit calculation that people engaged in around risky sex. This meant a greater focus on individual "risk factors," including the behavior of one's sexual partner, that could be altered through incentives.

Implicit in this is a critique of epidemiology. By studying groups of people to understand population-level health, epidemiology takes attention away from the way individuals make decisions about their health. In turn, there is a failure to recognize how incentives and information shape people's choices, and, in turn, their health. By centering on the rational individual, Philipson and Posner argue that one can treat the decisions made during the AIDS epidemic in the same way as decisions made in any other market context that economists study. They argue that a person who is contemplating sexual intercourse, or sharing a hypodermic needle, takes "optimal measures to adjust to the risk of infection."[46]

Following this logic, a new set of epidemiological experiments were set into motion involving economic incentives, giving people money in exchange for a behavior change. An incentives-based public health approach made sense if the root of most behaviors was rational.[47] The World Bank among other institutions took this approach seriously – interrogating its merits through a series of papers and reports. This mode of study, where populations were divided and studied with regard to incentives, was nascent in this time period, but would take on force with the rise of behavioral economics in the 1980s and 1990s. The core ideas that focused behavior change on incentives and choice would be revolutionary, altering the fields of public health and beyond.[48]

Like law and economics scholars who thought the idea that a sex act is the outcome of rational actors conducting a cost–benefit analysis could be applied universally to explain sex, feminists, too, relied on the narrative of the sex bargain to make a shared claim of women's subordination across race, context, and class. As the idea of the sex bargain took hold, it erased the notion that aspects of sex, marriage, and family might have local cultural dimensions.

Feminists sought to have the sex-subordination frame achieve status in both US and global governance responses to HIV. For feminists who understood the AIDS epidemic among women to be the outcome of sex subordination and sexual violence, the idea that women be held responsible for abuse and victimization was an incorrect way of resolving the issue of transmission of HIV between men and women. Ending sexual violence would require more government intervention, not less. For feminists who believed that women lacked the power to negotiate condom use, for example, public health interventions which, for example, left condoms out on a table for women to convince their partner to use were nearly useless without any structural intervention into the actual bargaining arrangement between men and women. These acts of sex in which women could not negotiate condom use had to be seen as what they were – acts of violence in which women could not consent to the sex that they wanted. In other words, while law and economics scholars emphasized the "private choices" aspect of negotiating sex, feminists sought to tear down the public/private distinction to allow the state into the home to alter how women were positioned there. They did so by proposing numerous ways governments could and should extend intervention into the home to shift the ability of women to bargain about sex and other areas of family life, including care work, in the context of their marriage.[49]

Feminism was also transforming epidemiology, and by the 1990s, a new subfield was taking shape: feminist epidemiology.[50] Feminist epidemiologists were interested in exploring questions of gender in the study of public health. Some specifically began to interrogate the relationship between sexual violence, gender inequality, and women's risk of HIV. Could feminists prove empirically that VAW bore a causal relationship to women's risk of contracting HIV? Drawing on dominance feminist arguments, epidemiologists set out to explore whether there was a causal relationship between sexual subordination (i.e., sexual and intimate partner violence) and HIV transmission. Given that the epidemic was ultimately a public health crisis, the idea that there could be empirical and scientific proof of causal links between behaviors and HIV transmission (or interventions and HIV prevention) had specific importance.

In the public health response to AIDS, which faced numerous funding shortfalls, greater attention and resources would be devoted to gender equality and ending VAW if there was indeed an empirical link. And, it would prove that men – channeling the patriarchal norms that drove them – were implicitly and explicitly responsible for the spread of HIV to women, given power differentials in sex.

By the mid to late 1990s, epidemiologists began to publish papers that described the connections between sex inequality, violence, and

HIV from an empirical and public health perspective. The growing scholarly and epidemiological literature on women and AIDS introduced the idea that women were at risk for numerous reasons, including "sex roles, social conditions, and socioeconomic conditions."[51] Many of these ideas were generated from US-based studies and advocacy.[52] An article in *Social Science and Medicine* in 1992, for example, makes female control of sexuality central to the success of behavior change programs in the context of HIV prevention in sub-Saharan Africa. The author states: "Control is thus an important dimension of women's power. Lack of access to, and control of, resources for decision-making, particularly in the sexual relationship, appears to be one key to the vulnerability of women and children in the AIDS epidemic."[53]

Epidemiologists also began to draw out links hypothesized to increase women's risk of HIV. First, through "forced or coercive sexual intercourse with an infected partner," second, because intimate partner violence may limit an ability to "negotiate safe sexual behaviors," and, third, by identifying "a pattern of sexual risk-taking among individuals assaulted in childhood and adolescence."[54] According to these studies, intimate partner violence, sexual harassment, and sexual coercion are endemic in women's lives and shape a woman's ability to negotiate when to have sex and advocate for condom usage.[55] Studies showed strong associations between intimate partner violence and rates of HIV. And, in turn, a new settlement on the issue of VAW and HIV emerged: that there is an association between the two – that women living with HIV have higher reported rates of violence, and that violence places women at an increased risk of HIV.[56]

In keeping with this perspective, nearly all of the studies at the intersection of violence and women's risk of HIV during this period called for an increased focus on VAW in the AIDS response. Following these studies, and the push by activists to take VAW more seriously, in 2000, the World Health Organization called for increased research on the intersection of violence and heterosexual HIV transmission, while deepening programmatic work on the linkages between gender, violence, and HIV transmission.

For feminist advocates, the epidemiological question had high stakes.[57] Showing that there was a connection between VAW and HIV transmission would route more public health money into a cause that was being treated as external to the HIV response. This challenged the assumption that HIV/AIDS funding and programming should prioritize getting medication to those people who had HIV or AIDS over prevention programs. And, within prevention advocacy, there was yet another fault line: Should prevention dollars be spent narrowly, say, on condoms, or more broadly, to address the social determinants of health that resulted in vulnerability to HIV transmission? These social determinants of health, according to those advocating for a broad understanding of prevention interventions, should include addressing gender-based violence and remedying other forms of gender inequality. For feminists, the narrow approach to prevention, which meant simply giving women condoms, ignored the issue of unequal bargaining power in sexual relationships. How were women to insist on condoms, feminists argued, when they couldn't control when and how they were having sex?

While this book does not extensively track the shifts in biological science, it is relevant to note the evolution in scientific research that contributed to the idea that women were particularly vulnerable to HIV, especially in moments of violence.[58] In other words, as victims, women's bodies were now a site of vulnerability to harm, and biological research into AIDS reflected this new thinking. Scientists began to hypothesize that the increasing numbers of women with HIV may be rooted in biological differences between men and women and established that viral contact with the cervix and vagina often resulted in greater exposure to a virus, and an increased likelihood of transmission from a man to a woman rather than in reverse.[59]

Soon, far from the popular perception from the 1980s that women might be resistant to AIDS, many began to conclude the opposite: that women were more vulnerable to contracting HIV. The idea that women were more biologically vulnerable to HIV quickly gained momentum as an additional explanatory force in terms of the rapid increase in diagnoses among women. By 1995, a publication of the Royal Tropical Institute, South Africa AIDS Information Dissemination Service, and the World Health Organization contained a section titled "Physiological Vulnerability" which exemplifies how the *biological* vulnerability of women to HIV would be described in the decades to come:

> Researchers estimate that women's risk of HIV infection from unprotected sex is at least twice that of men. Semen, which has high concentrations of virus, remains in the vaginal canal a relatively long time. Women are more exposed through the extensive surface area of mucous

> membrane in the vagina and on the cervix through which the virus may pass. In men, the equivalent area is smaller, mainly the entrance to the urethra in a circumcised man plus, in an uncircumcised man, the delicate skin under the foreskin.[60]

Furthering the idea that it was sexual violence that compounded the effect of biological vulnerability was new research suggesting that vaginal abrasions caused by rape, particularly in young women, further increased biological susceptibility to the virus. A new idea took shape: that women were physiologically and socially more vulnerable to HIV than men.

These epidemiological and biological ideas about women's vulnerability to HIV helped justify legal interventions to stem VAW. Feminist ideas began to make a greater appearance in the growing range of national and international law and policy documents on gender and HIV. The Beijing Conference Platform for Action exemplifies the influence of feminist ideas in global governance on HIV. The agreement, adopted by 189 countries, reflected feminist sex-subordination perspectives in speaking directly to connections between violence and discrimination against women and the spread of HIV. The document itself exemplifies the points above. It proposes a single story about women's risk of HIV, demonstrates the rise of sex bargaining through a discussion of power imbalances in the context of safe sex, and solidifies the idea that sexual violence drives women's risk of HIV and that there should be intervention into the home to remedy these issues:

> HIV/AIDS and other sexually transmitted diseases, *the transmission of which is sometimes a consequence of sexual violence*, are having a devastating effect on women's health, particularly the health of adolescent girls and young women. They often do not have the power to insist on safe and responsible sex practices and have little access to information and services for prevention and treatment. *Women, who represent half of all adults newly infected with HIV/AIDS and other sexually transmitted diseases, have emphasized that social vulnerability and the unequal power relationships between women and men are obstacles to safe sex, in their efforts to control the spread of sexually transmitted diseases*. The consequences of HIV/AIDS reach beyond women's health to their role as mothers and caregivers and their contribution to the economic support of their families. The social, developmental and health consequences of HIV/AIDS and other sexually transmitted diseases need to be seen from a gender perspective.[61]

By 2001, the United Nations General Assembly had held the first of three Special Sessions on HIV and AIDS. The declaration that emerged acknowledges women as a risk group for HIV/AIDS and highlights the role of gender inequality.[62] The declaration stresses "that gender equality and the empowerment of women are fundamental elements in the reduction of the vulnerability of women and girls to HIV/AIDS."[63] A recommendation calling for addressing gender inequality follows: "Ensure ... reduction of their vulnerability to HIV/AIDS through the elimination of all forms of discrimination, as well as all forms of violence against women and girls, including harmful traditional and customary practices, abuse, rape and other forms of sexual violence, battering and trafficking in women and girls."[64]

And, in 2005, *Science*, the peer-reviewed journal of the American Association for the Advancement of Science, published an article on women and AIDS highlighting both the social and biological factors contributing to women's vulnerability:

> *Social determinants of female vulnerability to HIV-1 include gender disparities, poverty, cultural, and sexual norms, lack of education, and violence. Women are also more susceptible to HIV-1 because of hormonal changes, vaginal microbial ecology and physiology, and a higher prevalence of sexually transmitted diseases.* Prevention strategies must address the wide range of gender inequalities that promote the dissemination of HIV-1.[65]

A new idea applicable to women around the world had taken shape: that women are biologically and socially more vulnerable to HIV than men due to violence.[66] The idea collapsed difference and location, and emerged as a universal idea of risk and vulnerability.[67] This idea was exemplified by a 2006 Center for Women's Global Leadership (CWGL) statement that said "women are facing a catastrophic assault on their bodies, rights and health as a result of the prevalence of both HIV and the unrelenting omnipresence of VAW on a global level. Each constitutes a crisis on its own. Yet, in the lives of thousands if not millions of women, these crises are not separable; they are fundamentally linked."[68]

From the perspective of feminists, CWGL's idea represented a new common sense in how and why women were at risk of contracting HIV: heterosexual sex. Given the gains made in fighting VAW, feminists were able to isolate one bad actor in the sex bargain: the man. Law and economics scholars were also focused in on the individual. Without worrying about the background political, economic, and legal issues that could result in power differentials, law and economics scholars zeroed in on the sex bargain as the outcome of two equal individuals. Together, law and economics scholars and feminists directed attention to the individual in the AIDS response through the sex bargain. Both these impulses fit within, and helped cement, a larger ideological shift taking place in public health: toward the individual and away from structural and social determinants of health.

### The Consequences

#### *Individual Responsibility, the Carceral Response*

The shifts in thinking inside public health and international financial institutions, attendant to law and economics, and the feminist attention to the sex bargain, catapulted the idea of individualism forward in the AIDS response. To be sure, some feminists had also long advocated for more attention to structural issues facing women, from poverty alleviation and property rights to welfare reform and addressing issues of race and class. But the individual responsibility frame for AIDS, bolstered by the idea of the sex bargain, fit neatly into the broader social and political moment of the 1980s, described in detail earlier in the chapter, in which social services were contracting alongside an expansion of criminal law.[69]

As has now been shown in a vast scholarly literature on feminism and the carceral state, feminist perspectives that rose to the top of feminist organizing were those whose views aligned with a steady turn away from structural solutions and toward the criminal justice system as a means to end sexual violence.[70]

Some dominance feminists believed that the failures of AIDS interventions could be attributed to the inability of women to negotiate safe sex or to counteract cultural constraints on men's willingness to utilize barrier methods like condoms. They fixed attention on women as victims of the epidemic. HIV became an opportunity to recast two issues – VAW and HIV – into a simplistic criminal law model, which attempts to fix social problems through a reductionist approach that describes the world in terms of "bad actors" and "aggrieved victims."[71] HIV became yet another reason for the public health response to focus on individual behavior change in development programming – whether through carceral or other means – and avoid the more complicated, structural, political, and economic forces that shape health outcomes. This is exemplified in a report by Human Rights Watch on Uganda:

> The accounts in this report reveal that Ugandan women are becoming infected with HIV, and will eventually die of AIDS, because the state is failing to protect them from domestic violence ... Human Rights Watch interviewed Ugandan women who confront an environment that sustains unequal power relations, contend with persistent societal pressure to tolerate violence, and whose husbands and extended family routinely subject them to coercion and emotional abuse ... Women were also powerless to protect themselves from infection and were unable to access HIV/AIDS services because their husbands physically attack and intimidated them, and did so with impunity ... the Ugandan government has failed in any meaningful way to criminalize, condemn, or prosecute violence against women in the home.[72]

The framing offered by Human Rights Watch requires understanding that women are passive recipients of sex with little to no ability to control or have agency in their own sexuality.[73] Individual responsibility – or in the case of the feminist frame, male responsibility – fit with the larger political moment. As the sex bargaining frame took hold, it was quickly absorbed into a nonstructural response to HIV, just as the VAW women's movement had been. The convergence deepened the push for criminal liability for HIV transmission. The 1994 Violence Against Women Act, for example, called for a revision of sentencing guidelines that "relate to offenses in which an HIV infected individual engages in sexual activity if the individual knows that he or she is infected with HIV and intends, through such sexual activity, to expose another to HIV."[74]

Combined with the push for criminal liability for gender violence, individual responsibility became key to understanding how to address the epidemic among women. In other words, it holds individuals, not institutions, accountable for women's vulnerability to HIV.

For feminists, the fight to maintain the victimhood of heterosexual women in the epidemic, and in turn the idea of a passive female sexuality as the foundation for feminist HIV interventions, often displaces a counternarrative that women can possess sexual agency. Positing women as victims of an exploitative heterosexuality requires us to frame men as enacting masculine patriarchal violence. Men are the primary mode of transmission between sex workers and wives and from girlfriend to girlfriend. Put in the language of dominance feminism, men, in living the privileges offered by patriarchy, become perpetrators in the spread of HIV. As reflected in the quote from Human Rights Watch, this gendered and often racialized trope, now about men, circulates widely in advocacy and journalistic accounts documents.[75]

As mentioned above, and discussed in detail in the next chapter, the criminal law focus encountered resistance and was not universally celebrated by feminists. By the late 1990s, many women's advocates, primarily women of color emerging from organizing on prison abolition, voiced skepticism about using criminal law to address violence in society. Scholars called for a turn toward redistributing social and economic goods and legal interventions that supported transformation over those that did not transfer material resources to battered women.[76] US organizations including Critical Resistance and INCITE!, both working on issues of communities of color, the former with regard to prison abolition and the latter on VAW, galvanized support for rethinking the use of criminal law while acknowledging tensions in progressive engagement with legal reform. They had limited success in pushing a critical perspective forward.[77] In a contest between feminist ideas, feminist groups critical of carceral approaches, many of whom were led by women of color, failed to gain traction in the 1980s and 1990s.[78] Instead, it was feminists and feminist ideas aligned with the pro-carceral perspective that reigned in the broader political discourse of the 1980s, that gained institutional and rhetorical power. The tensions between feminists, especially those around sexual agency, would come to travel through the AIDs response.

Another feminist position that directly challenged the dominance feminist sexual subordination frame also emerged in the 1980s, attacking the feminist idea that seemed to treat sex as largely heterosexual, dyadic, and hegemonic. Critical feminists, known now as pro-sex or sex-positive feminists, sought to understand the more complicated set of experiences around sex, including the mix of "pleasure and danger" that might drive a sexual encounter.[79] The basic idea that animated sex-positive feminism was that women might see or have experiences of pleasure in domination; that sex was not solely a site of subordination, but could be a site of agency and power.[80]

As the late 1990s approached, however, these critical feminist positions gained momentum with the public health evidence showing that anticarceral and pro-sex public health interventions were having real world impact in reducing HIV transmission. Detailed in the next chapter, these feminist disagreements would quickly shift into the AIDS law and policy world with life and death consequences.

*Silencing of Dissenting Feminisms*

In the context of AIDS activism, a universal narrative about women's risk had taken hold: Women were at risk due to violence, more specifically, sexual violence.[81] American feminists played a uniquely powerful role in crafting narratives of risk and vulnerability in the context of AIDS and sexual violence. The collapsing of global and local concerns into a master narrative about women's experiences with violence and AIDS did not go without cost to other competing feminist ideas and thus generated internal feminist critiques. I highlight two here.

The first grew outside of the AIDS context but held fast even in the context of public health. This was a feminist critique of a universalized narrative about women's lived experiences. While for some feminists the potential power of strategic alliance across country and culture is worth the costs of collapsing local difference for a global story, for others, there was a deep need to critique the universalization of women's experiences because of the stories and life experiences it masked.

The critique of universalization of a master narrative about women came largely from activists of color in the United States and the global south, critical race theorists, and scholars of Third World approaches to international law (TWAIL), who took on what was perceived to be an essentialist narrative about women's experiences. For TWAIL scholars and American critical race theorists, universalizing women's experiences came with costs. For Vasuki Nesiah, a leading TWAIL feminist scholar, for example, the foregrounding of gender issues came at the expense of other structural concerns that could be shaping women's lives. In a critique of MacKinnon, she calls out the overreliance on MacKinnon's "identification of oppressive features of women's lives across the globe – 'rape, domestic battery, and pornography'" which are then "used to frame the universal 'realities of women's condition.'" Nesiah highlights that the American feminist project in particular, in its attempts at universalization, has "complicity in masking global contradictions" by insisting upon the "universalization of female oppression." Underlying this critique was the idea that first-world feminists, primarily American feminists, often did not consider these wider structural concerns of third-world women. American legal scholar of race, Angela Harris, similarly argues against the essentialization of women's experiences in feminist legal theory. Critiquing legal scholars who paint a picture of universal and abstract ideas of feminism, she criticizes the essentializing of women's experiences, which inevitably leaves behind the complexity of women's experiences and silences some voices.[82]

The masking of complexity had life and death consequences in the AIDS context. Two examples demonstrate this. The first takes us back to the early days of the epidemic, as feminists began to narrow their agenda on women and AIDS to ending sexual violence and discussed it as a universal experience. But it was not the only risk factor women faced. The experience of African American women in the early part of the epidemic demonstrates how a universalized story about violence betrayed their experience. First, as African American women began to test positive at higher rates, one risk factor was the high rates of incarceration of African American men and women which led to higher rates of HIV, given transmission in prison.[83] This, in turn, led to community transmission as those released from prison had sex with others. Yet, most reproductive rights organizations largely did not take up the issue of HIV or incarceration. Second, as Cathy Cohen demonstrates in her work, injection drug use turned out to be a high-risk factor among communities of color, including women, early in the epidemic. (This also turned out to be the case in Eastern Europe and Russia.)[84] The dominance of the VAW narrative, however, created a blind spot: Missing from the agendas of most American feminist groups was the issue of incarceration in communities of color or of harm-reduction. To the contrary, there was a call for greater incarceration, lending support to the war on crime.

Feminist dissenters also noted that structural fixes were lost to the individualist focus of the AIDS response.[85] For these feminists ending coercion in bargaining required altering the bargaining endowments of women determined by the broader legal environment. These included what we think of as structural fixes: property and inheritance rights, labor protections, and the ability to contract in the market. But this was not the legal and programmatic work that lined up with the broader social and political moment, which had silenced these broader reforms in deference to a narrower mandate.[86]

Voices called for a broader perspective, including those from the Black women's health movement and AIDS movement. Activists raised concerns about systematic issues in public health that resulted in the loss of life for women – from the failings of maternal healthcare to infant mortality. In the context of AIDS, activists made connections between inequality and health outcomes, including the contributions of housing instability and lack of nutrition to contracting and dying of HIV faster. Yet, discussions about the deep structural change necessary to truly transform a woman's ability to seek adequate healthcare faded into the background, as the individual and her own capacity to take responsibility for her own health came to the fore.

The focus on sexual violence, as described earlier, aligned with the focus on the individual, at the cost of a focus on structural solutions in keeping with the broader ideological moment. In a competition between feminisms, and the feminists themselves, those willing to take on an ideological project that prioritized individual responsibility gained power and legitimacy in the AIDS response.[87]

5

# THE SEX WARS COME TO AIDS

## Risk and Consent

To get to the Indian town of Sangli, Maharashtra, from the United States (where many antitrafficking advocates depart for their trips), you would first take a sixteen-hour flight to Mumbai. Once you arrive in Mumbai, you must travel southeast 140 kilometers to the city of Pune. You would rent a car from Pune and drive another 400 kilometers, or five long hours, further south and further inland. While Sangli is known for being a producer of turmeric and is home to historic temples frequented by tourists, it is also, and perhaps most obviously, a busy truck stop: a pass-through point for drivers transporting goods throughout Maharashtra and Karnataka, the Indian state to its south. Its dusty streets are filled with metal parts merchants selling doorknobs and window hinges. In the late 1990s, Sangli also earned another reputation: It had some of the highest rates of HIV and AIDS in India. Not long after that, Sangli, a small town far from any major city, became the site of a transnational struggle over feminist conceptions of risk, consent, and exploitation.

The 2010 case of Ashabai, a local sex worker and HIV/AIDS peer educator arrested for trafficking young girls, demonstrates how a subset of American antitrafficking feminists shaped the regulatory environment on AIDS.[1] When she was arrested, Ashabai worked with an HIV/AIDS initiative called Sampada Grameen Mahila Sanstha (SANGRAM) and was a leader in Veshya Anyay Mukti Parishad (VAMP). Since its founding in 1992, SANGRAM has been held up as an example of how to effectively respond to the AIDS crisis. The organization brings together sex workers who meet in small community centers, clinics, and in brothels. They have organized against violent clients, distributed condoms, and cared for one another as the AIDS epidemic wreaked havoc on the community. But the work of SANGRAM went far beyond simple organizing around a risky vocation. Members fought to stop the discrimination against their children in local schools, created a library for their children, and made plans to help the aging sex workers around them.

In the days I spent with her, Ashabai sashayed around Sangli in her sari, her ears adorned in gold jewelry, her hair pulled back into a tight black braid, a large circular *bindhi* adorning her forehead. She winked at the local police officers as they passed by on their motorcycles and shouted words of solidarity to sex workers. Her sturdy and confident presence grounded the sex workers organizing in the area. It was due to efforts like Ashabai's that the soaring rates of HIV among sex workers rapidly began to decline.

As part of SANGRAM's efforts to organize sex workers, Ashabai ran a safe brothel that was part of a network of harm-reduction spaces promoting HIV prevention by distributing condoms, and equipping sex workers with the skills to use them, and by addressing the issue of violence against women (VAW). Inside the small building, constructed out of mud and cement and painted yellow and brown, Ashabai provided a safe place for women to congregate and sell sex safely. At lunchtime, sex workers gathered on the floor to eat. While some sex workers sold sex, others would care for their children and do chores.

Like many of the poor in India, sex workers do not have access to formal banking, making it impossible to receive loans to build homes, afford tuition, or pay medical bills. Instead, sex workers frequently loan each other funds when necessary, often in large amounts. But Ashabai's fate changed when her loan to a sex worker drew the wrath of an antitrafficking group.

Ashabai was approached in 2010 by an eighteen-year-old sex worker I will call Reshmi. Reshmi was seeking employment in a brothel, and she needed a loan of 10,000 rupees. VAMP policies do not allow an individual younger than eighteen to work as a sex worker in the brothel, but Reshmi's age qualified her. Ashabai gave Reshmi the loan and allowed her to work off the loan interest free as part of her stay in the brothel. Reshmi was able to pay off the loan and continued to work in the brothel.

An antitrafficking organization heard that a transaction had taken place in which Ashabai had loaned money that would be repaid by sex work. It planned a raid on the brothel with the federal police – going over the heads of the local police, with whom SANGRAM had established a good relationship. The purported goal of the raid was to rescue the young woman. According to sex workers in the brothel at the time of the raid, a man who posed as a client came in and asked for a girl. Reshmi came forward. The man posing as a client signaled the police, who then barged into the brothel, arrested Ashabai, and took Reshmi to a juvenile home – a locked facility a few miles away. The local government hospital certified that Reshmi was an adult, and the local magistrate transferred her to a government correction home.

Ashabai was arrested and released from detention a few days later. She was charged under the Immoral Trafficking (Prevention) Act (ITPA), Section 3–6, 1956 – the country's primary legislation addressing sex work and trafficking. Her purported crimes included keeping a brothel, living off the earnings of a sex worker, procuring or taking a person for the sake of prostitution, and detaining a person in a place where prostitution is taking place. Her arrest and time in detention destabilized the larger HIV intervention campaign and the community of sex workers.

Laws like ITPA, passed in countries all over the world, fueled by the US government's antitrafficking efforts, have also been pushed for and demanded by feminists and conservatives dedicated to using the police arm of the state to address sex-trafficking.[2] HIV interventions have come under attack, struggled, and sometimes collapsed against the growing pressure of a coalition of antitrafficking advocates that included carceral feminists and churches that see sexual violence (counting sex work in their capacious definition) as the locus of women's oppression.

To antitrafficking groups, Ashabai's provision of small loans, a safe place to sell sex, and condoms was not bettering women's health outcomes but furthering their exploitation. In other words, harm-reduction programs were aiding and abetting trafficking. Ashabai's arrest represents only one of the many casualties of feminist-led antitrafficking organizing. Through repeat attacks on sex work and harm-reduction services, programs offering AIDS prevention and care to vulnerable populations around the world including in the United States, Thailand, Cambodia, India, and Bangladesh have shuttered. And, because the definition of trafficking continues to expand, sex workers like Ashabai frequently end up in jail or detention centers. Far from being rescued, they are punished repeatedly for selling sex to survive financially.

Feminists are not unified on how to conceptualize or understand women's risk of AIDS and split on how to manage exposures to the virus. For sex work advocates and feminists who believed sex workers could have agency, changing the conditions that sex workers bargained in meant that transmission of HIV could be reduced. From this perspective, a fair bargain, one that involved safe sex, was possible. But, for anti-sex-work and carceral antitrafficking feminists, the best way to reduce the harms of sex work was to eliminate it by arresting and punishing clients and others profiting off the sex industry. To them, there was no such thing as a fair sex bargain; sex work was coercion and violence all the way down. Criminal law was the preferred mode of regulating a sex market.

These debates mapped onto another division occurring inside the public health community in the late twentieth century: harm reduction versus harm elimination. Each of these frames calls upon opposing legal solutions to address the idea of harm associated with selling sex. The difference lies in competing ideas of harm and exploitation. For harm-reduction practitioners and activists, it is not transacting sex itself that is necessarily the risk. The risks associated with selling sex come from the criminalization of the purchase and sale of sex. These criminal laws create conditions that hamper public health efforts to make selling sex safer.[3] For harm-reduction advocates, decriminalizing sex work and enabling state protection is key to improving public health programs and outcomes. Contrary to harm-reduction principles, antitrafficking advocates argue for harm elimination. The harm and risk are in transacting sex itself.[4] They want the state to mobilize criminal law to prevent prostitution by prosecuting and punishing people who buy sex, not women who sell sex.[5] This position avoided the possibility that an appropriate response to the AIDS epidemic should include the clients of sex workers beyond arrest.

The stake's of this debate are high: Sex workers are central to the AIDS response. Since the beginning of the epidemic, epidemiologists noted that sex workers were at high risk of contracting HIV. In the worst moments of the epidemic, some groups of sex workers in AIDS-endemic regions had an HIV prevalence of over 50 percent. Mobilizing sex workers and decriminalizing sex work became one of the most effective strategies in fighting HIV transmission.

Sex work proved to be one of the most controversial issues for feminists, and that manifested in the feminist response to AIDS – resurrecting feminist fights on sex and sexuality but raising the stakes significantly with new and potentially deadly consequences. In the context of the epidemic, it was not only the logic of feminist law reformers that mattered. Epidemiologists and public health practitioners weighed in on the debates about legal reforms. The laws, in turn, shaped the questions epidemiologists were asking about the relationship between sex and HIV transmission.

American stakeholders were uniquely influential in the AIDS response. The US government has historically been the largest funder of HIV/AIDS globally. Hundreds of millions of dollars have been channeled from the United States into aid-dependent countries since 2003, with the aim of restructuring gender and health interventions. By engaging with foreign policy institutions, feminist ideas about risk and harm traveled the world, structuring public health interventions and altering health outcomes.

Following Chapter 4, which documented the rise and contestation of sex bargains as the primary frame for thinking about how women are at risk for AIDS, this chapter delves deep into the heart of feminist conflict around sexual agency. It tracks the powerful and central ways feminist ideas became embedded in the global AIDS response and how feminists turned their attention to US foreign policy and global governance institutions with the specific goal of harm reduction or harm elimination.

## THE NINETEENTH CENTURY AND EARLY TWENTIETH CENTURY

Understanding contemporary feminist advocacy for and against sex work requires a detour to the nineteenth century. In recounting this history, I focus on how the idea of disease wove in and out of debates on regulating prostitution. Feminist activism from this period acts as a reference point for feminists still today.

An early moment of feminist organizing on prostitution and disease began with the Contagious Diseases Acts (CDAs) of 1864, 1866, and 1869. Passed by the British government, the Acts attempted to regulate prostitution in England and in the colonies for the purpose of controlling the spread of venereal disease.[6] The CDAs mandated checkups for women, who were ordered by a judge to submit to periodic examinations, and prostitutes were targeted.[7] Those who were found to have a venereal disease were detained at the hospital and treated.[8] Supporters of the CDAs often cited the health of British troops as a key reason for the requirement.[9]

The regulation of women's sexuality for the protection of public health rubbed feminists the wrong way.[10] In the late 1860s, Josephine Butler founded the Ladies National Association (LNA) in Britain to fight the CDAs.[11] Butler argued that the medical regulation of prostitution, alongside the brothel system, exploited women's sexuality "for the gain of men and the state."[12] Butler and other abolitionists opposed the disrespectful manner in which medical exams were conducted, some arguing that the CDAs left poor women at the mercy of the police, who could easily exploit the Acts for the purposes of harassment.[13] As described by historian Jessica Pliley, Butler and her compatriots argued for the "reclaimability of all prostitutes, whom she considered to be the victims of sexist circumstances and male abuse."[14] They argued that instead of focusing on women, it was men who should be targeted and be forced to remain chaste and learn to control their sexual desires.[15] John Stuart Mill, perhaps one of the more well-known opponents of the CDAs, argued that "the wives and daughters of the poor are exposed to insufferable indignities on the suspicion of a police officer."[16] The vast mobilization of activists through media, letter-writing campaigns, and protest beginning in 1869 led to the eventual repeal of the Acts in 1888.[17]

Despite this feminist victory, concerns over venereal disease continued to drive the regulation of prostitution in the UK and the US. In the United States, progressive reformers and physicians decided in 1905 that the goal of the movement to end the spread of sexually transmitted infections (STIs) should be the "complete repression of prostitution."[18] The fear of prostitution and disease had racial and eugenicist overtones. As legal scholar Kerry Abrams writes, Chinese women bore the brunt of these efforts. Seen to be "harbingers of disease," the United States banned Chinese women from entering.[19] Legal challenges simply resulted in the Supreme Court's legitimation of this idea.

With ideas about race and racial purity front and center in the national discourse in the early 1900s, American concerns about prostitution took on a new dimension: the fear of white slavery, a moral panic about the prospect of white women being transported to brothels.[20] The fear of white slavery motivated a range of legal and regulatory interventions.[21] In 1910, for example, Congress passed the Mann Act, also known as the White-Slave Traffic Act, aimed at curbing the transport of any woman or girl for the purposes of prostitution or debauchery.[22] While the Mann Act reflected the idea that women selling sex were victims, it continued to facilitate a punitive approach to sex work by channeling resources toward law enforcement. In the same period with the national conversation in the United States, the idea of white slavery shaped a series of international conventions and treaties, including the International Convention for the Suppression of the White Slave Traffic[23] and the 1921 Convention for the Suppression of Traffic in Women and Children.[24]

The desire to manage STIs through controlling sex work continued through the 1900s, raising the ire of women involved in campaigns to curb the spread of venereal disease. In 1910, the New York State Legislature, for example, passed laws seeking to end the spread of disease by focusing on prostitutes and calling for medical examination and mandatory treatment of women found guilty of soliciting. While social hygienists were supportive, on moral and health grounds, of eradicating prostitution and testing and treating sex workers for disease, like the British feminists before them, women's groups were angry that women were the primary targets of laws aiming to end the spread of venereal disease. This new generation of feminists argued that women were being punished for spreading disease, while men largely escaped responsibility.[25]

Concerns for soldiers serving in World War I and World War II provided further motivation to discourage transacting sex. Empowered by the Mann Act and state and city efforts, law enforcement cracked down on women selling sex. These arrests did not work: They had little effect on the incidence of STIs. Historians have noted that by the end of World War I, large numbers of men in the army carried STIs.[26]

## SEXUAL REVOLUTION

By the 1960s and 1970s, the American political atmosphere around sex, and in turn around STIs, began to transform with the sexual revolution, second-wave feminism, and the sex workers' rights movement.

Histories of the women's movements from the 1960s and 1970s are plenty.[27] They track the divides of feminists as they navigated how and where to place critiques of capitalism and race in their feminist projects, along with feminist disagreements on housework, sex, sexuality, and gender identity. The complexity of this history makes any summary necessarily incomplete.

Understanding how divergent modes of feminism eventually became a powerful force shaping ideas of sex work and prostitution in the context of AIDS, however, requires recounting the growing tension among feminists on questions of sex work that grew out of this moment.

One divide would be particularly important for the HIV response: between carceral antitrafficking feminists who saw prostitution as inherently an act of objectification of women and, therefore, furthering the subjection of women and another camp of sex-positive feminists and sex workers who wanted to complicate understandings of sex and power.

This split has many roots, but one began with the commitment of feminists to end VAW.[28] While radical feminist perspectives differed slightly, many shared a commitment to the idea that prostitution was a form of objectification and oppression of women.[29] Feminist organizations of the 1970s, including Women Against Violence Against Women (WAVAW) and Women Against Violence in Pornography (WAVP), sought to end the degradation of women through the imagery of pornography. They protested by the thousands in the streets.[30] Radical feminists, including Catharine MacKinnon and Andrea Dworkin, fought for laws outlawing pornography. It was a sustained campaign to rid the world of prostitution and pornography. Many radical feminists claimed the mantle of "abolitionist," freeing women from sexual slavery as previous movements had done for African Americans.[31]

Against this radical feminist backdrop was the rise of the sex worker's movement. The sex worker's movement sought to decriminalize the sex industry, make working conditions safer for the people in it, and unionize its workers. The movement understood that exploitation in the sex industry did and could occur, but it also saw the potential for safe working conditions and consensual sex.

On Mother's Day in 1973, Margo St. James, a sex worker, formed COYOTE (Call Off Your Old Tired Ethics), the first sex worker organization in the United States. She declared 1973 "the year of the whore." One of the organization's primary goals was to decriminalize sex work. The organization won support from anti-racist groups and activists like Flo Kennedy, the noted civil rights leader.

Despite attempts by sex workers and radical feminists to build bridges, tensions between these groups existed from the outset. One tension that would eventually travel into AIDS programming and policy was the idea, put forward by sex worker organizations, that while violence and exploitation was rife in the sex industry, there was the possibility of equality in sex markets and in the transaction of sex. For abolitionist feminists, there was no such thing as equality in a sex market: "Prostituted women" were being exploited.

The early moments of this split are documented in a written exchange between radical feminist organizers of an international conference on sex trafficking and sex worker advocates tucked away in the COYOTE archives. Three feminists, Kathleen Barry, Charlotte Bunch, and Shirley Castley, began to organize what would become the Global Feminist Workshop to Organize Against Traffic in Women. The event was to take place in Rotterdam in the Netherlands. In 1982, Bunch and her colleagues wrote to Margo St. James and Priscilla Alexander, as members of the National Task Force on Prostitution representing sex workers, to invite them to Rotterdam to attend the gathering. As described in the letter, the purpose of the meeting was to gather an international advisory group for an intensive workshop focused on ending trafficking and slavery. The conference was organized under the umbrella of the International Women's Tribute Centre, Inc. in New York.

Priscilla Alexander replied on behalf of herself and Margo St. James. The tone was warm and engaging. Speaking from the perspective of a sex work advocate, Alexander's response sought to nuance the claim of prostitution as trafficking and slavery, contending that there was a need to both learn more about trafficking and exploitation *and* understand how prostitutes could be supported. She asked, for example, whether laws designed to protect women were instead punishing them, noting the similarity of laws being proposed in the United States to the nineteenth-century CDAs. She also warned that the focus must stay on customers to be tested for "venereal disease." Alexander was also concerned about "how to 'empower' the women who work as prostitutes."

In a response, Bunch clarified that the workshop would not be on "prostitution per se" but rather on the topic of "female sexual slavery."[32] This framing would assume a different set of questions, away from the issues of empowerment and improving the conditions of labor for sex workers that Alexander was interested in, and instead focus on the question of "forced prostitution."[33]

This divide between sex workers who wanted to make their industry safer and abolitionist feminists who saw women as victims of the exploitation by others in the sex market would deepen with time.

Between 1982 and 1986, several events would cement the split between radical feminists and sex workers.

In April 1982, a group of feminists organized what is now known as the Barnard Conference.[34] Professor Carole Vance, the academic organizer of the conference and co-editor of the book that emerged from the gathering, *Pleasure and Danger: Exploring Female Sexuality*, describes in a reflection piece that the conference was set to explore a range of issues including the "diversity of women's sexual experiences," "the complex meaning of sexual images," and "the terror aroused by sexuality." It aimed to complicate the radical feminist claim that sex always equaled subordination. Anti-pornography feminists, including WAVP, WAVAW, and New York Radical Feminists, protested the Barnard Conference as anti-feminist and harmful to women. Staff at Barnard University who supported the conference lost their jobs. The university confiscated conference materials.[35] This moment of deep ideological division came with material consequences for the feminists involved, especially those organizing the conference, and came to be known as the sex wars.[36] It pitted an emerging group of sex-positive feminists, who sought to explore the complicated relationship between agency, consent, and sexuality, against radical feminists who saw sexuality as the crux of women's subordination and sex work as emblematic of this oppression.

As this fight played out in New York City, in Rotterdam, despite the earlier outreach, Margo St. James would later note that Barry decided that she would no longer appear on stage with a sex worker. Radical feminists were alienating sex workers: the very women they sought to rescue.[37] St. James decided she had to correct the wrong-headed path feminism had taken toward prostitution. In reflecting on her organizing on and for sex workers, she remarked: "Getting the feminists to support prostitutes' rights was a difficult job in the States. One of the reasons I came to the continent here was to beat Dworkin and MacKinnon to the punch, and save you all from Kathleen Barry and her 'sexual slavery.'"[38]

The next year, Barry, Bunch, and Castley published the report from their Rotterdam meeting on human trafficking, titled *Report of the Global Feminist Work to Organize against Traffic in Women*. Despite the earlier invitation to sex worker rights organizations and their participation at the conference,[39] the report revealed that some sex worker groups – those that supported women who were doing sex work – would no longer be partners in the new push to end sex trafficking. In the report, Barry states:

> In examining the relationship between the feminist movement with prostitute organizations we face the serious question of how to support and work with individual women in prostitution without supporting the institution, something that will place us in opposition to the prostitute organizations which do not support the institution. It also raises problems about the role of pimps in supporting some prostitute organizations, something which is obviously incompatible with feminist work against the traffic in women.[40]

Sex workers responded. In 1985, the World Charter for Prostitutes' Rights – one of the first charters of its kind – called for decriminalization of "all aspects of adult prostitution resulting from individual decision."[41] The charter was the product of the first of the two World Whores' Congresses, held in 1985.[42] The charter makes demands on behalf of sex workers including the decriminalization of prostitution, shelter, privacy, freedom of association, and the ability to marry and have children.[43]

As these feminist positions for and against the transacting of sex were concretizing, the circumstances around the debates changed rapidly. A new deadly sexually transmitted virus, HIV, was spreading through the population. While HIV initially played little role in structuring feminist debates about prostitution, given that it did not exist, the progression of HIV through the population gave new life and deadly consequences to this feminist fight.

## NEW ALLIANCES

As confusion about the AIDS virus in the 1980s was sweeping the nation, law became more central to the AIDS response.[44] With the war on drugs and crime in full swing, and cuts in the welfare state and public health funding, governments increasingly relied on criminal law as a route to better public health outcomes. HIV emerged as a significant public health threat just as resources to actually respond to drivers of disease spread were shifting to crime control. The AIDS crisis provided new fodder for ever-increasing criminal enforcement against individuals.[45]

Outside of hemophiliacs, who were largely understood as the epidemic's innocent victims, the criminal and punitive legal responses to HIV bore down on those at high risk for contracting HIV and those who had HIV. Gay sex was already illegal, and anti-gay rhetoric took center stage. States passed laws criminalizing intentional transmission of HIV,[46] HIV-positive Haitians were detained in Guantanamo Bay,[47] new sentencing guidelines punished drug use more harshly, and gay men became the target of increased public health surveillance. Prostitution, already criminalized, took on a new dimension. Those arrested were no longer simply engaging in an illegal activity; they were now threatening to spread a new deadly disease.[48]

Inside public health, and against the carceral logic that was quickly colonizing social services, a new frame was growing in prominence: harm reduction.[49] Because many activities that exposed people to HIV were criminalized – including gay sex, injection drug use, and sex work – harm-reduction advocates fought against using criminal law in the public health response. This was especially important, as the specter of criminality that hung over public health interventions in these communities impacted the ability of public health workers to do outreach without being implicated in aiding and abetting a crime.

The difference between these two approaches (carceral vs. harm reduction) was the idea of risk. Motivating the carceral response was the idea that through crime control the government could entirely eliminate a risk category, whether through laws criminalizing sodomy or the purchase of sex. You could abolish the harm altogether. Harm-reduction advocates saw things differently; they took a pragmatist perspective and sought to manage risk by focusing on the sites of potential HIV exposure.

Within the public health community, the harm-reduction frame dominated. The harm-reduction frame was originally pushed by advocates and activists who called for needle exchange and safe injection sites in lieu of the punitive approach of the war on drugs. Civil liberties organizations championed the cause of harm reduction. By the 1990s, harm reduction was widely accepted by public health officials as the most effective means to address drug use. And in 1990, the first international harm-reduction conference took place.[50] In 1995, the *American Journal of Public Health* published recommendations to redefine the American drug policy that advocated for harm reduction.[51] US Surgeon General Jocelyn Elders came forward supporting the exploration of legalization as a means to address drug use.[52] In global fora, a health and human rights movement gained momentum with the appointment of civil rights champion Jonathan Mann as the first director of the new World Health Organization (WHO) Global AIDS Programme in 1986.[53] Harm-reduction principles became institutionalized in global governance and US public health advocacy.[54]

The harm-reduction philosophy merged well with the growing sex worker movement.[55] While formal harm-reduction programs remained focused on drug use, harm reduction as a principle became increasingly central to the sex work response to HIV.[56] Local and global sex worker activist groups were early adopters of harm-reduction principles to address issues arising from sex work.[57] Sex workers mobilized harm reduction to resist being characterized as vectors of the HIV epidemic and came to be seen as change agents in the face of the HIV epidemic. Building on the preexisting sex worker movement, sex workers aimed to reframe their status as victims, rather than vectors, of the HIV crisis. It worked. Just as with drug users, the pragmatist principles of harm reduction enabled public health practitioners to focus on the harms surrounding transactional sex and not the sex itself.[58] Public health practitioners began to see sex workers as victims of the epidemic, subject to harms including sickness, violence, discrimination, prosecution, debt, and exploitation (including trafficking).[59]

Sex-positive feminists supported sex workers in their efforts to organize in the era of AIDS.[60] This growing union of harm reduction, sex workers, and sex-positive feminism galvanized funding for sex worker initiatives that supported improving the lives of sex workers.[61] New organizations and initiatives took shape. In 1990, sex workers founded the Global Network of Sex Work Projects (then the Network of Sex Work Projects). They would go on to publish a guide *Making Sex Work Safe* in 1997.[62] The growing global sex worker movement took on harm reduction as part of its mantle.[63]

While inside the public health arena harm reduction was the mainstream perspective, outside of public health the antiprostitution feminist fight was reshaping itself into a powerful new movement: carceral antitrafficking feminists (CAFs). They allied with conservatives and a pro-crime-control agenda to achieve their goal of liberating women from sexual slavery.

Kathleen Barry tells the story of the rise of the antitrafficking movement of the 1980s and 1990s in her 1995 book *The Prostitution of Sexuality*. Her history is rooted in Josephine Butler's fight against the CDAs.[64] While she praises Butler's radical feminist activism, Barry writes that Butler had a weakness: Butler saw a distinction between "forced" and "free" prostitution.[65] For Barry, that distinction hid the "everyday business of industrial capitalism, a prostitution industry." It wouldn't be until the 1980s and 1990s that "feminism could build on Butler's equality campaigns and focus on fundamental change in the sexual values and power that give men unlimited, unrestrained sexual access, including the purchase of women."[66] For Barry, the antitrafficking movement should reject the forced and free distinction. She describes how her contemporary allies, including Catharine MacKinnon and Andrea Dworkin, fought for anti-pornography ordinances and helped to build and support a global movement against the prostitution of women. Barry writes that it was during this period that she helped found the Coalition Against Trafficking in Women (CATW), the first international organization to fight trafficking in women. With CATW, antitrafficking activists began to participate at the United Nations, with the intent to spread the radical feminist message to other women in the world.[67] In the 1980s, Barry would become the first founding director of the Coalition Against Trafficking in Women. CATW would be a leading voice against harm-reduction programs for sex workers.

Carceral antitrafficking feminists found political allyship in unlikely places. Conservative politicians and the religious right were also focused on ending sexual slavery. Termed neo-abolitionists by Janie Chuang, the coalition was building a base.[68] While radical feminists were skeptical about the possibilities of law, the law still provided a toolkit, one that they were willing to use. The primary tool for "rescuing" prostituted women and ending prostitution became criminal sanctions and penalties levied against participants in the sex industry, excluding the women in sex work. The Rotterdam report helped lay the foundation for a carceral approach. Barry writes in her book that the "Abolitionists press for the vigorous prosecution of pimps because they force women into prostitution or prevent them from escaping it."[69]

Now acknowledged for their carceral turn,[70] the radical feminist emphasis on crime and punishment fit well with the American war on crime, and often mirrored the broader push toward criminalization by feminists in the context of domestic violence.[71]

CAFs banded together with conservatives and religious organizations to influence antitrafficking lawmaking, both domestically and internationally. In each instance, this alliance aimed to make the definition of trafficking as broad as possible. The outcome was two important documents for framing the legal intervention into sex work and sex trafficking: the Victims of Trafficking and Violence Protection Act

(TVPA) of 2000 and the Protocol to Suppress, Prevent, and Punish Trafficking in Persons, Especially Women and Children (Palermo Protocol).

In 2000, the United States passed the TVPA.[72] CAFs had advocated for a broad definition of trafficking that would include all forms of commercial sex work. Sex-positive feminists wanted to mitigate the expansion of the definition of sex trafficking beyond situations of force, fraud, or coercion. In the end, the TVPA capaciously defines sex trafficking as "the recruitment, harboring, transportation, provision, or obtaining of a person for the purposes of a commercial sex act."[73] It states that forms of commercial sex that are induced by "force, fraud, or coercion" are severe forms of sex trafficking.[74] [75]

Feminists also carried these definitional tensions into negotiations for a new UN crime control treaty. Negotiations began in 1999 and culminated in the Palermo Protocol in 2000.[76] The issue of how to regulate prostitution was fraught. As documented by many scholars, feminist fights over the definition of trafficking were present at the treaty negotiations.[77] On one side were the abolitionist feminists, including those of CATW, who kept with the organization's mission to include all forms of prostitution in the definition of trafficking. On the other was the "human rights caucus," and antitrafficking groups that did not want to conflate all forms of sex work with sex trafficking and wanted to ensure that other forms of labor exploitation were included. The final definition states that trafficking in persons is the:

> recruitment, transportation, transfer, harbouring or receipt of persons, by means of the threat or use of force or other forms of coercion, of abduction, of fraud, of deception, of the abuse of power or of a position of vulnerability or of the giving or receiving of payments or benefits to achieve the consent of a person having control over another person, for the purpose of exploitation. Exploitation shall include, at a minimum, the exploitation of the prostitution of others or other forms of sexual exploitation, forced labour or services, slavery or practices similar to slavery, servitude or the removal of organs.

Documentation of the meeting itself suggests that the definition of sex trafficking in the Palermo Protocol was intended to leave the regulation of prostitution up to the state. As Jo Doezma notes, however, in her summary of the meeting, while the text ought to be read as intentionally ambiguous it has the effect of "banishing" the sex worker to "the margins of the text."[78]

These feminist debates occurring in the streets and at conferences, and having real effect through the law, would soon make their way into the response to HIV and AIDS.

## THE SEX WARS COME TO AIDS: THE RETURN TO "DISEASE"

As shown in Chapters 1 and 2, by the mid 1990s, it was clear AIDS was impacting women in large numbers. Feminist organizations fell into two camps that mapped onto the harm-reduction and harm-elimination frames offered by public health.

In the first camp were the harm-reduction feminist organizations. They included feminist organizations, individual feminists, and feminist-adjacent organizations (like sex worker organizations, some of whom identified as feminists) who saw AIDS as central or, at minimum, important to their own organizing. They were organizations of women who worked with poor women, worked with sex workers, and saw that feminism had to be a part of the growing harm-reduction movement. I will call these groups harm-reduction feminists. They advocated against the use of criminal law to address the concerns of the sex industry and felt it drove participants underground. In a public health response context, this was counterproductive because it meant at-risk communities were inaccessible.

In the second camp were the CAFs. They advocated for laws to prosecute and punish people involved in the sex industry as purchasers of sex or those who benefitted from the sex industry (e.g., managers). They hoped that through arresting bad actors in the sex industry and "ending demand" for sex work, the world would see a collapse of sex markets. This group was made up of feminist organizations, including CATW, and individual feminists who saw AIDS as an outcome of women's inequality. Arguably, for many of these organizations, AIDS was not the central issue of concern but provided a strategic opportunity to forward a radical feminist agenda. They sought to eliminate sex trafficking by criminalizing both demand (the clients) and living off the earnings of sex work (pimping). This group, continuing forward with the radical feminist agenda of the 1970s, continued as abolitionist feminists.

CAFs believed in harm elimination.[79] For the abolitionist feminists, the harm-reduction movement, including the feminists and sex workers in it, was forwarding the subordination of women. The language of Kathleen Barry describes the views taken by CAFs on the issue of women and AIDS.

> Prostitution may be the only high-risk AIDS context in which high-risk sex is promoted, despite the costs in human lives. Creating the illusion of controlling venereal disease in order to promote the prostitution market was the original basis of regulated prostitution … But prostitution alone and its normalization does not account for the increase in AIDS among women. Men's promiscuous sexual behavior with multiple partners in polygamous societies and in sexually liberal societies, as well as in prostitution, establish the epidemiological base for the spread of HIV/AIDS …. At no time in patriarchal history has the outbreak of venereal diseases massively transported to and from prostitutes by customers been a cause for helping women get out of prostitution. Prostitution itself, that is, the prostitution of sexuality, is not considered harmful because the women in prostitution are considered to be an expendable population to be thrown away when no longer useful to the sex industries. AIDS prevention, which should be oriented toward getting women out of prostitution, is reduced to a massive marketing of condoms to keep the sex industry and condom manufacturers going.

Barry's position, taken by CAFs working in the AIDS space, ran counter to that of an emerging orthodoxy within public health: that condoms work and that providing safe resources to sex workers would help stop the spread of AIDS among women. Against the public health sensibility, CAFs felt that harm-reduction was making things worse for women, not better.

## THE ANTIPROSTITUTION LOYALTY OATH

These two feminist positions came to a head as new AIDS legislation was introduced in the United States. The legislation offered an opportunity to influence national-level policymaking on prostitution around the world.

President Bush announced the President's Emergency Plan for AIDS Relief (PEPFAR), a commitment to address the global HIV epidemic which would result in over 100 billion dollars to HIV/AIDS relief. This announcement led to the United States Leadership Against HIV/AIDS, Tuberculosis, and Malaria Act ("Leadership Act"), which became law in May 2003.[80] This law made the United States the largest government donor for HIV and AIDS globally.

The legislation was immediately contentious.[81] Proposed amendments pushed by the Congressional Pro-Life Caucus alerted left-leaning activist groups of the need to engage with the Leadership Act.[82] These amendments included the application of the "global gag rule," which prevented organizations from performing abortions if they received US dollars,[83] prioritization of abstinence-only sex education,[84] and funding provisions for faith-based organizations.[85]

During this time, Republicans proposed another amendment to the Leadership Act that has come to be known as the "antiprostitution loyalty oath" (APLO).[86] CAFs and conservatives supported the introduction of the APLO.[87] The amendment mandated that organizations receiving funding through the Leadership Act must have a policy explicitly opposing prostitution and sex trafficking. It banned organizations from promoting or advocating for the legalization or practice of prostitution or sex trafficking. In fact, the Leadership Act incorporated the abolitionist feminist position toward sex work and prostitution: "Prostitution and other sexual victimization are degrading to women and children and it should be the policy of the United States to eradicate such practices."[88] The idea enshrined a core carceral antitrafficking position: that a woman's risk of contracting HIV during a sexual transaction could only be mitigated if sex markets were abolished. The Act states: "No funds made available to carry out this Act, or any amendment made by this Act, may be used to promote or advocate the legalization or practice of prostitution or sex trafficking."

Further, the legislation states that Leadership Act fund recipients must have a policy opposing prostitution and sex trafficking, what came to be known as the "pledge requirement": "No funds made available to carry out this Act, or any amendment made by this Act, may be used to provide assistance to any group or organization that does not have a policy explicitly opposing prostitution and sex trafficking."

The CAF conflation of sex work and trafficking not only positioned these feminists in opposition to the harm-reduction position, it indicted both the harm-reduction activists for engaging in sex trafficking, and the feminist and sex work advocates that were seeking to make sex work safer. In other words, supporters of the APLO argued that harm-reduction services that included giving women condoms, treating them for STIs, or enabling them to practice sex work safely, were aiding and abetting in trafficking. Support for this antitrafficking frame necessarily called upon crime control agencies to stop what was a *crime*: trafficking another human being. Delivering public health services in the mode of harm reduction was a crime.

Harm-reduction advocates argued the opposite. Rather than arrest people, especially the vast numbers of public health peer educators and the clients of sex workers, supporters of harm reduction sought increased access to condoms and supported forming sex workers' collectives.[89] The collectives were an integral part of the HIV response and seen as one of the most effective ways to address HIV amongst sex workers.[90] In these collectives, sex workers engage in community building and empowerment activities, alongside an informal regulation of the local industry.[91] For example, sex workers might identify violent clients so that others could ban them from brothels and protect other sex workers from harm by acting as guards.

Advocacy by sex-positive feminists, public health agencies, funders, and nonprofits, including the Open Society Institute and Global AIDS Alliance, failed. The APLO became part of the Leadership Act. In 2003, the year the Leadership Act was passed, the Department of Health and Human Services (HHS) mandated that all funding recipients had to have a policy "explicitly opposing prostitution and sex trafficking."

Next on the agenda for CAFs and conservatives was ensuring that the APLO would be implemented. Doing so would ensure the defunding of harm-reduction organizations working with sex workers. Alongside other efforts, in 2005, two years after the passage of the Leadership Act, feminists cosigned a letter with the Christian Medical and Dental Association, Alabama Physicians for Life, World Relief, and the Traditional Values Coalition. The letter urged President Bush to enforce the APLO and stop policies that legalized, regulated, or tolerated prostitution. They reframed public health interventions for and by sex workers as supporting prostitution and, in turn, supporting the trafficking of women and children:

> Under the guise of anti-trafficking or anti-HIV/AIDS activities, some NGOs incredibly continue to prop up the practice of prostitution instead of rescuing the victims. Despite the fact that Congress has required any organization receiving certain federal grants to produce assurances that the organization opposes prostitution and sex trafficking, many of these NGOs are now imploring you to ignore this mandate.[92]

The government continued to implement the APLO. The consequences were grave: Sex worker programs were shuttered, sex workers were arrested under the guise of ending sex trafficking, mothers who were sex workers were separated from their children, and many were denied HIV care and treatment in detention.[93] For harm-reduction feminists and public health practitioners, these outcomes were both horrifying and preventable. Providing condoms, organizing sex workers, educating clients, and even working with the police had proven to be effective strategies in preventing the transmission of HIV.

### Alliance for the Open Society Institute versus USAID: Feminism in the Courts

Litigation ensued. While ideas about sex, women, and gender were integral to the way feminists saw the law being implemented, the legal battle took place on the terrain of the First Amendment of the US Constitution. In August 2005, DKT International, a provider of HIV/AIDS services, sued the United States Agency for International Development (USAID) in the US District Court for the District of Columbia. The suit alleged First Amendment violations, arguing that DKT was being compelled to take the US government's position on prostitution, contravening its ability to effectively deliver public health services. The organization sought to be neutral on the question of prostitution and asserted that it was its First Amendment right to do so. The US government responded that organizations do not have the right to make any statement they want as recipients of government funds. The US Congress may insist that its mission is accomplished and may do so by placing conditions on aid money. Here, that goal is the eradication of prostitution. The government argued that the pledge requirement was a part of accomplishing this goal.[94]

On September 23, 2005, the Alliance for Open Society International (AOSI) and coplaintiffs the Open Society Institute, Pathfinder International, the Global Health Council, and Interaction, also sued USAID arguing that the pledge requirement under PEPFAR violated First Amendment protections against compelled government speech. As in *DKT*, the primary claim of the AOSI and their copetitioners was that the pledge requirement was a clear violation of First Amendment protections of free speech under the US Constitution.

Feminist advocates from both sides saw the litigation and the Leadership Act as an opportunity to channel their viewpoint into the administration of US funds and have a global impact.[95] On November 15, 2006, in *DKT v. USAID*, international sex-positive feminist organizations, including the Women's Rights Project of the American Civil Liberties Union (ACLU), the Centre for Health and Gender Equity, the Center for Reproductive Rights, and the International Women's Health Coalition, filed an amicus brief in support of DKT's motion for preliminary injunction.[96] The brief argued that, in addition to the First Amendment violations, the existence of the Anti-Prostitution Pledge meant that sex workers were being further stigmatized, driven away from health programs, and were not being reached in key HIV interventions.

CAFs did not file a brief in *DKT* but their ideas were present in the litigation through their advocacy.[97] On April 9, 2003, for example, Donna Hughes testified to the Subcommittee of East Asian and Pacific Affairs for the Senate Foreign Relations Committee on the "Trafficking of Women and Children in East Asia and Beyond."[98]

> We can better reduce the spread of HIV by rescuing trafficking victims and ending the sexual slave trade that creates a demand for more victims. In every case, U.S. policies should encourage the arrest and prosecution of traffickers and pimps and the permanent closure of the brothels.
>
> There are billions of dollars being spent on HIV/AIDS prevention and treatment, and a significant portion of it is directed for prevention in "high risk" groups, such as women and children in prostitution. There should be appropriate restrictions or requirements for how aid organizations and their personnel respond when they suspect that anyone they come in contact with is abused, exploited, or enslaved.[99]

In responding to DKT, USAID cites Donna Hughes to claim that women who are trafficked are at higher risk for HIV, which is a "death sentence for victims."[100]

CAFs did submit an amicus brief in support of the prostitution pledge in *AOSI v. USAID*. The brief was filed by CATW and Equality Now on behalf of eighteen organizations, including Apne Aap in India, Coalition Against Trafficking in Women, Asia Pacific, and Standing Against Global Exploitation ("the SAGE Project").[101] In the brief, the amici argued that organizations opposed to legalizing prostitution are more effective in the long run, because the eradication of the sex industry will lead to a reduction of HIV/AIDS.[102] In keeping with the abolitionist position, the amicus brief highlights the exploitative nature of prostitution:

> The harms of prostitution are so profoundly linked to gender, class, and racial inequality as to make the prostitution industry one of the world's most extreme systems of discrimination. Its victims are overwhelmingly female and overwhelmingly poor. They are made vulnerable by the disadvantaged status of women in many regions, by the childhood sexual abuse for which girls are disproportionately targeted, and by the desperation induced by poverty.[103]

Their brief goes on to argue that it is necessary to address HIV while "condemning the industry of prostitution." In turn, it is necessary to work toward "harm-elimination" rather than simply "harm-reduction." Organizations, they argue, should be supportive of condom distribution and education but only as they condemn the act of prostitution.[104]

Sex-positive feminists and sex worker rights groups filed their own amicus brief in support of AOSI and other plaintiffs. The brief was submitted by the Women's Rights Project of the ACLU on behalf of amici, including the Center for Health and Gender Equity (CHANGE), International Women's Health Coalition, the Center for Reproductive Rights, and a variety of public health organizations (including AIDS Action, Planned Parenthood Federation of America, and the Foundation for AIDS Research). The brief argues that sex workers are integral to successful HIV programs and that the abolitionist position alienates the most marginalized women, in turn preventing HIV programs from effectively reaching sex workers.[105]

In 2006, harm-reduction advocates, including sex-positive feminists and sex workers, were successful in court, receiving an injunction against the application of the APLO.[106] Justice Victor Navarro of the District Court of the Southern District of New York held that the law undermined the ability of public health organizations to freely speak in the context of public health interventions. This created, per the legal standard necessary, an irreparable harm, including an inability to work with governments that refused to sign the pledge and an inability to explore the connections between legalization and sex work in the context of the epidemic.[107]

USAID responded by saying that it would soon publish guidelines responding to those concerns. In 2007, HHS published guidance clarifying that if an organization was an "independent organization affiliated with a recipient of Leadership Act funds, the independent organization did need not to have a policy explicitly opposing prostitution and sex trafficking for the recipient to maintain compliance with the policy requirement."[108] This satisfied the US government concern that a pro-sex work position, contrary to the government's, would be imputed to it. At first glance, the requirements seemed attainable. To be found to have "objective integrity and independence" from an organization receiving Leadership Act money the organization had to show it was a legally separate entity: that it received no Leadership Act funds, and that it was physically and financially separate from the affiliated organization. But an organization could not simply keep separate accounting. HHS regulations allowed the agency to examine organizational relationships on a "case-by-case basis and based on the totality of the facts" using several factors including "the existence of separate personnel, management, and governance"; "the existence of separate accounts, accounting records, and timekeeping records"; "the degree of separation from facilities, equipment and supplies, the extent to which signs and other forms of identification which distinguish the Recipient from the affiliated organization are present, and signs and materials that could be associated with the affiliated organization or restricted activities are absent"; and "the extent to which HHS, the U.S. Government and the project name are protected from public association with the affiliated organization and its restricted activities in materials such as publications, conference and press or public statements."

For harm-reduction organizations, these guidelines were not acceptable. The rules would continue to defund critical sex worker services and place unreasonable demands on organizations. Many of the sex worker projects were hanging on by a financial thread. Nonprofits were unable to pay staff, relied on volunteer labor, and often operated in run-down facilities. The idea that an organization would be able to split into two and create an entirely different entity with its own staff and budget was unreasonable and unlikely. The effect was that sex worker groups were simply going to continue to be denied funding by the largest donor on HIV – the US government – and be unable to function as necessary.

USAID appealed the injunction put into place by Judge Navarro at the District Court. While the government's appeal was pending, HHS continued to draft and contest regulations.

The 2007 guidelines were opened up for notice and comment in 2008, allowing for feedback from the public. There was clear public concern and opposition from nongovernmental organizations and elected officials. Congressman Henry Waxman and Congresswoman Barbara Lee submitted joint comments on the proposed rule, writing that it was vague, would produce a chilling effect on organizations, and that the separation requirements would be burdensome.[109] Despite these critiques, the rule was finalized in 2008 and went into effect in early 2009.

In November 2009, the federal government once again issued a rule for notice and comment. Under new draft guidelines that year, organizations were still required to have a policy opposing sex trafficking and prostitution. This did not satisfy feminist harm-reduction advocates who felt that the requirement itself compelled speech – particularly for US organizations – and undermined effective public health interventions.[110]

Sex-positive, harm-reduction feminists organized responses to the proposed rule, highlighting the mismatch between the rule and the injunction issued by the Second Circuit, and called for HHS to stop implementation of the APLO. With that call, they were directly challenging the constant urging of abolitionists to further push for its implementation. In their letter, CHANGE and Human Rights Watch (HRW),[111] for example, argued that the new guidelines did not acknowledge that US-based organizations were now exempt from the Act's requirements. CHANGE and HRW stated their concerns:

> US anti-HIV/AIDS and anti-trafficking efforts – as well as the human rights of individuals targeted by these efforts – will be severely undermined by the Leadership Act's "anti-prostitution pledge" requirement, which requires recipients of funding to have a "policy opposing prostitution and sex trafficking." We oppose this requirement because it wrongly restricts free speech, and because it is irreconcilable with best practices in public health.

In a separate letter, the International Women's Health Coalition, Ipas USA, and the International Planned Parenthood Federation also joined public health organizations expressing concern about the anti-prostitution pledge.[112] The letter sought clarification as to what the pledge meant by "opposing prostitution" and noted that organizations were unsure whether they could engage in activities that benefitted sex workers and reduced the spread of HIV. Drawing on ideas generated from harm reduction, the letter called for reducing criminal penalties associated with sex work:

> Researching the pros and cons of various legal regimes and their impact on HIV transmission among sex workers; [a]dvocating for reducing or eliminating criminal penalties against sex workers in order to encourage them to help identify traffickers or to address extortion of police; and [h]elping sex workers form collectives and unions in order to better protect themselves from police and community violence and abuse and enable them to access health services.[113]

A third letter was submitted by 170 individuals and organizations, including the Sex Worker Outreach Project, Global Network of Sex Worker Projects, Scarlet Alliance in Australia, Sex Workers Interest Organization in Denmark, and Syndicat du TRAvail Sexuel (STRASS) of France.[114] The individual and organizational signatories also criticized the US government for violating the human rights of sex workers and pointed out the many ways in which the APLO interfered with public health practice.

On April 13, 2010, now with Barack Obama as president, HHS issued final regulations. The new regulations did not benefit from the progressive turn in national politics. Instead, they reiterated the US government goal of ensuring that "the Government's position opposing prostitution and sex trafficking is not undermined." The rule also reinforced the abolitionist position taken on by the US government, demanding that funding announcements and agreements with funding recipients included a clause "that states that the recipient is opposed to prostitution and sex trafficking because of the psychological and physical risks they pose for women, men, and children … the rule also … eliminates the requirement for an additional certification by funding recipients."[115] The definition of commercial sex work remained vague; and to the detriment of harm-reduction projects, sex work was conflated with sex trafficking. HHS did, however, acknowledge the need for "greater flexibility in finding alternative channels for protected expression in diverse areas for diverse populations." In turn, it offered what it claimed was a more flexible way of affiliating with organizations potentially in violation of the pledge requirement: Rather than require certification, HHS would examine affiliations on a case-by-case basis.[116] The regulations went into effect on May 13, 2010. Advocates argued that they clarified little about how the antiprostitution pledge should be implemented, and recipients voiced confusion.

As the regulations were being altered, the litigation continued. In 2011, the Second Circuit again decided for the petitioners and against the government, concluding that the requirements went far beyond what the Supreme Court had previously held to be permissible restrictions on funding, and that the plaintiffs clearly suffered an injury from the pledge requirement. Importantly, the court held that the government rule promulgated in 2010 did not solve the First Amendment issue produced by APLO, in that a US-funded agency still had to take the US government's position.[117]

The government appealed again and in 2012 the US Supreme Court agreed to hear *AOSI v. USAID* to consider the constitutionality of the antiprostitution pledge requirement on First Amendment grounds. AOSI continued to argue that the pledge requirement compelled government speech and was therefore unconstitutional. The US government argued that the requirement was necessary to the goal of the government to end prostitution and sex trafficking. The case was argued before the Supreme Court in April 2013.

Sex-positive feminists did not have an explicit presence in the briefs filed before the US Supreme Court. Abolitionists did, however. In keeping with their claims before the lower courts, abolitionists continued their fight to use criminal law to end sex work. Once again, AOSI argued that the pledge requirement undermined its First Amendment rights since it was compelled to take the US government's position on prostitution and trafficking. AOSI contended that the pledge limited its ability to engage in outreach with sex worker groups and, in turn, its ability to effectuate good public health programming. The group argued that because engaging with sex workers was a best practice in public health, opposing prostitution would undermine its ability to work. In a moment signifying the importance of US lawmaking on global governance and financing on AIDS, UN Joint Program on HIV and AIDS (UNAIDS) also filed a neutral amicus arguing that sex workers represent a population at risk of HIV infection and that to be effective, organizations working with them needed "flexibility, funding, and support."[118] Further, UNAIDS argued that the loss of funds suffered by HIV/AIDS organizations would contribute to a resource-poor environment, hampering efforts to prevent HIV transmission amongst sex workers. Although UNAIDS did not argue for decriminalization or legalization in its brief, it focused on the importance of the role of the legal environment in implementing services for sex workers.[119]

Against the arguments of AOSI, CATW filed a brief on behalf of forty-six organizations – including Apne Aap, Equality Now, and the Hunt Alternatives Fund – arguing that the APLO should be upheld:

> In order to work effectively against the harms inflicted by prostitution, including exposure to HIV/AIDS, it is essential to identify the industry of prostitution and sex trafficking for what it is: a global marketplace in which organized criminal entities and other profiteers reap billions annually from the sexual exploitation and enslavement of the most vulnerable women and children in the world, and as a system of abuse, of exploitation, of discrimination, of violence.

Despite this language, in a footnote CATW clarifies that it does not presume that all individuals in the sex industry are controlled "by a trafficker," yet the group also notes that most people in the sex industry cannot exit due to "addiction, trauma and other psychological injury, and subtle and not-so-subtle tactics of coercion employed by sex industry profiteers." To CATW, prostitution and sex trafficking are "inherently harmful."[120]

Based on this, CATW insists that "opposing the legalization and legitimization of prostitution lies at the heart of any program aimed at eradicating HIV/AIDS." By restricting PEPFAR funds, the harm-elimination goal will be achieved. CATW clarifies that while penalties should not be placed on "prostituted persons" the US government should urge messaging which allows for the prosecution of "pimps and johns." Given its position on criminalization, CATW demands that advocating for the legalization of prostitution should not be permissible with US government funds.

In 2013, nearly ten years after the law was first passed, the US Supreme Court ruled that of the two restrictive conditions of the APLO, the pledge requirement violated the First Amendment. The holding only partially liberated US-based harm-reduction, sex worker and sex-positive feminist organizations from the constraints of the PEPFAR funding. The Leadership Act continued to prevent organizations from advocating for the legalization of prostitution. This meant that harm-reduction organizations could not advocate for the legalization of sex work, undermining their ability to bring about necessary legal reforms.

HHS responded with interim guidelines in 2014 saying that it would no longer apply the Leadership Act's pledge requirement against US organizations, only against foreign NGOs.[121] In 2017, the Trump administration issued guidelines for recipients of USAID money devoted to HIV and AIDS, reinforcing that the US government is opposed to prostitution and trafficking, and requiring non-US government organizations to comply with the provisions of the pledge requirement.

Confusion remained, however. Organizations that received contracts with USAID to do public health work often worked in partnership with foreign-based affiliates of US-based entities. Did the APLO apply to these organizations registered outside the United States even if they were a subsidiary of a US-based organization? That question forced the US Supreme Court to revisit the case again in 2020. The four organizations that sued argued that as US-based organizations they rely heavily on their foreign affiliates and that the positions taken by the foreign affiliates at the behest of the US government could be imputed to the

US-based organizations, undermining their work on HIV/AIDS and their First Amendment rights. The Supreme Court disagreed. Writing for the majority, Justice Brett Kavanaugh stated that foreign organizations and affiliates are not protected by the First Amendment of the US Constitution. The pledge requirement for foreign organizations and affiliates would stand: The US government could force them to have a policy against prostitution and sex trafficking if they were taking US dollars to do AIDS relief.

From the perspective of harm-reduction feminists and sex workers, while US-based organizations were finally freed from the pledge requirement, foreign-based organizations remained subject to the US government position on prostitution and sex trafficking. The second condition of the Leadership Act, that organizations could not advocate for the legalization of prostitution and sex trafficking, still severely limited the ability of harm-reduction advocates and sex workers to advocate for legal transformation in their own national context. While CAFs lost ground on mandating that all organizations including US-based organizations receiving funds would have to take the abolitionist feminist position, the continued application of the law to aid-receiving countries would accomplish some of their goals: shuttering and silencing sex worker focused harm-reduction interventions.

## INTERNATIONAL ADVOCACY: UN AND HUMAN RIGHTS

Tensions in feminist camps between harm reduction and harm elimination were also present in international governance. Over a decade before the Supreme Court ruling, in 2002, UNAIDS offered a technical advisory document on HIV and sex work, stressing the need to decriminalize sex work and involve sex workers in condom promotion and safer sex outreach.[122] The UNAIDS technical advisory document explicitly called for the decriminalization of sex work and the development of programs not just for sex workers but for all players in sex work:

> It is essential that these strategies be implemented concurrently so that they can strengthen and complement one another – i.e., using peer education and outreach approaches while ensuring the provision of basic health and social services and *moving to decriminalize sex work.* By using this approach, "creating supportive environments" becomes a

> predictable outcome. The most effective actions design an appropriate mix of interventions into a community-development-oriented programme that is geared not just towards sex workers but towards *all players* in sex work.[123]

In 2004, the WHO continued the promotion of harm reduction for sex workers by highlighting the role of sex workers in the implementation of HIV projects and collaborating with sex worker networks to publish a tool kit laying out key principles to effective and sustainable sex worker programs, including:[124] "ensuring that interventions do no harm"; "recognizing that sex workers are usually highly motivated to improve their health and well-being"; making "sex workers are part of the solution"; "building capacities and leadership among sex workers in order to facilitate effective participation and community ownership"; and "recognizing the role played in HIV transmission by clients and third parties, i.e., targeting the whole sex work setting, including clients and third parties, rather than only sex workers."[125]

WHO and the Global Coalition on Women and AIDS, a project of UNAIDS, also published a shorter document entitled *Violence against Sex Workers and HIV Prevention*, which states that the criminalization of sex work leads to violence against sex workers. Sex worker rights activists provided input into the document.[126] In 2006, UNAIDS and the Office of the High Commissioner for Human Rights published the *International Guidelines on HIV/AIDS and Human Rights* ("International Guidelines"), which declared that among other structural factors, the decriminalization of sex work was necessary to reach sex workers in the response to HIV:

> With regard to adult sex work that involves no victimization, criminal law should be reviewed with the aim of decriminalizing, then legally regulating occupational health and safety conditions to protect sex workers and their clients, including support for safe sex during sex work. Criminal law should not impede provision of HIV prevention and care services to sex workers and their clients. Criminal law should ensure that children and adult sex workers who have been trafficked or otherwise coerced into sex work are protected from participation in the sex industry and are not prosecuted for such participation but rather are removed from sex work and provided with medical and psycho-social support services, including those related to HIV.[127]

These reforms were tenuous victories for sex workers in the context of AIDS governance. They acknowledged that the entire sex market could be aided by harm-reduction interventions and prioritized the choice and agency of sex workers. They were soon challenged by American CAFs.

In 2006, UNAIDS sponsored a Global Consultation on Sex Work and AIDS in Rio de Janeiro.[128] Attendees included members of UN agencies and NGOs from sex worker organizations, including the Asia-Pacific Network of Sex Workers, the Latin American and Caribbean Network of Sex Workers, and the Global Network of Sex Workers (NSWP). Abolitionists had gained influence following their victories of the early 2000s – including the TVPA and the APLO in PEPFAR – and abolitionist activists attended the meeting at the urging of the US government. Until 2006, CAFs had not been involved in discussions on HIV and sex work at UNAIDS. But this time, both sex worker organizations and abolitionist feminists gave presentations.[129] Melissa Farley, an abolitionist, spoke about "'healing' from prostitution" and a "harm-elimination" rather than a harm-reduction approach.[130] Farley also spoke of the need to reduce demand for sex work through the use of felony-level charges against clients of sex workers.[131] As documented by Anna-Louise Crago in her article *The Curious Sex Worker's Guide to the UNAIDS Guidance Note*, the participation of abolitionist feminists and their allies shifted the thinking of UNAIDS on the decriminalization of sex work:

> The United States sent 4 people to the meeting. Three worked with the government and one was an antiprostitution activist. The Americans were very against sex work or harm reduction projects. They supported criminalizing clients and "rescuing" women from sex work. They also had a very intimidating presence. One UN person told me that after they said in the meeting that there was a difference between sex work and trafficking, their boss at the head office in another country received an angry call from the U.S. government almost immediately. When the UN people had a meeting after the consultation, the Americans sat nearby and appeared to be listening in and taking notes.[132]

Reports published by sex worker activist attendees from the Sex Worker's Rights Advocacy Network suggested that the US government also placed pressure on UN officials to adopt an abolitionist position.[133]

In 2007, only a year after the issuance of the International Guidelines and five years after UNAIDS issued a technical advisory document suggesting that sex work be decriminalized, UNAIDS issued a new

Guidance Note prepared by the UN Population Fund (UNFPA). The 2007 *Guidance Note on HIV and Sex Work* retreated from a sex worker rights perspective advocating decriminalization and focused instead on providing alternatives to sex work and ending demand for sex work.[134] As signaled by the shift in perspective, the new Guidance Note on sex work was the product of interventions from abolitionists and marked the product of a struggle between abolitionist and sex-positive feminists with and within UNAIDS. In this new 2007 Guidance Note, decriminalization was not mentioned once, in contrast to the numerous United Nations documents produced before the Guidance Note. Further, unlike previous documents, the 2007 Guidance Note explicitly suggested that most sex workers are trafficked into sex work:

> A significant number of women and girls are trafficked into sex work, knowingly or unknowingly, with the promise of a better life for themselves and their families. The increasing feminization of migration and the involvement of families, kin networks and local communities in the movement of women and girls, blurs the difference between trafficking and sex work. The figures on the proportion of women trafficked into sex work and those people entering sex work of their own volition, regardless of the reason for doing so, are often disputed and result in significantly different political, legal and policy approaches and outcomes.[135]

This reversal led to a multipronged advocacy effort from harm-reduction feminists and allies, including the Canadian HIV/AIDS Legal Network, the Open Society Institute, and the Global Working Group on Sex Work Policy, as well as the NSWP. At the April 2008 Programme Coordinating Board meeting of UNAIDS, several NGO representatives lobbied UNAIDS to move closer to returning to its 2002 stance on sex work. Another UNAIDS Guidance Note was released in 2009, and though it mentions law as a barrier to accessing care and the need for positive steps toward a nondiscriminatory legal system for sex work, it stops short of calling for decriminalization.[136] This Guidance Note retained many elements of the abolitionist position, in particular, the conflation of sex work with trafficking:

> A number of complex factors may also contribute to entry into sex work. For sex workers, these factors range along a continuum that extends from free choice to forced sex work and trafficking. Trafficking, which represents the denial of virtually all human rights, involves the recruitment, transportation, transfer, harbouring or receipt of persons, by means of threat or use of force or other forms of coercion, abduction, or

> fraud, of deception, of abuse of power or the giving or receiving of payment or benefits to achieve the consent of a person having control over another person, for the purposes of exploitation. Women and girls are the primary victims of trafficking for sex work, although a smaller number of men and boys are also trafficked into sex work. This Guidance Note affirms the right of any sex worker to leave sex work if she/he so wishes and to have meaningful access to options for employment other than sex work.[137]

Perhaps to counter the document's strong abolitionist focus, at the release of the Guidance Note, Michel Sidibé, the executive director of UNAIDS, established an advisory group co-chaired by NSWP and UNAIDS "to support and advise UNAIDS (Secretariat and Cosponsors), from a perspective that is informed by human rights principles, the best available evidence and the lived experience of sex workers."[138] The group was to be guided by the experiences of sex workers, and punitive laws became an important area of focus[139] and work on four thematic areas, including: the removal of punitive laws, policies, and practices; reduction of demand; the conflation of human trafficking and sex work; and economic empowerment.[140]

In 2012, UNAIDS released an updated Guidance Note that was partly the outcome of the consultative process in 2009.[141] The 2012 guidelines called for the decriminalization of various aspects of the sex industry including the purchase and sale of sex.[142] The updated Guidance Note states:

> States can take many actions to establish legal and policy environments that are conducive to universal access to HIV services for sex workers. Among these are the following: States should move away from criminalising sex work or activities associated with it. Decriminalisation of sex work should include removing criminal laws and penalties for purchase and sale of sex, management of sex workers and brothels, and other activities related to sex work. To the degree that states retain non-criminal administrative law or regulations concerning sex work, these should be applied in ways that do not violate sex workers' rights or dignity and that ensure their enjoyment of due process of law.[143]

While actively acknowledging that trafficking is a problem that must be addressed, the UNAIDS 2012 Guidance Note[144] specifically distinguished its recommendations on sex work from the Palermo Protocol definition of trafficking. The Guidance Note distinguishes the harms associated with sex work from the sale of sex itself:

> However, it is important to understand that being trafficked is often a temporary situation: people who are trafficked do not necessarily remain in situations of powerlessness and coercion. For example, individuals who have been trafficked into the sex industry, or those who find themselves tricked or coerced once within the sex industry, can find their way out of situations of coercion but remain in sex work operating more independently and usually with support from their fellow sex workers, their clients, their intimate partners and their managers or agents.[145]

In addition to the sex-worker-led advisory group, several key events between 2008 and 2012 bolstered the strength of both borrowing harm-reduction principles for sex work and calling for decriminalizing sex work and related practices. In 2008, prominent Indian attorney Anand Grover became the UN Special Rapporteur for the Right to Health.[146] In 2010, Grover submitted an official report that specifically highlighted challenges that the criminalization of sex work and related practices posed to realizing the right to health.[147]

That same year the United Nations Development Program (UNDP) established an independent Global Commission on HIV and the Law.[148] The purpose of the commission was to assess legal and regulatory barriers to slowing the HIV epidemic, with three primary areas of focus: criminal laws, laws pertaining to women's rights, and intellectual property law. Advisory group members produced reports on areas of concern to the commission to guide the commissioners' recommendations.[149] Importantly, the Global Commission hosted a series of regional meetings that brought together activists, NGOs, and academics to discuss regional issues pertaining to law and human rights.[150] Organizations submitted reports to be considered in the drafting of key recommendations.[151] Ultimately, the commission recommended the decriminalization of all consensual adult sex.[152]

In 2012, UNAIDS released a report in partnership with the United Nations Population Fund, the WHO, and the NSWP titled *Prevention and Treatment of HIV and Other Sexually Transmitted Infections for Sex Workers in Low- and Middle-Income Countries: Recommendations for a Public Health Approach*.[153] The document placed its recommendations in two tiers: "good practice recommendations" and "evidence-based recommendations."[154] Good practice recommendations were "overarching principles derived not from scientific evidence but from common sense, ethics and human rights principles."[155] With regard to good practice, the report recommends that "all countries should work toward decriminalization of sex work and elimination of the unjust application of non-criminal laws and regulations against sex workers."[156] In doing so, the report cites the report of the Global Commission on HIV and the Law.[157]

## SHIFTING EPIDEMIOLOGY: THE RISE OF ANTITRAFFICKING LITERATURE IN AIDS RESEARCH

In each chapter of this book, the legal debates have shaped the epidemiological environment, and in the context of a public-health-based ideological battle, epidemiology has altered the ability of legal actors to legitimate their legal and political claims. The same is true for the feminist debates on sex work and trafficking. A look at the epidemiological literature suggests a shift in this literature on how to understand risk and consent, and the spread of HIV. While this nascent literature has provided some grounding for legal claims that have been made to justify a capacious definition of sex trafficking, it also reveals how little evidence was required for carceral feminists and conservatives to unleash an ideological project grounded in aid conditions to undermine the most effective programs in AIDS prevention.

Until 2000, the peer-reviewed literature on HIV did not explore the question of how sex trafficking related to HIV. Most studies examined how sex work or prostitution related to HIV transmission. The search terms "sex trafficking" and "HIV" in the Pub-Med database of peer-reviewed public health articles revealed that prior to 2000, there was only one article linking sex trafficking and HIV.[158] The article, however, was a critique of the conflation of sex trafficking and sex work in the context of HIV programming.

The lack of research linking sex trafficking to HIV undermined the ability of abolitionist feminists to claim that it was necessary to abolish the sex industry through the use of criminal law. Public health research was necessary. The studies began churning out in 2000, as attention to antitrafficking programming was growing both in the US and internationally. Between 2000 and 2021, forty-two peer-reviewed articles on sex trafficking and HIV were published.

The primary claim emanating from the literature on sex trafficking and HIV is that sex-trafficked women and girls are at high risk for contracting HIV.[159] To make this claim, however, requires defining trafficking in a consistent way. While several studies cite the Palermo Protocol definition of trafficking as a reference point, the studies themselves reveal a nonstandardized use of the term sex trafficking.[160]

Researchers for a study by Gupta et al. in the *International Journal of Gynaecology and Obstetrics*, for example, decided whether or not a sex worker was trafficked based on her age entering sex work or if she reported being "lured, forced, or cheated" into sex work.[161] In another instance, a study looked at case records of a "major non-governmental organization" providing rescue, shelter, and care of minor girls "held against their will in brothels in Mumbai."[162] In yet another study, Goldenberg et al. considered women with "involuntary" or adolescent entry into sex work to be sex trafficked in accordance with the Palermo Protocol definition.[163] Several studies also claim that women trafficked into sex work have a greater vulnerability to contracting HIV than those who voluntarily enter the sex industry.[164]

While the goal of understanding how sex-trafficked individuals might be at particular risk of HIV is important, it may be equally necessary to consider how varied definitions of sex trafficking may muddy our understanding of who is or is not being trafficked and, in turn, how the data should or should not be interpreted to justify legal intervention. Casting the net of exploitation broadly also results in a broader evidence base for justifying the carceral solution offered by mainstream approaches to sex trafficking.

As this literature continues to grow, so does the literature on sex work and HIV.[165] Importantly for harm-reduction advocacy, the public health literature supports decriminalization of sex work. In 2012, for example, the leading public health journal, *The Lancet*, stated:

> Discriminatory laws and policies, stigma, violence, and social exclusion all impede efforts to reach sex workers and their clients with effective HIV prevention, treatment, care, and support programmes. Individual-level behaviour change in the form of traditional peer education, condom promotion, and screening for sexually transmitted infections does not work without substantial community mobilisation, leadership, and participation of sex workers themselves to tackle the social and structural factors that influence their vulnerability.[166]

Despite sex worker organizations actively acknowledging trafficking as an issue in the sex industry, the epidemiological research on sex work often avoids the question of coercion. It focuses on the ability to deliver health services to sex workers, the effectiveness of sex worker outreach and programming, and the related health outcomes. The lack of engagement with the trafficking definition could be based on a variety of factors. One might be acknowledgment that the line between sex work and trafficking is too difficult to discern at times, or that even if a woman is trafficked she may benefit from harm-reduction services, given the dearth of other available social interventions. A second reason might be a flaw in the way public health studies are conducted: They look narrowly at specific harms and assume away structural concerns or coercion that might emanate from issues such as poverty. A third reason might be the underlying contradiction between the crime control framework that the definition of sex trafficking rests on and the emphasis on the decriminalization model in research with and on sex workers.

It is clear from the data that the production of public health knowledge centers on sex workers and, in turn, decriminalization for the sake of harm reduction. Yet the antitrafficking frame continues to grow. Despite the dominance of the idea that decriminalization is necessary to stop the spread of HIV, sex workers, their clients, and others within the industry are arrested and prosecuted at the expense of life-saving public health interventions.[167]

# CONCLUSION

## Governing the Unknown: Legal–Scientific Settlements

On January 31, 2020, the US government issued an emergency declaration about a new public health emergency: COVID. This new pandemic raised old questions in the contemporary moment.[1] How do we determine legal rules to stop the spread of disease in the face of scientific uncertainty? How do knowledge claims – around disease, illness, health – shape the distribution of material resources?

This conclusion offers the frame of *legal–scientific settlements* as a way to understand the interactions between law, science, and social movements in public health crises.[2] The term legal–scientific settlement describes how the stabilization of particular truth-claims results in new legal and regulatory regimes. I use the term "settlement" to reflect the contingency and possibility for disruption. In these moments of legal–scientific settlement, law and science are coproductive of new facts and new knowledge ecosystems that are then generative of distributional outcomes.[3] Legal–scientific settlements reflect negotiations between law and new scientific and epidemiological claims refracted through the political and economic context in which they are developed. As reflected by the story of feminist AIDS activists, legal–scientific settlements are important *because* they have distributional effects: material, social, and cultural.[4]

### REMAKING LAW, REMAKING SCIENCE

As HIV travelled from person to person lawmakers struggled to govern in a moment of scientific uncertainty. The virus spread as the idea of personal responsibility further entrenched itself into the politics and economics of healthcare: People ought to take care of their own health. As personal responsibility narratives took hold, so did the idea that the state does not owe a duty to provide necessary healthcare services, especially to those who do not deserve them.[5] The stigma around gay sex and drug use moved people who had HIV quickly into the category of undeserving. A growing emphasis on criminal law would result in a crime control paradigm for many of the groups deemed at risk for HIV and harm-reduction programs were de-emphasized. [6] The result was sickness and death.

Who would be deemed as most in need and deserving of healthcare in a floundering public health system? A technocratic approach might suggest that this would be scientifically determined by the epidemiological data. This data would presumably be collected in a methodologically thorough and neutral way scientifically revealing how services and funding should be prioritized. In these accounts, as scientists and epidemiologists gained more knowledge, legislators and regulators were able to transform laws accordingly to better target the epidemic.

Studying feminist social movement activism in the AIDS response reveals the deep obfuscation of activism's role in shaping public health responses in technocratic accounts. This book remedies this erasure by showing how activists and lawyers helped shape a new legal order that would alter how scientists and public health institutions responded to AIDS. This shifted how money, resources, and power are distributed within the ideological framework offered by the current political and economic frameworks.

Feminists saw an inextricable connection in how the legal rules on disability were making and reinforcing the scientific vision of who has AIDS. It was a legal–scientific settlement that excluded women and needed to be disrupted. As the AIDS epidemic roiled on feminists saw that shifting science and law could create opportunities for remaking the world according to a feminist imaginary. As this book documents, whether it was the Centers for Disease Control and Prevention (CDC) definition of AIDS or mobilizing evidence in the context of harm and consent in sex work and trafficking, feminist advocates successfully transformed the ideas and institutions that produced knowledge about risk and vulnerability to HIV. Reflecting what Janet Halley and her co-authors have called governance feminism, they remade the world from both inside and outside institutions.[7] The focus on science and epidemiology was intentional. The goals of feminist reformers were not only to change what we know – they were to alter the material distribution of resources in the context of a withering welfare state. They fought the ideology of individual responsibility that repeatedly failed women during the AIDS epidemic.

Feminists were not the first, nor the last, to take on legal–scientific settlements in service of redistributing resources through altering legal rules. The idea of challenging legal–scientific settlements has many origins, not least W. E. B. DuBois' 1906 book *The Health and Physique of the Negro American*. DuBois questioned the belief held by experts of the day that there was something specific to African Americans that made them less healthy and more likely to die of illnesses like tuberculosis that were circulating rapidly through the American population. He challenged the racialized science that was increasingly taking hold in medicine in the early 1900s, arguing that "[t]he Negro death rate and sickness are largely matters of [social and economic] condition[s] and not due to racial traits and tendencies." DuBois saw that to change the distribution of services and provide more healthcare for African Americans, it was necessary to take on a legal–scientific settlement dictating that the problem of poor health was innate to Black people. This idea justified denying healthcare and maintained a race and class hierarchy.

From DuBois to the Black Panthers and the New Left, feminists continued a tradition that sought to remake institutions and ideas, based on a recognition that the distribution of resources flows from law and knowledge being intertwined, one legitimating the other.[8] The critique of experts, DuBois and beyond, would inspire and motivate scholars and activists to disrupt political–scientific settlements for at least over a century.

In the context of AIDS, despite a shared sense that it was necessary to disrupt legal–scientific settlements, feminists were not always unified in their strategy or goals. Feminists often disagreed, holding competing theories of how to best address women's subordination. There were, and are, deep feminist disagreements about harm reduction and public health, about sex and sexuality, and about race and gender. At the heart of these disagreements was often the question of how to accurately portray the subjugation of women and how to understand liberation. The debates on sex work and trafficking in Chapter 5 clearly illustrate this point. Competing camps of feminists, each with their own feminist projects, fought for recognition of their own worldview in order to shape the distribution of resources to one ideological project or another. At stake was not only money, but life and death, and a virus that moved more quickly where resources to prevent and manage its transmission were scarce.

Feminists engaged in the project, and sometimes competing projects, of defining who women are, what puts them at risk, and how we ought to understand a disease as a phenomenon related to sex and gender. In "Making Up People," philosopher of science Ian Hacking shows how a diagnosis not only gives a preexisting issue a label, it has the effect of producing people: "Who we are is not only what we did, do, and will do but also what we might have done and may do. Making up people changes the space of possibilities for personhood."[9] To make people anew, to make them "at risk," can be an act of resistance and world-making. Feminist advocates pushed to remake the science of women in a fight for material resources.

**New Illness, New Formations, New Legal–Scientific Settlement**

COVID further revealed the severe effects that decades of state restructuring that depleted the welfare and public health systems would have on the management of a new pandemic. As COVID surged, there was limited state/public health capacity to effectively collect and aggregate data on COVID infections for epidemiological analysis, and little to no infrastructure to roll out basic services, including COVID testing.

AIDS activism laid the groundwork for the social movement response to COVID. As before, government failure to appropriately respond to the COVID pandemic resulted in social movement activism. Activists recognized that the fight for redistribution of resources would require questioning/challenging how scientific questions were being framed by experts. They feared a legal–scientific settlement that would obscure the realities of the COVID pandemic.

The movement of Long COVID activists has parallels to the feminist struggles of the 1980s. Long COVID advocates were afflicted by a condition that was being dismissed.[10] They pushed back against the notion that COVID was a simple illness like the flu or pneumonia that would last no more than two weeks. By organizing patient groups and using first-person accounts, Long COVID sufferers published their stories in medical journals.[11] Others recognized themselves in the first-person accounts and began to make the case that they, too, had been suffering for weeks or months after a prior COVID infection. News media then began to pick up on these accounts.

Patient advocates and their allies knew that without the declaration of a medical condition that had been validated by science, necessary legal protections would not be afforded to them.[12] Being classified as having a chronic condition could help people access medical care and treatment, receive insurance coverage, and claim disability benefits. As with AIDS, the scientific and epidemiological understandings of COVID directly related to the distribution of material resources.

In November 2020, Anthony Fauci, Director of the National Institutes of Allergy and Infectious Diseases during AIDS and COVID, noted that it was time to begin exploring a new condition that describes physical consequences that continue from a COVID infection. This development reflected months of advocacy by patient groups, and a burgeoning scholarly and medical literature. Feminists, activated in this context, and with data that women report Long COVID symptoms more frequently than men, called for greater attention to women in the study of Long COVID, while cautioning against the biologization of gender through research on women.[13]

To be sure, while some stakeholders and social movements mobilized basic science and epidemiology to demand a more robust public health response, from vaccines to social welfare support, challenges to scientific authority would also come from individuals and organizations with conflicting ideological projects. Many stakeholders set out to disrupt legal–scientific settlements from mask efficacy to vaccine safety and reliability by claiming the preservation of liberty and freedom. Their redistributionist impulse diverged from advocates who sought more state services and care. Corporate entities, like Delta Airlines, sought to boost business. It worked to rewind the ten-day quarantine period to five days and sought to reduce postinfection isolation times to address worker shortages and keep individuals traveling.[14] Along with other players, and against the flight attendants' union, it lobbied the CDC to change the rules around quarantine and isolation.[15] Masking was portrayed by some activists as an act of state overreach and control, despite evidence that face coverings effectively prevented disease transmission.[16] A successful campaign to challenge public health authority seemed inspired by a desire to galvanize voters in the name of liberty and freedom. It is still not possible to assess the true impact of these rule shifts: Did more people contract COVID? Did more people die from COVID? As various actors step into fray, scientific uncertainty produces opportunities to legally govern in a way that redistributes the losses and gains of a crisis.

Though this book focuses on how feminists utilized science and epidemiology in service of law reform for women's health during AIDS, the reality is that competing projects to remake scientific and epidemiological settlements long predate COVID as well. In the early 2000s, for example, the George W. Bush administration directed the CDC to emphasize the failure rates of condoms and the positive role of abstinence in stopping the spread of HIV and sexually transmitted infections (STIs).[17] There were political benefits to pushing this perspective: It justified providing greater resources to the faith-based organizations who were willing to work on an abstinence-only agenda and sated the appetites of social conservatives who long advocated for abstinence.

These fights to disrupt legal–scientific settlements, either from the left or the right, have all been similarly erased from narratives of disease management that foreground apolitical scientific discovery. The occlusion of the political contributes to the contemporary sensibility that the politics of scientific disruption that are taking place during COVID are a new phenomenon and that they are only counterproductive to scientific and social progress.

The World Health Organization pronounced the COVID pandemic over on May 5, 2023. Though bodies no longer pile up in freezers near major city hospitals in the United States, the virus continues to travel rapidly from person to person. As this book is published, some newspapers continue to publish weekly death counts. Most of the world remains unvaccinated and many people continue to fall sick. In January 2023, a *New York Times* headline announced that "scientists see a diminished threat" in the newest surge of COVID cases. "We are in good shape," an expert on COVID reassured readers. A few paragraphs later the article offers a statistic without comment: 1,200 people die of COVID each week. This is not a viral state of nature; it is the outcome of a legal–scientific settlement that distributes disability and death.

HIV also continues to spread. Forty years into AIDS, public health institutions have yet to declare that the epidemic is over. There is no vaccine or cure. Alarming statistics tell a troubling story: As of 2023, 17 percent of the South African population aged 15–49 are testing positive for HIV. In the United States, one in two gay Black men will be diagnosed with HIV in his lifetime and girls aged thirteen to nineteen constitute the majority of new AIDS cases.

We await the next pandemic even as we cannot escape the current ones. Each impending public health crisis brings new legal–scientific settlements. Social movements, with competing political and material interests, will continue to challenge the notion that law and science reflect the deepest commitment to reason. The outcomes of these struggles will dictate who will survive and how.

# NOTES

## A NOTE ON METHODS

1. David Garland, *What Is a "History of the Present"? On Foucault's Genealogies and Their Critical Preconditions*, 16(4) PUNISHMENT AND SOC. (Oct. 3, 2014), https://doi.org/10.1177/1462474514541711. Garland reads Foucault to describe a genealogy as "a method of writing critical history: a way of using historical materials to bring about a 'revaluing of values' in the present day. Genealogical analysis traces how contemporary practices and institutions emerged out of specific struggles, conflicts, alliances, and exercise of power, many of which are nowadays forgotten."
2. David Garland, *What Is a "History of the Present"? On Foucault's Genealogies and Their Critical Preconditions*, 16(4) PUNISHMENT AND SOC. (Oct. 3, 2014), at 372.
3. Sheila Jasanoff writes that STS enables "new ways of querying how knowledge and belief are constructed, proof and evidence validated, meaning conferred on inanimate things, and material objects made to function in harmony with human bodies and collectives. Put differently, STS provides a distinctive gaze on modernity, and it does so by problematizing the productions of science (or, more broadly, knowledge) and technology in ways that complement the work of other disciplines without diminishing their contributions to social theory". Sheila Jasanoff, *The Floating Ampersand*, 2 ENGAGING SCI., TECH., AND SOC. 227–237 (2016).
4. On background rules and distribution see generally Robert Hale, *Coercion and Distribution in a Supposedly Non-Coercive State*, 38 POLITICAL SCI. Q. 470–494 (1923); DAVID KENNEDY, WORLD OF STRUGGLE: HOW POWER, LAW, AND EXPERTISE SHAPE GLOBAL POLITICAL ECONOMY (2016). On a feminist distributional analysis, see Janet Halley, *Distribution and Decision: Assessing Governance Feminism*, in GOVERNANCE FEMINISM: AN INTRODUCTION (Janet Halley et al. eds., 2018). On law and distribution, see LIBBY ADLER, GAY PRIORI: A QUEER CRITICAL LEGAL STUDIES APPROACH TO LAW REFORM (2018) and Karl Klare, On Socialism and Critical Legal Theory, LPE Blog, November 9, 2020.
5. *See generally* SADIYA HARTMAN, WAYWARD LIVES, BEAUTIFUL EXPERIMENTS: INTIMATE HISTORIES OF RIOTOUS BLACK GIRLS, TROUBLESOME WOMEN, AND QUEER RADICALS (2019).

## INTRODUCTION: "WOMEN DON'T GET AIDS, THEY JUST DIE FROM IT"

1. Interview by Aziza Ahmed with Patricia Nalls, Executive Director, The Women's Collective, in Washington, DC (2019).
2. Interview by Dr. Victoria Harden, Director, NIH (National Institutes of Health) Historical Office and the DeWitt Stetten, Jr. Museum of Medical Research and Dr. Caroline Hannaway, NIH Historical Consultant, with Thomas Quinn, Medical Doctor, Johns Hopkins Medical School, Baltimore, MD (Dec. 1996); Centers for Disease Control, Morbidity and Mortality Weekly Report (1982); Lawrence Altman, *Rare Cancer Seen in 41 Homosexuals*, N.Y. Times (July 3, 1981), www.nytimes.com/1981/07/03/us/rare-cancer-seen-in-41-homosexuals.html; James Curran & Harold Jaffe, *AIDS: The Early Years and the CDC's Response*, 60 CDC: Supplements 64–69 (2011); *see* Lawrence Altman, *New Homosexual Disorder Worries Health Officials*, N.Y. Times (May 11, 1982), www.nytimes.com/1982/05/11/science/new-homosexual-disorder-worries-health-officials.html. Altman highlights that scientists are calling the disorder GRID – Gay Related Immunity Disorder. Gay Men's Health Crisis, Records 1975–1978, 1982–1999 (on file with the New York Public Library Humanities and Social Sciences Library Manuscripts and Archives Division); George Oswald et al., *Attempted Immune Stimulation in "Gay Compromise Syndrome"*, 382 Brit. Med. J. 1082 (1982). There was also conflation between gay identity and risk of HIV. In 1982, for example, the CDC stated that most cases of HIV had one of several identifiable "risk factors," naming "male homosexuality" as one of them. *Morbidity and Mortality Weekly Report*, Sept. 24, 1982 ("Only a small percentage of cases have none of the identified risk factors male homosexuality, intravenous drug abuse, Haitian origin, and perhaps hemophilia A"); *see* Russell Robinson, *Racing the Closet*, 61 Stanford L. Rev. 1464 (2009) (discussing how Black men were implicated in public discussions on the spread of HIV); *see generally* Wendy Parmet, *Stigma, Hysteria, and HIV*, 38 Hastings Center Report 1 (2008).
3. John Langone, *Misunderstanding AIDS*, Discover Magazine (Dec. 1985); Collections of the Smithsonian's National Museum of American History, division of Medicine and Science; Paula Treichler, How to Have a Theory in an Epidemic: Cultural Chronicles of AIDS (1999).
4. Lindsay Knight, UNAIDS: The First 10 Years (2008). ("The doctors' expectations for the conference were not met. Some participants aggressively refused to accept that HIV could be transmitted through heterosexual intercourse. 'In a non-scientific way they were saying … these men must be closet gays, and transmission from women to men is impossible,' Piot recalled.") Michael Fumento, The Myth of Heterosexual AIDS (1989) at 46.

5. Feminist legal scholars have long been arguing that feminists have transformative power in institutions. *See* Janet Halley et al., *From the International to the Local: Four Studies in Governance Feminism*, 29 Harv. J. L. and Gender 335 (2006). For work on law and expertise, see David Kennedy, World of Struggle: How Power, Law, and Expertise Shape Global Political Economy (2016). On risk, see Ulrick Beck, Risk Society: Towards a New Modernity (1992). *See also* Tom Baker & Jonathan Simon, Embracing Risk: The Changing Culture of Insurance and Responsibility (2002); Sheila Jasanoff, *Songlines of Risk*, 8 Environmental Values 135–152 (1999).
6. For scholarship about law and distribution, see David Kennedy, World of Struggle: How Power, Law, and Expertise Shape Global Political Economy (2016); Karl Klare, *Judicial Deradicalization of the Wagner Act and the Origins of Modern Legal Consciousness, 1937–1941*, 62 Minn. L. Rev. 265 (1978); Duncan Kennedy, *The Stakes of Law, or Hale and Foucault!*, 4 Legal Stud. F. 327 (1991); Janet Halley, *Distribution and Decision: Assessing Governance Feminism*, in Governance Feminism: An Introduction (Janet Halley et al. eds., 2018). For a critique of identity as a frame in legal reform projects, see Martha Fineman, *Equality and Difference – The Restrained State*, 66 Ala. L. Rev. 609 (2015) (describing vulnerability theory as moving away from discrimination and toward thinking about power and privilege through institutions and relationships).
7. For debates on the role of law and social movements in social change, see generally Duncan Kennedy, *The Critique of Rights in Critical Legal Studies*, in Left Legalism, Left Critique (Wendy Brown and Janet Halley eds., 2002); Janet Halley et al., Governance Feminism: An Introduction (2018); Amna Akbar, Sameer M. Ashar, & Jocelyn Simonson, *Movement Law*, 73 Stan. L. Rev. 821 (2021); Libby Adler, Gay Priori: A Queer Critical Legal Studies Approach to Law Reform (2018); Kathy Abrams, Open Hand, Closed Fist: Practices of Undocumented Organizing in a Hostile State (2022); Michael McCann, Rights at Work: Pay Equity Reform and the Politics of Legal Mobilization (2004); Gerald Rosenberg, The Hollow Hope: Can Courts Bring about Social Change? (2008); Lucie White & Jeremy Perelman, Stones of Hope: How African Activists Reclaim Human Rights to Challenge Global Poverty (2010); Catherine Albiston, *The Dark Side of Litigation as a Social Movement Strategy*, 96 Iowa L. Rev. Bulletin 61 (2011); Gwendolyn Leachman, *From Protest to Perry: How Litigation Changed the LGBT Movement's Agenda*, 47 UC Davis L. Rev. 1667 (2014);

Veena Dubal, *Winning the Battle, Losing the War: Assessing the Impact of Misclassification Litigation on Workers in the Gig Economy*, WISCONSIN L. REV. 739 (2017); DOUG MCADAMS, SIDNEY TARROW, & CHARLES TILLY, DYNAMICS OF CONTENTION (2001). On how gender, race, and class shape the possibilities of law reform for greater participation, see Lucie White, *Subordination, Rhetorical Survival Skills, and Sunday Shoes: Notes on the Hearing of* Mrs. G, 38 BUFFALO L. REV. 1 (1990); Scott Cummings, *Movement Lawyering*, 5 UNIVERSITY OF ILLINOIS L. REV. 1645 (2017); Lani Guinier & Gerald Torres, *Changing the Wind: Notes toward a Demosprudence of Law and Social Movements*, 123 YALE L. REV. 8 (2014); BRUCE ACKERMAN, WE THE PEOPLE: THE CIVIL RIGHTS REVOLUTION (2014).

8. *See generally* BEN HURLBUT, EXPERIMENTS IN DEMOCRACY: HUMAN EMBRYO RESEARCH AND THE POLITICS OF BIOETHICS (2016).
9. For another discussion about the relationship between science and law, see Aziza Ahmed, *Medical Evidence and Expertise in Abortion Jurisprudence*, 41 AM. J. L. AND MED. 85 (2015). For an example of arguments for the separation of science and regulation, see Marcia McNutt et al., The National Academies of Science, Engineering, and Medicine, *Statement by NAS, NAE, and NAM Presidents on Report of Banned Words at CDC* (Dec. 2017), www8.nationalacademies.org/onpinews/newsitem.aspx?RecordID=12182017.
10. Sheila Jasanoff defines coproduction as "how knowledge-making is incorporated into practices of state-making, or of governance more broadly, and, in reverse, how practices of governance influence the making and use of knowledge … Knowledge, in particular, is seen as crystallizing in certain ontological states – organizational, material, embodied – that become objects of study in their own right." Like law and social movements scholars who focus on the constitutive relationship between law and and its application, STS scholars are often interested in how scientific change happens or how we come to understand world-making. While there are divergent strands of STS, that of science, technology and society (ST&S), ST&S overlaps with legal scholars who are interested in the constitutive role of law – in other words, how the law creates the world around it. For ST&S scholars this insight means understanding that law and science constitute one another. Sheila Jasanoff, *The Idiom of Co-production*, in STATES OF KNOWLEDGE: THE CO-PRODUCTION OF SCIENCE AND SOCIAL ORDER (Sheila Jasanoff ed., 2004).
11. The literature on the sociology of science and medicine offers a rich history of how social movements contribute to the shift in legal regulation for health. *See generally* ALONDRA NELSON, BODY AND SOUL: THE BLACK PANTHER PARTY AND THE FIGHT AGAINST MEDICAL

DISCRIMINATION (2011); STEVEN EPSTEIN, INCLUSION: THE POLITICS OF DIFFERENCE IN MEDICAL RESEARCH (2007).

12. My prior work touches on these themes. *See generally* Aziza Ahmed, *Medical Evidence and Expertise in Abortion Jurisprudence*, 41 AM. J. L. AND MED. 85 (2015).
13. Sheila Jasanoff, *The Idiom of Co-production*, in STATES OF KNOWLEDGE: THE CO-PRODUCTION OF SCIENCE AND SOCIAL ORDER (Sheila Jasanoff ed., 2004).
14. The social studies of science and medicine argue that science and knowledge production is not value-neutral, instead it emerges from our social world – law, activism, and science constitute one another. For a history of critical theories of science and technology, see generally Sheila Jasanoff, *A Field of Its Own: The Emergence of Science and Technology Studies*, in THE OXFORD HANDBOOK OF INTERDISCIPLINARITY (Robert Frodeman & Julie Thompson Klein eds., 2012). For a contemporary example of how STS has influenced legal scholarship, see Sally Engle Merry, *Measuring the World: Indicators, Human Rights, and Global Governance*, 52 CURRENT ANTHROPOLOGY S83 (2011); Kevin E. Davis, *Benedict Kingsbury, & Sally Engle Merry, Indicators as a Technology of Global Governance*, 46 L. & SOC'Y REV 71, 73–74 (2012). One of the leading scholars of feminist critiques of science is Donna Haraway, *Situated Knowledges: The Science Question in Feminism and the Privilege of Partial Perspective*, 14 FEMINIST STUD. 575 (1988).

## 1 "WE ARE NOT IMMUNE": A NEW BRANCH OF THE FEMINIST WOMEN'S HEALTH MOVEMENT

1. Kathy Boudin, *The Resilience of the Written Off: Women in Prison as Women of Change*, 29 WOMEN'S RIGHTS LAW REPORTER 15 (2007) at 18.
2. James Feron, *Kathy Boudin Given 20 Years to Life in Prison*, N.Y. TIMES (May 4, 1984), www.nytimes.com/1984/05/04/nyregion/kathy-boudin-given-20-years-to-life-in-prison.html; David Gilbert, *From Weather Underground Activist to Life in Prison*, OPENDEMOCRACY (December 26, 2014), www.opendemocracy.net/en/transformation/from-weather-underground-activist-to-life-in-prison/.
3. Elizabeth Kolbert, *The Prisoner*, NEW YORKER (July 16, 2001), http://archives.newyorker.com/?i=2001-07-16#folio=044.
4. Interview by Aziza Ahmed with Kathy Boudin (phone), in New York, NY (2019).
5. MEMBERS OF THE ACE (AIDS COUNSELING AND EDUCATION) OF THE BEDFORD HILLS CORRECTIONAL FACILITY et al., BREAKING THE WALLS OF SILENCE: AIDS AND WOMEN IN A NEW YORK STATE MAXIMUM SECURITY PRISON 5 (1988). *See also* CELESTE WATKINS-HAYES, REMAKING A LIFE: HOW WOMEN LIVING WITH

HIV CONFRONT INEQUALITY (2019) (documenting the story of other women who became activists out of this moment).

6. Kathy Boudin et al., *ACE: A Peer Education and Counseling Program Meets the Needs of Incarcerated Women with HIV/AIDS Issues*, 10 J. ASS'N NURSES AIDS CARE 90–98 (1999).
7. It is worth noting here that not much is known about the women in Bedford Women's Prison. The most developed account comes from GENA CORREA, WOMEN AND AIDS: THE INVISIBLE EPIDEMIC (1992).
8. GENA CORREA, WOMEN AND AIDS: THE INVISIBLE EPIDEMIC (1992).
9. For historical accounts of AIDS see generally RANDY SHILTS, AND THE BAND PLAYED ON (1988); DAVID FRANCE, HOW TO SURVIVE A PLAGUE (2016); DEBORAH GOULD, MOVING POLITICS: EMOTION AND ACT-UP'S FIGHT AGAINST AIDS (2009); CATHY COHEN, THE BOUNDARIES OF BLACKNESS: AIDS AND THE BREAKDOWN OF BLACK POLITICS 96–97 (1999); CELESTE WATKINS-HAYES, REMAKING A LIFE: HOW WOMEN LIVING WITH HIV CONFRONT INEQUALITY (2019).
10. On background rules and distribution see generally Robert Hale, *Coercion and Distribution in a Supposedly Non-Coercive State*, 38 POLITICAL SCI. Q. 470–494 (1923); DAVID KENNEDY, WORLD OF STRUGGLE: HOW POWER, LAW, AND EXPERTISE SHAPE GLOBAL POLITICAL ECONOMY (2016). On a feminist distributional analysis see Janet Halley, *Distribution and Decision: Assessing Governance Feminism*, in GOVERNANCE FEMINISM: AN INTRODUCTION (Janet Halley et al. eds., 2018); LIBBY ADLER, GAY PRIORI: A QUEER CRITICAL LEGAL STUDIES APPROACH TO LAW REFORM (2018).
11. *See generally* WENDY KLINE, BODIES OF KNOWLEDGE: SEXUALITY, REPRODUCTION, AND WOMEN'S HEALTH IN THE SECOND WAVE (2010); MICHELLE MURPHEY, SEIZING THE MEANS OF REPRODUCTION (2012).
12. Rebecca Dresser, *Seeking White, Male Body for Medical Research*, The Hastings Center (1992).
13. WENDY KLINE, BODIES OF KNOWLEDGE: SEXUALITY, REPRODUCTION, AND WOMEN'S HEALTH IN THE SECOND WAVE (2010); JENNIFER NELSON, MORE THAN MEDICINE: A HISTORY OF THE FEMINIST WOMEN'S HEALTH MOVEMENT (2015).
14. Framing theory – drawn from the sociology of social movements – is instructive in understanding the power of this feminist explanation. As described by sociologists of social movements Robert Benford and David Snow, frames allow individuals to interpret, assess, and experience their world through a specific explanatory lens. *See* Robert D. Benford & David A. Snow, *Framing Processes and Social Movements: An Overview and Assessment*, 26 ANN. REV. SOC. 611, 614–615 (2000). In the scholarship on law and social movements, Amy Kapczynski argues that framing is essential to understand transformations in intellectual property law. Amy

Kapczynski, *The Access to Knowledge Mobilization and the New Politics of Intellectual Property*, 117 YALE L. J. 804 (2008).

15. *See generally* STEVEN EPSTEIN, INCLUSION: THE POLITICS OF DIFFERENCE IN MEDICAL RESEARCH 17 (2007). Steven Epstein is careful to highlight the difference between the activist claim of exclusion and the reality that racial minorities had long been serving as research subjects. The biological underpinnings of "difference" activism by advocates for women and racial minorities creates the need to examine what Epstein calls "biopolitical citizenship," or the desire for political participation in the context of "biomedical technologies and authorities reproducing and transforming practices of social stratification and exclusion – as well as the role of others in resisting those authorities."
16. In her book, Alice Echols argues that nineteenth-century feminists deployed a similar argument – that women were both "same" and "different." ALICE ECHOLS, DARING TO BE BAD: RADICAL FEMINISM IN AMERICA 1967–1975 (1989). On the fight against medical racism see ALONDRA NELSON, BODY AND SOUL: THE BLACK PANTHER PARTY AND THE FIGHT AGAINST MEDICAL DISCRIMINATION (2011).
17. The founding of the Our Bodies Our Selves collective and 1973 publication of the *Our Bodies Our Selves* work played an important role in generating information about women's bodies. WENDY KLINE, BODIES OF KNOWLEDGE: SEXUALITY, REPRODUCTION, AND WOMEN'S HEALTH IN THE SECOND WAVE 1–5 (2010). This was the start of a new line of thinking about women's health: That alongside the male scientific medical establishment, it was women who could speak to their own bodies.
18. Reva Siegel, *Abortion as a Sex Equality Right*, in MOTHERS IN LAW: FEMINIST THEORY AND THE LEGAL REGULATION OF MOTHERHOOD (Martha Fineman and Isabel Karpin eds. 1995); Reva Siegel, *Equality and Choice: Sex Equality Perspectives on Reproductive Rights in the Work of Ruth Bader Ginsburg*, 25 COLUM. J. GENDER & L. 63 (2013).
19. DEIRDRE OWENS COOPER, MEDICAL BONDAGE: RACE, GENDER, AND THE ORIGINS OF AMERICAN GYNECOLOGY (2017).
20. DEIRDRE OWENS COOPER, MEDICAL BONDAGE: RACE, GENDER, AND THE ORIGINS OF AMERICAN GYNECOLOGY (2017).
21. *See* Donna Haraway, *Situated Knowledges: The Science Question in Feminism and the Privilege of Partial Perspective*, 14 FEMINIST STUD. 581 (1988).
22. Donna Haraway, *Situated Knowledges: The Science Question in Feminism and the Privilege of Partial Perspective*, 14 FEMINIST STUD. 581 (1988).
23. Mary Jo Frug argued that sex differences are semiotic – "constituted by a system of signs that we produce and interpret" as "anatomically determined and psychologically predictable." Mary Jo Frug, *A Postmodern*

*Feminist Legal Manifesto (An Unfinished Draft)*, 105 HARV. L. REV. 1045 (1992). For feminist critique in the context of health activism, see Gillian Einstein & Margrit Shildrick, *The Postconventional Body: Retheorising Women's Health*, 69 SOC. SCI. & MED. 293, 294 (2009) (arguing that postmodernism has something to offer women's health practitioners, despite its "unalign[ment] with current women's health practice" in its present state).

24. Ellen Kuhlmann & Birgit Babitsch, *Bodies, Health, Gender: Bridging Feminist Theories and Women's Health*, 25 WOMEN'S STUD. INT'L F. 433, 434–435 (2002) (arguing that Judith Butler and Donna Haraway, amongst other scholars, pushed the limits of feminist understandings of the body, moving beyond binary frames).
25. *See generally* DOROTHY ROBERTS, FATAL INVENTION: HOW SCIENCE, POLITICS, AND BIG BUSINESS RE-CREATE RACE IN THE 21ST CENTURY (2012); JONATHAN KAHN, RACE IN A BOTTLE: THE STORY OF BIDIL AND RACIALIZED MEDICINE IN A POST-GENOMIC AGE (2012).
26. JENNIFER NELSON, MORE THAN MEDICINE: A HISTORY OF THE FEMINIST WOMEN'S HEALTH MOVEMENT 15–56 (2015).
27. JENNIFER NELSON, MORE THAN MEDICINE: A HISTORY OF THE FEMINIST WOMEN'S HEALTH MOVEMENT 57–90 (2015).
28. Reva Siegal argues that abortion liberalization was initially led by public health practitioners prior to feminist engagement in the issue. Feminists eventually turned to the issue of decriminalizing abortion with the view that the illegality of abortion was a symbol of an unjust and unequal society. Siegal goes on to argue that these feminist arguments, however, shaped the contour of the opposition to abortion as well. Reva Siegal, *Abortion and the "Woman Question": Forty Years of Debate*, 89 INDIANA L. J. 1367–1370 (2014).
29. For historics of feminist intervention in law see generally LINDA GORDON, THE MORAL PROPERTY OF WOMEN: A HISTORY OF BIRTH CONTROL POLITICS IN AMERICA (2002); Deborah Dinner, *The Costs of Reproduction: History and the Legal Construction of Sex Equality*, 46 HARV. CIVIL RIGHTS-CIVIL LIBERTIES L. REV. 415 (2011); SERENA MAYERI, REASONING FROM RACE: FEMINISM, LAW, AND THE CIVIL RIGHTS REVOLUTION (2011).
30. There is a well-developed literature on the role of litigation in forwarding women's rights. In the context of reproductive rights, Robin West argues that there are costs to a strategy for reproductive rights focused on constitutional law in that the abortion rights are framed as negative rights and may undermine the reproductive justice demand that the state play a role in supporting pregnancy and family. In turn, the court-based strategy for achieving reproductive rights have "ill served"

progressive politics. Robin West, *From Choice to Reproductive Justice: De-Constitutionalizing Abortion Rights*, 118 Yale L. J. 1394 (2009). Outside of the context of reproductive rights, Catherine Albiston notes that litigation strategies have the potential to "deradicalize and subtly reshape social movements in undesirable ways" and maintain the status quo. Catherine Albiston, *The Dark Side of Litigation as a Social Movement Strategy*, 96 Iowa L. Rev. Bull. 61 (2011). Reva Siegal argues, in a related but different mode, that Supreme Court cases on reproductive rights have channeled debates on the topic. Reva Siegal, *Abortion and the "Woman Question": Forty Years of Debate*, 89 Indiana L. J. 1367–1370 (2014). Catharine MacKinnon offered an early critique of *Roe v. Wade*, arguing that it was the product of male supremacy and that its holding under privacy doctrine justified *Harris v. McRae*. Catharine Mackinnon, *Roe v. Wade: A Study in Male Ideology*, *in* Abortion Controversy 25 Years After (Louis Pojman ed., 1998) ("abortion's availability is frames, and is framed by, the conditions under which men, worked out between themselves, will grant legitimacy to women to control the reproductive consequences of intercourse"). The role of Supreme Court decisions in delimiting counterarguments has become a key point of debate in the related field of law and sexuality. *See* Teemu Ruskola, *Gay Rights versus Queer Theory: What Is Left of Sodomy After* Lawrence v. Texas, 23 Soc. Text 235 (2005); Katherine Franke, *The Domesticated Liberty of* Lawrence v. Texas, 104 Colum. L. Rev. (2004); Janet Halley et al., Governance Feminism: An Introduction (2018).

31. Linda Greenhouse, Becoming Justice Blackmun: Harry Blackmun's Supreme Court Journey (2006).
32. The constitutional questions were controversial, however. Not just from the perspective of a progressive/conservative divide on abortion but amongst progressives. Feminist scholars raised important questions following *Roe*. Robin West, *From Choice to Reproductive Justice: De-Constitutionalizing Abortion Rights*, 118 Yale L. J. 1394 (2009).
33. *See* Khiara Bridges, The Poverty of Privacy Rights (2017) (discussing how constitutional law failed to protect the reproductive freedoms of poor women despite a robust commitment to the right of privacy). *See* Naomi Cahn & June Carbone, *The Blue Family Constitution*, J. Am. Acad. Matrim. Laws. 529–530 (2022) (discussing the enforcement of the "class line" in reproductive rights). Instead, criminal law was often deployed in service of regulating the poor woman. Many of those subject to these criminal laws are women of color, especially Black and Latina women. *See generally* Michele Goodwin, Policing the Womb: Invisible Women and the Criminalization of Motherhood (2020).

34. Kaaryn Gustafson, *The Criminalization of Poverty*, 99 J. CRIM. L. AND CRIMINOLOGY (2009).
35. Interview by Lorretta Ross with Byllye Avery, Founder, the Black Women's Health Project, in North Hampton, MA (2005).
36. CATHY COHEN, THE BOUNDARIES OF BLACKNESS: AIDS AND THE BREAKDOWN OF BLACK POLITICS 96–97 (1999).
37. ALICE ECHOLS, DARING TO BE BAD: RADICAL FEMINISM IN AMERICA 1967–1975 (1989).
38. ALICE ECHOLS, DARING TO BE BAD: RADICAL FEMINISM IN AMERICA 1967–1975 244–245 (1989) ("cultural feminism held out the possibility that women could build a culture, a space, uncontaminated by patriarchy.").
39. DEBORAH GOULD, MOVING POLITICS: EMOTION AND ACT-UP'S FIGHT AGAINST AIDS Kindle edition. (2009).
40. DEBORAH GOULD, MOVING POLITICS: EMOTION AND ACT-UP'S FIGHT AGAINST AIDS Kindle Location 108. Kindle edition. (2009).
41. DEBORAH GOULD, MOVING POLITICS: EMOTION AND ACT-UP'S FIGHT AGAINST AIDS Kindle location 116–117. Kindle Edition. (2009).
42. On identity, race, and fights for inclusion in medical care and research, see generally ALONDRA NELSON, BODY AND SOUL: THE BLACK PANTHER PARTY AND THE FIGHT AGAINST MEDICAL DISCRIMINATION (2013); RUHA BENJAMIN, PEOPLE'S SCIENCE: BODIES AND RIGHTS ON THE STEM CELL FRONTIER (2013); STEVEN EPSTEIN, INCLUSION: THE POLITICS OF DIFFERENCE IN MEDICAL RESEARCH (2007).
43. The terms legal change "from below" or "bottom up" are widely used in law social movements scholarship. For two examples see Tomiko Brown-Nagin's description of a "bottom up" approach as "focused on activists as much as on the law and lawyers" and on the Supreme Court as well as lower courts. TOMIKO BROWN-NAGIN, COURAGE TO DISSENT: ATLANTA AND THE LONG HISTORY OF THE CIVIL RIGHTS MOVEMENT 10–11 (2011). In the literature on law, human rights, and social movements the term "from below" has been used to describe how grassroots actors utilize human rights to mobilize social change. *See* Boaventura de Sousa Santos & Cesar A. Rodriguez-Garavito, *Law, Politics, and the Subaltern in Counter-Hegemonic Globalization*, in LAW AND GLOBALIZATION FROM BELOW: TOWARDS A COSMOPOLITAN LEGALITY (Boaventura de Sousa Santos & Cesar A. Rodriguez-Garavito eds., 2005). In his critique of Gerald Rosenberg's book THE HOLLOW HOPE: CAN COURTS BRING ABOUT SOCIAL CHANGE, Michael McCann describes bottom-up analysis as "dispute-centered" studies of law that place emphasis on "social struggles" and center the role of nonjudicial actors as "practical legal agents." Michael McCann, *Reform Litigation on Trial*, 17 L. AND SOC. INQUIRY 715 (1992).

44. Ruha Benjamin discusses a political sociology of science that considers political–scientific hybrids and social inclusion in science. RUHA BENJAMIN, THE PEOPLE'S SCIENCE: BODIES AND RIGHTS ON THE STEM CELL FRONTIER (2013).
45. *See* Robert D. Benford & David A. Snow, *Framing Processes and Social Movements: An Overview and Assessment*, 26 ANN. REV. SOC. 611, 614–615 (2000). (Explaining that the use of the verb framing "denotes an active, processual phenomenon that implies agency and contention at the level of reality construction." In turn collective action frames are partly constructed to "negotiate a shared understanding of some problematic condition or situation … in need of change.")
46. The *Cosmopolitan* article ignited protests from the ACT UP Women's Caucus who protested the article for propagating misinformation about AIDS. Interview by Sarah Schulman with Maxine Wolfe, activist, ACT UP Oral History Project in New York, NY (May 25, 2007); CAROLE CAMPBELL, WOMEN, FAMILIES, AND HIV/AIDS: SOCIOLOGICAL PERSPECTIVE ON THE EPIDEMIC IN AMERICA (1999).
47. MICHAEL FUMENTO, THE MYTH OF HETEROSEXUAL AIDS: HOW A TRAGEDY HAS BEEN DISTORTED BY MEDIA AND PARTISAN POLITICS (1990).
48. Documentation by Maxine Wolfe on History of Women's Caucus (on file with Lesbian Herstory Archive, Maxine Wolfe Collection, Box 2, Folder 1).
49. Documentation by Maxine Wolfe on History of Women's Caucus (on file with Lesbian Herstory Archive, Maxine Wolfe Collection, Box 2, Folder 1).
50. ACT UP, *Reproductive Rights and AIDS: The Connections*, in Women, AIDS, and Activism 199 (1990).
51. ACT UP, *Reproductive Rights and AIDS: The Connections*, in WOMEN, AIDS, AND ACTIVISM 199–201 (1990).
52. Interview by Sarah Schulman with Maxine Wolfe, activist, ACT UP Oral History Project, in New York, NY (May 25, 2007). ("When we carried our first signs about women, we were told by everybody that it was never going to be women. That's what we were told. Everybody thought it was always going to be a really small number. There was no heterosexual transmission.")
53. Linda Anderson and Samantha Winchester, *Off Our Backs* (Apr. 1988) (on file with Lesbian Herstory Archive, Maxine Wolfe Collection, Box 2, Folder 2).
54. ACT UP, *Shea Stadium Women's Action: As Told by Maxine Wolfe*, https://actupny.org/diva/CBstory-shea.html.
55. Interview by Sarah Schulman with Maxine Wolfe, activist, ACT UP Oral History Project, in New York, NY at 90 (May 25, 2007); ACT UP,

*Shea Stadium Women's Action: As Told by Maxine Wolfe*, https://actupny.org/diva/CBstory-shea.html.

56. Interview by Sarah Schulman with Terry McGovern, HIV Officer at the Ford Foundation, ACT UP Oral History Project, in New York, NY at 18 (May 25, 2007). Many women who had HIV often sought support from gay men's groups and organizations.
57. Bedford Hills Correctional Facility, New York State Archives, www.archives.nysed.gov/creator-authority/bedford-hills-correctional-facility.
58. Interview by Sarah Schulman with Terry McGovern, HIV Officer at the Ford Foundation, ACT UP Oral History Project, in New York, NY at 11 (May 25, 2007).
59. Jonathan Kagan et al., *A Brief Chronicle of the CD4 as a Biomarker for HIV/AIDS: A Tribute to the Memory of John F. Fahey*, 6 Immunopathological Diseases and Therapy 55–64 (2015).
60. The World Health Organization did not require HIV testing until 2013.
61. The AIDS case definition has changed over time. The AIDS case definition in 1982 focused on men who have sex with men and included opportunistic diseases that were indicative of problems with the immune system. By 1985, HIV was found to be the cause of AIDS. In turn, the 1985 update to the case definition added more opportunistic diseases to the broader list. A person would have been found to have AIDS if they presented with one of these opportunistic infections and a positive serologic or virologic test. However, in the absence of test results, patients who met other criteria in the definition (presentation of an opportunistic disease known to cause AIDS) would still be categorized as having AIDS. The 1987 case definition specifies twenty-three AIDS-defining conditions associated with severe immune deficiency caused by HIV. It continued to allow practitioners to make a diagnosis of AIDS based on clinical observations rather than on the basis of a laboratory test. It did not include any severe manifestations of HIV as found in women. The revised definition released in 1993 held that a person had AIDS if they (1) had a CD4 count of 200 or below and (2) had one of an enumerated list of illnesses. The 2008 AIDS case definition required a person to have been diagnosed with an HIV test, a CD4 count of less than 200, a CD4 count of less than 14 percent of all lymphocytes, and/or the existence of an opportunistic infection. Today, due to advances in technology, the CDC uses algorithmic testing alongside clinical manifestations to confirm HIV diagnosis and categorize individuals into subtypes of HIV and stage of HIV infection. Centers for Disease Control and Prevention, *Revision of CDC Case Definition of Acquired Immunodeficiency Syndrome for National Reporting*, 34 Morbidity & Mortality Weekly Rep. 373–375

(1985); Centers for Disease Control and Prevention, *Revision of CDC Definition of Acquired Immunodeficiency Syndrome*, 36 Morbidity and Mortality Weekly Report S1–15 (1987); Richard M. Selik et al., *Revised Surveillance Case Definition for HIV Infection – United States, 2014*, 63 Morbidity and Mortality Weekly Rep. 1 (2014).

62. Cathy Cohen, The Boundaries of Blackness: AIDS and the Breakdown of Black Politics 124 (1999) (citing Gerald Oppenheimer, *Causes, Cases, and Cohorts: The Role of Epidemiology in the Historical Construction of AIDS*, in AIDS: The Making of a Chronic Disease 49–83 [Elizabeth Fee & Daniel Fox eds., 1992]).
63. Terry McGovern, S. P. v. Sullivan*: The Effort to Broaden the Social Security Administration's Definition of AIDS*, 21 Fordham Urb. L. J. 1083, 1091–1093 (1994); *see also* M. Maiman et al., *Cervical Cancer as an AIDS Defining Illness*, 89 Obstetrics & Gynecology 76, 76–80 (1997). I am indebted to Terry McGovern for providing more detail about some of these key historical moments.
64. Cathy Cohen, The Boundaries of Blackness: AIDS and the Breakdown of Black Politics 123 (1999). Cohen is engaged with the work of Gerald Oppenheimer, see generally Gerald Oppenheimer, *Causes, Cases, and Cohorts: The Role of Epidemiology in the Historical Construction of AIDS*, in AIDS: The Making of a Chronic Disease (Elizabeth Fee & Daniel Fox eds., 1992).
65. Cathy Cohen, The Boundaries of Blackness: AIDS and the Breakdown of Black Politics 123 (1999).
66. Cathy Cohen, The Boundaries of Blackness: AIDS and the Breakdown of Black Politics 125 (1999).
67. For a helpful primer on the distinction between the two, see Karen Tani, *Disability Benefits as Poverty Law: Revisiting the "Disabled State"*, 170 U. Pa. L. Rev. 1687, 1690–1691 (2022).
68. Presumptive disability can be issued to a claimant who meets financial requirements and whose disability is contained on a specified list of disabling impairments. They are provided with immediate benefits as they await initial determinations on their applications. Presumptive disability determinations are made at local social security offices and the Office of Disability Determinations. They are paid for a maximum of three months. *S.P. v. Sullivan*, 90 Civ. 6294 (Plaintiff's Memorandum of Law in Support of Class Certification at 6–7, Oct. 31, 1990).
69. Obstacles That Prevent Women and Children With HIV-Related Disabilities From Qualifying For Social Security Disability Insurance and Supplemental Security Income, 102 Cong. 102–99 (1992) (Statement of Gwendolyn S. King, Commissioner of Social Security, US Department of Health and Human Services) ("The SSA's first recognition of AIDS as disabling was in the July 1984 SS Ruling 84–19, 'Evaluation of Acquired

Immune Deficiency Syndrome and corresponding Program Operations Manual Systems ('POMS')' section DI 00401.537."). *S.P. v. Sullivan*, 90 Civ. 6294 (Plaintiff's Memorandum of Law in Support of Class Certification at 6–7, Oct. 31, 1990). (a) ("Social Security Ruling 84–19 was superseded in October of 1986 by Ruling 86–20, an apparent recognition by the Secretary that increased medical knowledge regarding HIV infection required revised standards for evaluation of HIV related disability." "Social Security Ruling 86–20 expanded the number of opportunistic infections which would support a finding of AIDS, and added a section permitting a finding of disability based on AIDS Related Complex ('ARC')").

70. The definition of a disability in the Social Security Act is the inability to engage in any substantial gainful activity by reason of any medically determinable physical or mental impairment which can be expected to result in death, or which has lasted or can be expected to last for a continuous period of not less than twelve months.
71. *S.P. v. Sullivan*, 90 Civ. 6294 (Plaintiff's Memorandum of Law in Support of Class Certification at 6–7, Oct. 31, 1990). (Describing the process for accessing disability: "Determinations of disability are made, in the first instance, by state agencies under contract with the Secretary. In New York state, the Office of Disability Determinations (ODD), an agency of the New York State Department of Social Services, is charged with making initial disability determinations. If the application is denied at the initial level, and claimant requests reconsideration, ODD is also charged with that determination. A claimant whose application has been denied at the initial and reconsideration levels by ODD may request a hearing before an administrative law judge (ALF) employed by the Secretary, and if still dissatisfied may request review of the ALJ's decision before the Secretary's Appeals Council. Unlike initial and reconsideration determinations, 'presumptive' disability determinations can be made at local Social Security offices as well as by ODD, and are not subject to appeal. The Secretary enforces the federal policies, practices, standards, and procedures by reviewing the state's individual disability determinations and by overriding any such determination which the Secretary decides does not conform and by maintaining the power to assume the state agency's functions if he finds too high a rate of 'error' in its determinations. The Secretary issues various substantive policy statements and instructional materials which state agencies, such as the ODD in New York State, must use in disability determinations. The Secretary hires, trains, and issues instructional materials to the employees at Social Security's local offices who make initial determinations and decisions on presumptive disability determinations, as well as to the ALJs, Appeals Council members, and other Office of Hearings and Appeals employees who process disability

cases and perform disability adjudications. Among the instructional materials issued by the Secretary to direct his employees in the application of the Secretary's policies, practices, standards, and procedures for making decisions about entitlement to disability benefits are a compilation known as the Program Operation Manual System ('the POMS') and Social Security Rulings. The POMS are not binding on adjudicators above the state agency level. Neither Social Security Rulings nor the POMS are subject to the notice and comment requirement of the Administrative Procedure Act or are published in the Federal Register. Upon information and belief, most claimants for disability benefits are unaware of the existence of the POMS and the Social Security Rulings.")

72. This chapter deals with SSDI and SSI as administered by Health and Human Services. For an overview of how disability in SSDI and SSI relates to areas of disability law from an anti-discrimination perspective, see Chai Feldblum, *Definition of Disability under Federal Anti-Discrimination Law: What Happened – Why – And What Can We Do about It*, 21 BERKELEY J. EMP. & LAB. L. 91 (2000).
73. The administrative state has long functioned to regulate sex and gender. For an excavation of how administrative law regulates sex and gender, see Jacob E. Gersen & Jeannie Suk Gersen, *The Sex Bureaucracy*, 104 CAL. L. REV. 881 (2016); Melissa Murray & Karen Tani, *Something Old, Something New: New Reflections on the Sex Bureaucracy*, 7 CAL. L. REV. ONLINE 122 (2016). On the regulation of sexuality through civil and administrative channels, see Melissa Murray, *Rights and Regulation: The Evolution of Sexual Regulation*, 116 COLUM. L. REV. 573 (2016). *See* Dean Spade, *Documenting Gender*, 59(1) HASTINGS L. J. 731 (2008).
74. *SP, MC, JM, LK, PS on Behalf of Themselves and All Others Similar Situated v. Sullivan*, 90 Civ. 6294, Complaint (Oct. 1, 1990).
75. *SP, MC, JM, LK, PS on Behalf of Themselves and All Others Similar Situated v. Sullivan*, 90 Civ. 6294, Complaint at 14 (Oct. 1, 1990). ("Although the APA generally requires publishing of proposed rules, and a period of notice and comment prior to the adoption of final rules, the Secretary invoked one of the Act's exceptions which provides for dispensing with such procedures if they are unnecessary or contrary to the public interest. Thus, the secretary accepted notice and comment during the 60-day period from February 11–April 12, 1985, after adopting the interim regulations.")
76. *SP, MC, JM, LK, PS on Behalf of Themselves and All Others Similar Situated v. Sullivan*, 90 Civ. 6294, Complaint at 14 (Oct. 1, 1990).
77. Protest Flyers (on file with Lesbian Herstory Archive, Maxine Wolfe Collection, Box 3, Folders 19–22).

78. Interview by Sarah Schulman with Linda Meredith, HIV Officer at the Ford Foundation, ACT UP Oral History Project, in New York, NY at 29 (March 10, 2013).
79. Meeting on the expansion of the AIDS Surveillance case definition, CDC 347 (1992).
80. Interview by Sarah Schulman with Linda Meredith, HIV Officer at the Ford Foundation, ACT UP Oral History Project, in New York, NY at 17 (March 10, 2013).
81. Background Briefings (on file with Lesbian Herstory Archive, Maxine Wolfe Collection, Box 3, Folders 19–22).
82. Bail Records and Documentation of the Event (on file with Lesbian Herstory Archive, Maxine Wolfe Collection, Box 3, Folders 19–22).
83. Bail Records and Documentation of the Event (on file with Lesbian Herstory Archive, Maxine Wolfe Collection, Box 3, Folders 19–22).
84. Interview by Sarah Schulman with Terry McGovern, HIV Officer at the Ford Foundation, ACT UP Oral History Project, in New York, NY at 18 (May 25, 2007).
85. Transcript of Dialogue with Fauci after Our Presentation (July 27, 1990) (on file with Lesbian Herstory Archive, Maxine Wolfe Collection, Box 2, Folder 6).
86. Transcript of Dialogue with Fauci after Our Presentation (July 27, 1990) (on file with Lesbian Herstory Archive, Maxine Wolfe Collection, Box 2, Folder 6 and Box 2, Folders 3 and 3A).
87. The primary ACT UP people involved with the conference advocacy and organizing were Linda Meredith, Melinda Daniels, and Lorrie Sprecher from ACT-UP DC and Risa Denenberg, Heidi Dorow, Garance Franke-Ruta, and Maxine Wolfe from ACT UP New York.
88. Letter from Linda Meredith to Anthony Fauci (July 27, 1990) (on file with Lesbian Herstory Archive, Maxine Wolfe Collection, Box 2, Folder 6).
89. Anthony Fauci Reply Letter (on file with Lesbian Herstory Archive, Maxine Wolfe Collection, Box 2, Folder 6).
90. Anthony Fauci Reply Letter (on file with Lesbian Herstory Archive, Maxine Wolfe Collection, Box 2, Folder 6).
91. The ACT UP Network Women's Issues Committee at the December ACTG Meetings (January 31, 1992) (on file with Lesbian Herstory Archive, Maxine Wolfe Collection, Box 2, Folder 1).
92. *NIAID AIDS Agenda* (on file with Lesbian Herstory Archive, Maxine Wolfe Collection, Box 2, Folder 6).
93. Founding Document (on file with Lesbian Herstory Archive, Maxine Wolfe Collection, Box 3, Folders 19–22). Other members include Victoria Coffman, Camille Lore, Lorrie Sprecher, Wendy Sharp, Melinda Daniels, Linda Meredith, Ann Steinecke, and Sarah Wolfe.

94. Background Report (on file with Lesbian Herstory Archive, Maxine Wolfe Collection, Box 3, Folders 19–22). In this document, in a section titled "Background on: Life Force 'Women Fighting AIDS, Inc.,'" Life Force discusses that it gets support from the Bushwick Health Center, the Brooklyn AIDS Task Force, WARN, the SUNY Health Science Center at Brooklyn, the Caribbean Women's Health Association, and the American Red Cross.
95. Phone Interview by Aziza Ahmed with Bylle Avery, Founder, National Black Women's Health Project, in Cape Cod, Mass. (2019).
96. Background Report (on file with Lesbian Herstory Archive, Maxine Wolfe Collection, Box 3, Folders 19–22). ("Training for these community educators includes an intensive study of current facts about HIV/AIDS, family planning, health care, reproductive health, sexually transmitted diseases, stress reduction, and safer sex techniques. Also included are education techniques for imparting information, group facilitation, group dynamics and active listening. Life Force educators are trained to network with appropriate health and social services for referrals and crisis intervention." "A range of community service organizations, and public agencies offer support and cooperation to Life Force. Among them are the Bushwick Health Center, the Brooklyn AIDS Task Force, WARN, the SUNY Heath Science Center at Brooklyn, the Caribbean Women's Health Association, and the American Red Cross.")
97. Interview by Sarah Schulman with Alexandra Juhasz, activist, ACT UP Oral History Project, in New York, NY (May 25, 2007). ("you couldn't imagine one more, kind of, embodying everything different than what ACT UP was in Brooklyn AIDS Task Force. Brooklyn AIDS Task Force was an underfunded social service organization – staffed entirely by black women in some tawdry building that served, you know, a large number of Haitian people in Brooklyn at the time, that did support groups and HIV education and really nitty gritty stuff – getting people housing and public – getting them attached to entitlement programs they need to be attached to. And, it's very much about serving an under – working class and under class population of people who were really needing services. It was like a band-aid – the Brooklyn AIDS Task Force was, but they had their pulse on a completely – their fingers on the pulse of another AIDS, another AIDS … if you wanted to think about women and AIDS, you needed to be thinking about poverty, race in urban America. And, how was I going to cross that divide. And, that was a very different thing than thinking about what it meant to be a white gay man with AIDS. It just was like two different things – two different sets of concerns, two different questions. And, at certain times they intersected, and in a lot of times, they didn't. It was really about, you know, a different set of social justice issues that are not addressed to this day.")
98. Initially, organizing in the Black community on issues of AIDS came from Black LGBT organizations including the National Black Gay

and Lesbian Leadership Forum and the National Taskforce on AIDS. Cathy Cohen, The Boundaries of Blackness: AIDS and the Breakdown of Black Politics 97–103 (1999). Cohen documents how Black politicians got involved but their involvement was not consistent. For example, Black and Latino elected officials opposed a needle exchange program that would have benefitted Black and Latino communities. Cathy Cohen, The Boundaries of Blackness: AIDS and the Breakdown of Black Politics 103 (1999).

99. It is not unusual to hear women diagnosed early in the HIV epidemic discuss seeking and receiving support from support groups of largely gay men. *See, e.g.*, Jeff Berry, *One-on-One with Dawn Averitt Bridge*, Positively Aware (July 2009); Mary Fisher & Dawn Averitt Bridge, *Leading Ladies*, POZ 34 (March 2010).
100. *Implications of the Revised CDC Definition, Hearing Before the National Commission on AIDS*, 102nd Cong. (Dec. 10, 1991) (statement of Terry McGovern).
101. Linda Singer, Erotic Welfare: Sexual Theory and Politics in the Age of Epidemic 83 (1993).
102. Important to note is that while the idea of exclusion generated feminist energy and cohesion in the context of regulatory change amongst women in organizations like ACT UP and beyond, it generated both alliances and conflict between men and women involved in AIDS activism. Lewis Grossman, *AIDS Activists, FDA Regulation, and the Amendment of America's Drug Constitution*, 42 Am. J. of L. & Med. 687 (2016) (describing the support of men in ACT UP having women recognized as a risk group); interview by Sarah Schulman with Terry McGovern, HIV Officer at the Ford Foundation, ACT UP Oral History Project, in New York, NY at 18 (May 25, 2007).

## 2 LITIGATING RISK: THE LAW AND POLITICS OF DISEASE IN THE ADMINISTRATIVE STATE

1. Terry McGovern, working with MFY Legal Services, recruited lawyers from Cardozo Bet Tzedek Legal Services, the Center for Constitutional Rights, and Lambda Legal Defense Fund to support the litigation efforts. *SP v. Sullivan*, 90 CIV. 6294 4 (1990).
2. Although this chapter focuses on the women's issues in the lawsuit, the class of plaintiffs could be broken down to four subclasses: women who were disabled by HIV-related illness, current and former intravenous drug users disabled by HIV-related illness, children who were disabled by HIV-related illness, and poor persons disabled by HIV-related illness. *SP v. Sullivan*, 90 CIV. 6294 4 (1990).

3. Interview by Sarah Schulman with Terry McGovern, HIV Officer at the Ford Foundation, ACT UP Oral History Project, in New York, NY at 20 (May 25, 2007). ("The way I always tried to practice is, you can't, you're not going to win on just a lawsuit, if you're talking about something that's more about a social movement, as far as I'm concerned. And I think in some cases if the government really, really feels like it can ignore the population, the demonstrations may not be enough. And in this case, I think having to actually answer in court really shook them up. But the day that, one of the days that the federal court refused to dismiss the case, the government littered us with papers and tried to basically kind of outwork us; the judge in the case read from some *Times* article about a demonstration. And so they really, really worked together.")
4. *See also Matthews v. Eldrige*, 424 U.S. 319 (1976).
5. Names were hidden and are fictionalized here. *SP, MC, JM, LK, PS on Behalf of Themselves and All Others Similar Situated v. Sullivan*, 90 Civ. 6294, Complaint at 19 (Oct. 1, 1990).
6. *SP, MC, JM, LK, PS on Behalf of Themselves and All Others Similar Situated v. Sullivan*, 90 Civ. 6294, Amended Class Action Complaint at 25 (Oct. 29, 1990).
7. Plaintiff was a later addition to the class.
8. Office of Technology Assessment, The CDC's Case Definition of AIDS: Implications of the Proposed Revisions (1992). *See also SP, MC, JM, LK, PS on Behalf of Themselves and All Others Similar Situated v. Sullivan*, 90 Civ. 6294, Complaint at 26 (Oct. 1, 1990).
9. *SP, MC, JM, LK, PS on Behalf of Themselves and All Others Similar Situated v. Sullivan*, 90 Civ. 6294, Complaint at 20 (Oct. 1, 1990).
10. Names were hidden and are fictionalized here. *SP, MC, JM, LK, PS on Behalf of Themselves and All Others Similar Situated v. Sullivan*, 90 Civ. 6294, Complaint at 19 (Oct. 1, 1990).
11. *SP, MC, JM, LK, PS on Behalf of Themselves and All Others Similarly Situated v. Sullivan*, 90 Civ. 6294, Complaint at 28 (Oct. 1, 1990).
12. The plaintiffs sought several other outcomes including payments of presumptive disability to all claimants with proof of HIV infection and a physician report stating that the claimant is unable to work.
13. *SP, MC, JM, LK, PS on Behalf of Themselves and All Others Similar Situated v. Sullivan*, 90 Civ. 6294, Complaint at 11 (Oct. 1, 1990); *S.P. v. Sullivan*, Amended Class Action Complaint; *S.P. v. Sullivan*, Document F at 15.
14. *S.P. v. Sullivan*, 90 Civ. 6294; APA 5 USC Sec. 551 set seq., Amended Class Action Complaint.

15. *SP, MC, JM, LK, PS on Behalf of Themselves and All Others Similar Situated v. Sullivan*, 90 Civ. 6294, Complaint at 11 (Oct. 1, 1990); *S.P. v. Sullivan*, Amended Class Action Complaint at 37–39.
16. Flyers and Notes (on file with Lesbian Herstory Archive, Maxine Wolfe Collection, Box 3, Folders 19–22); Interview by Sarah Schulman with Terry McGovern, HIV Officer at the Ford Foundation, ACT UP Oral History Project, in New York, NY at 18 (May 25, 2007).
17. Image (on file with Lesbian Herstory Archive, Maxine Wolfe Collection, Box 3, Folders 19–22).
18. Linda Meredith, Press Release (1990) (on file with Lesbian Herstory Archive, Maxine Wolfe Collection, Box 3, Folders 19–22).
19. Image (on file with Lesbian Herstory Archive, Maxine Wolfe Collection, Box 3, Folders 19–22).
20. Interview by Sarah Schulman with Linda Meredith, activist, ACT UP Oral History Project, in New York, NY at 13–14 (Mar. 10, 2013).
21. Image (on file with Lesbian Herstory Archive, Maxine Wolfe Collection, Box 3, Folders 19–22).
22. Image of Protest Flyer for HHS Action (Oct. 2, 1990) (on file with Lesbian Herstory Archive, Maxine Wolfe Collection, Box 3, Folders 19–22).
23. Image of Protest Flyer for HHS Action (Oct. 2, 1990) (on file with Lesbian Herstory Archive, Maxine Wolfe Collection, Box 3, Folders 19–22).
24. Other chants included: "Men with AIDS get benefits, just because they don't have tits!" and "Women with AIDS won't wait till later, we're not your fucking incubator!"
25. The protests were funded by ACT UP and ACT UP members. Interview by Sarah Schulman with Terry McGovern, HIV Officer at the Ford Foundation, ACT UP Oral History Project, in New York, NY at 18 (May 25, 2007). ("Well, they had money because they, the men who were members of ACT UP had a lot more money, certainly, than the clients I was seeing. So, yeah, the resources were incredible. That was the other thing that I didn't, that I neglected to mention. The creativity, the press capabilities, talking about why the lawsuit was successful, you're sitting on Avenue A, doing this lawsuit. And then Robin Hauser and Laurie Cotter come, and they're the press people from ACT UP. And they sit with me for half an hour, and they write this press release. And then we file the lawsuit; we're in Washington. And it's on the front page of the New York Times. That was ACT UP. Those were, it was also that the lawsuit was credible, and for the first time, I think part of the strategy that was unique to the press was that they could speak to women who had gone through this training and could really describe the way in which they were being denied disability, not just, like, make this generalized complaint. But the level of resources that ACT UP

brought to this thing was incredible. So you had people who had many, many resources, to begin with. So it brought everything to a whole new level.")

26. ACT UP Documentation (on file with Lesbian Herstory Archive, Maxine Wolfe Collection, Box 3, Folders 19–22).
27. Documentation of Testimony (on file with Lesbian Herstory Archive, Maxine Wolfe Collection, Box 3, Folders 19–22).
28. Congressional Record, E3087, Oct. 2, 1990.
29. Interview by Sarah Schulman with Terry McGovern, HIV Officer at the Ford Foundation, ACT UP Oral History Project, in New York, NY (May 25, 2007).
30. *Baltimore Sun*, Oct. 3, 1990 (Image).
31. *USA Today*, Oct. 3, 1990 (Image).
32. Transcription of Meeting by Activists (on file with Lesbian Herstory Archive, Maxine Wolfe Collection, Box 3, Folder 25).
33. Transcription of Meeting by Activists (on file with Lesbian Herstory Archive, Maxine Wolfe Collection, Box 3, Folder 25).
34. Transcription of Meeting by Activists (on file with Lesbian Herstory Archive, Maxine Wolfe Collection, Box 3, Folder 25).
35. Transcription of Meeting by Activists (on file with Lesbian Herstory Archive, Maxine Wolfe Collection, Box 3, Folder 25).
36. Transcription of Meeting by Activists (on file with Lesbian Herstory Archive, Maxine Wolfe Collection, Box 3, Folder 25) (according to the ACT UP transcription, one CDC official stated, "I mean we'll be able to do it – we can do it three years beyond, but when we start talking about changing the case definition we get a lot of screams from scientists, from all kinds of places, saying we can't track trends every time you do this because it threw everybody apart for awhile").
37. Transcription of Meeting by Activists (on file with Lesbian Herstory Archive, Maxine Wolfe Collection, Box 3, Folder 25). (Gary Noble: "Again, it gets back to the reason for changing that. There is a whole spectrum, all the way from reporting anyone with HIV infection, with or without symptoms, as you know, it can be based on CD4 cell counts, it could be based on any number of things, but if we did that we would be laughed out of the country for inflating the epidemic and the curve and simply trying to bring more money to AIDS research. There has to be a rationale.")
38. Transcription of Meeting by Activists (on file with Lesbian Herstory Archive, Maxine Wolfe Collection, Box 3, Folder 25). (Bert Peterson, Women's Health and Fertility, CDC: "That raises a concern because if we talk about case definition because if there is a woman who is infected today and has candida vulvar vaginitis today, and yet would we want to say that she has AIDS?")

39. Transcription of Meeting by Activists (on file with Lesbian Herstory Archive, Maxine Wolfe Collection, Box 3, Folder 25).
40. Transcription of Meeting by Activists (on file with Lesbian Herstory Archive, Maxine Wolfe Collection, Box 3, Folder 25).
41. Transcription of Meeting by Activists (on file with Lesbian Herstory Archive, Maxine Wolfe Collection, Box 3, Folder 25) (ACT UP: "I don't think we can afford to wait for years for you to do the studies of causal relationships").
42. Transcription of Meeting by Activists (on file with Lesbian Herstory Archive, Maxine Wolfe Collection, Box 3, Folder 25).
43. Transcription of Meeting by Activists (on file with Lesbian Herstory Archive, Maxine Wolfe Collection, Box 3, Folder 25). The quote differs slightly according to the source.
44. Transcription of Meeting by Activists (on file with Lesbian Herstory Archive, Maxine Wolfe Collection, Box 3, Folder 25).
45. ACT UP Demands for December 3rd Demonstration at the CDC (Chip Rowan) (on file with Lesbian Herstory Archive, Maxine Wolfe Collection, Box 3, Folders 19–22). (Note that ACT UP New York had a much longer list of demands. It sought the addition of a much longer list of opportunistic and indicator diseases with atypical outcomes in immunocompromised people. Its list included chronic pelvic inflammatory disease unresponsive to conventional therapy, repeat episodes of endometritis, salpingitis, tubovarian abscess leading to multiple pelvic adhesions and chronic pelvic pain, chronic refractory vaginal thrush, anal, vulvar, or vaginal condylomas, genital ulcers that are unresponsive to conventional therapy, and other health issues.)
46. ACT UP, Women, AIDS, and Activism vii (1990).
47. ACT UP, Women, AIDS, and Activism 6 (1990).
48. ACT UP, Women, AIDS, and Activism 6 (1990).
49. ACT UP, Women, AIDS, and Activism 9 (1990). ("White supremacy is a set of institutions (supported by a set of racist ideas) that ensures that white people continue to have access to the labor and other resources of the various communities of color. Political, economic, and cultural control of these communities is often necessary for this to occur. Violence against people of color and official tolerance of and/or initiation of such violence remain institutionalized practices that perpetuate racism. Violence against people of color is not only perpetrated by young white men on the street, it also reaches into the highest levels of our government. For example, despite undisputed statistical evidence that a Black person is four times as likely to receive the death penalty as a white person convicted of a similar crime, the U.S. Supreme Court found that the death penalty is 'not inherently racist' and does not violate the equal protection provision of the Fourteenth Amendment.")

50. ACT UP, WOMEN, AIDS, AND ACTIVISM 32 (1990).
51. ACT UP, WOMEN, AIDS, AND ACTIVISM 33 (1990).
52. ACT UP, WOMEN, AIDS, AND ACTIVISM 39 (1990).
53. Reviews of ACT UP, *Women, AIDS, and Activism*: Merle Knight, *Review*, 7 (6) ON OUR BACKS 36 (July/Aug. 1991) and Maria Erlien, *Review*, SOJOURNER: THE WOMEN'S FORUM (on file with Lesbian Herstory Archive, Maxine Wolfe Collection, Box 2, Folder 8).
54. Merle Knight, *Review*, 7 (6) ON OUR BACKS 36 (July/Aug. 1991) (on file with Lesbian Herstory Archive, Maxine Wolfe Collection, Box 2, Folder 8).
55. Maria Erlien, *Review*, SOJOURNER: THE WOMEN'S FORUM (on file with Lesbian Herstory Archive, Maxine Wolfe Collection, Box 2, Folder 8).
56. Donna Minkowitz, Village Voice (Feb. 19, 1991) (on file with author).
57. Meeting Flyers, Agendas, and Schedules (on file with Lesbian Herstory Archive, Maxine Wolfe Collection, Box 2, Folder 5A).
58. Meeting Flyers, Agendas, and Schedules (on file with Lesbian Herstory Archive, Maxine Wolfe Collection, Box 2, Folder 25).
59. Meeting Flyers, Agendas, and Schedules (on file with Lesbian Herstory Archive, Maxine Wolfe Collection, Box 2, Folder 6A).
60. Meeting Flyers, Agendas, and Schedules (on file with Lesbian Herstory Archive, Maxine Wolfe Collection, Box 2, Folder 6A).
61. Resignation Note (on file with Lesbian Herstory Archive, Maxine Wolfe Collection, Box 2, Folder 6A (the person appointed as staff was Caitlyn Ryan)).
62. Meeting Flyers, Agendas, and Schedules (on file with Lesbian Herstory Archive, Maxine Wolfe Collection, Box 2, Folder 6A).
63. Interview by Aziza Ahmed with James Curran, Dean, Emory School of Public Health, in Atlanta, GA (2019); Email communication between Aziza Ahmed and James Curran (June 7, 2025).
64. Documentation of Conference (on file with Lesbian Herstory Archive, Maxine Wolfe Collection, Box 2, Folder 25).
65. ACT UP, TREATMENT AND RESEARCH AGENDA FOR WOMEN WITH HIV INFECTION (1992).
66. ACT UP, TREATMENT AND RESEARCH AGENDA FOR WOMEN WITH HIV INFECTION (1992).
67. ACT UP, TREATMENT AND RESEARCH AGENDA FOR WOMEN WITH HIV INFECTION (1992).
68. Treatment and Research Agenda for Women with HIV Infection (on file with Lesbian Herstory Archive, Maxine Wolfe Collection, Box 2, Folder 6A).
69. Treatment and Research Agenda for Women with HIV Infection (on file with Lesbian Herstory Archive, Maxine Wolfe Collection, Box 2, Folder 6A).

70. Interview by Aziza Ahmed with Ruth Berkelman, formerly with CDC, in Atlanta, GA (2019).
71. Interview by Sarah Schulman with Terry McGovern, HIV Officer at the Ford Foundation, ACT UP Oral History Project, in New York, NY at 20–21 (May 25, 2007).
72. Social Security and AIDS Disability Act of 1991, H.R. 2299, 102nd Congress (1991).
73. *Obstacles That Prevent Women and Children With HIV-Related Disabilities From Qualifying For Social Security Disability Insurance and Supplemental Security Income*, 102nd Cong. 102–99 (1992) (statement of Constance Morella).
74. Letter from Constance Morella to Linda Meredith (Jan. 11, 1991) (Image) (on file with author).
75. Department of Health and Human Services, 56 C.F.R. 65,702 (1991).
76. Letter from Terry McGovern to Lorraine Novinski (on file with Lesbian Herstory Archive, Maxine Wolfe Collection, Box 3, Folders 19–22).
77. *Obstacles That Prevent Women and Children With HIV-Related Disabilities From Qualifying For Social Security Disability Insurance and Supplemental Security Income*, 102nd Cong. 102–99 (1992) (statement of Phyllis Sharpe).
78. The AMA often came out against the broadening of SSA benefits because it felt it was an encroachment of socialized medicine. KEITH WAILOO, PAIN: A POLITICAL HISTORY (2014).
79. *Obstacles That Prevent Women and Children With HIV-Related Disabilities From Qualifying For Social Security Disability Insurance and Supplemental Security Income*, 102nd Cong. 102–99 (1992) (statement of Lonnie Bristow).
80. *Obstacles That Prevent Women and Children With HIV-Related Disabilities From Qualifying For Social Security Disability Insurance and Supplemental Security Income*, 102nd Cong. 102–99 (1992) (statement of Gordan Nary, PAAC).
81. *Obstacles That Prevent Women and Children With HIV-Related Disabilities From Qualifying For Social Security Disability Insurance and Supplemental Security Income*, 102nd Cong. 102–99 (1992) (statement of Gwendolyn S. King, Commissioner of Social Security).
82. As noted by historian Keith Wailoo in his book *Pain: A Political History*, the SSA's claim to objectivity was a move to deny complaints in the context of a politically charged moment in which poor, sick individuals were accused of falsifying illness to get benefits. KEITH WAILOO, PAIN: A POLITICAL HISTORY 99 (2014).
83. *Obstacles That Prevent Women and Children With HIV-Related Disabilities From Qualifying For Social Security Disability Insurance and Supplemental*

*Security Income*, 102nd Cong. 102–99 (1992) (statement of Gwendolyn S. King, Commissioner of Social Security).

84. *Obstacles That Prevent Women and Children With HIV-Related Disabilities From Qualifying For Social Security Disability Insurance and Supplemental Security Income*, 102nd Cong. 102–99 (1992) (statement of Gwendolyn S. King, Commissioner of Social Security).
85. Phone Interview by Aziza Ahmed with James Curran, Dean, Emory School of Public Health, in Atlanta, GA (2019).
86. Interview by Sarah Schulman with Terry McGovern, HIV Officer at the Ford Foundation, ACT UP Oral History Project, in New York, NY (May 25, 2007).
87. Phone Interview by Aziza Ahmed with James Curran, Dean, Emory School of Public Health, in Atlanta, GA (2019).
88. Office of Technology Assessment, The CDC's Case Definition of AIDS: Implications of the Proposed Revisions I–4 (1992).
89. The OTA report acknowledges this quite explicitly. Office of Technology Assessment, The CDC's Case Definition of AIDS: Implications of the Proposed Revisions II-5 (1992). ("The new AIDS case definition is expected to increase the number of HIV infected persons considered to have AIDS. This increase in the number of AIDS cases will affect allocations of Federal funds and will have implications for the privacy of the individuals with AIDS whose names will be reported to the State and local health departments.") These issues were also reported in the press. *See* Gale Scott, *City Will Expand AIDS Definition: Move Could Nearly Double Caseload*, N.Y. Newsday (Nov. 13, 1992).
90. Phone Interview by Aziza Ahmed with James Curran, Dean, Emory School of Public Health, in Atlanta, GA (2019).
91. Interview by Sarah Schulman with Maxine Wolfe, activist, ACT UP Oral History Project, in New York, NY at 90 (May 25, 2007).
92. Interview by Sarah Schulman with Terry McGovern, HIV Officer at the Ford Foundation, ACT UP Oral History Project, in New York, NY at 34 (May 25, 2007).
93. Hard copy of meeting transcription "Meeting on the Expansion of the AIDS Surveillance Case Definition, CDC" at 3, Atlanta, GA (1992) (on file with author).
94. Hard copy of meeting transcription "Meeting on the Expansion of the AIDS Surveillance Case Definition, CDC" at 5, Atlanta, GA (1992) (on file with author).
95. Hard copy of meeting transcription "Meeting on the Expansion of the AIDS Surveillance Case Definition, CDC" at 17, Atlanta, GA (1992) (on file with author).

96. Hard copy of meeting transcription "Meeting on the Expansion of the AIDS Surveillance Case Definition, CDC" at 21, Atlanta, GA (1992) (on file with author).
97. Hard copy of meeting transcription "Meeting on the Expansion of the AIDS Surveillance Case Definition, CDC" at 21, Atlanta, GA (1992) (on file with author).
98. Hard copy of meeting transcription "Meeting on the Expansion of the AIDS Surveillance Case Definition, CDC" at 34, Atlanta, GA (1992) (on file with author).
99. Hard copy of meeting transcription "Meeting on the Expansion of the AIDS Surveillance Case Definition, CDC" at 66, Atlanta, GA (1992) (on file with author).
100. Hard copy of meeting transcription "Meeting on the Expansion of the AIDS Surveillance Case Definition, CDC" at 68, Atlanta, GA (1992) (on file with author).
101. Hard copy of meeting transcription "Meeting on the Expansion of the AIDS Surveillance Case Definition, CDC" at 38, Atlanta, GA (1992) (Peter Kerndt, Director of the AIDS Epidemiology Program at the Los Angeles County Department of Health Services, argued that expanding the definition would complicate disease surveillance) (on file with author).
102. Hard copy of meeting transcription "Meeting on the Expansion of the AIDS Surveillance Case Definition, CDC" at 203, Atlanta, GA (1992) (Kathryn Anastos, physician and Director of the HIV Primary Care Services at Bronx Lebanon Hospital in New York City) (on file with author).
103. Hard copy of meeting transcription "Meeting on the Expansion of the AIDS Surveillance Case Definition, CDC" at 209, Atlanta, GA (1992) (on file with author).
104. Hard copy of meeting transcription "Meeting on the Expansion of the AIDS Surveillance Case Definition, CDC" at 216, Atlanta, GA (1992) (on file with author).
105. Hard copy of meeting transcription "Meeting on the Expansion of the AIDS Surveillance Case Definition, CDC" at 72, 77, Atlanta, GA (1992) (on file with author).
106. Hard copy of meeting transcription "Meeting on the Expansion of the AIDS Surveillance Case Definition, CDC" at 300–301, Atlanta, GA (1992) (on file with author).
107. Hard copy of meeting transcription "Meeting on the Expansion of the AIDS Surveillance Case Definition, CDC" at 313, Atlanta, GA (1992) (on file with author).
108. Hard copy of meeting transcription "Meeting on the Expansion of the AIDS Surveillance Case Definition, CDC" at 313, Atlanta, GA (1992) (on file with author).

109. Hard copy of meeting transcription "Meeting on the Expansion of the AIDS Surveillance Case Definition, CDC" at 316, Atlanta, GA (1992) (on file with author).
110. Hard copy of meeting transcription "Meeting on the Expansion of the AIDS Surveillance Case Definition, CDC" at 332, Atlanta, GA (1992) (on file with author).
111. Hard copy of meeting transcription "Meeting on the Expansion of the AIDS Surveillance Case Definition, CDC" at 357, Atlanta, GA (1992) (on file with author).
112. Hard copy of meeting transcription "Meeting on the Expansion of the AIDS Surveillance Case Definition, CDC" at 360, Atlanta, GA (1992) (on file with author).
113. Hard copy of meeting transcription "Meeting on the Expansion of the AIDS Surveillance Case Definition, CDC" at 363–365, Atlanta, GA (1992) (on file with author). His comments also addressed the specific concerns raised by advocates around cervical cancer. He pointed out that the terminology itself was confusing with some advocates using CIN (cervical intraepithelial neoplasia) and dysplasia and others discussing grades of cancer.
114. Centers for Disease Control, *1993 Revised Classification System for HIV Infection and Expanded Surveillance Case Definition for AIDS among Adolescents and Adults* (1993), www.cdc.gov/mmwr/preview/mmwrhtml/00018871 .htm. The CDC also added pulmonary tuberculosis and recurrent pneumonia as advocated by activists. Terry McGovern, *S.P. v. Sullivan: The Effort to Broaden the Social Security Administration's Definition of AIDS*, 21 FORDHAM URB. L. J. 1083, 1094 (1994); Emma Brick-Hezeau, *Who Gets a Say? Women and the AIDS Crisis*, 4 (2) WOMEN LEADING CHANGE: CASE STUDIES ON WOMEN, GENDER, AND FEMINISM 29–40 (2019) (documenting the relationship between Katrina Haslip and Terry McGovern and their struggle to change the definition of AIDS).
115. *See* OFFICE OF TECHNOLOGY ASSESSMENT, THE CDC'S CASE DEFINITION OF AIDS: IMPLICATIONS OF THE PROPOSED REVISIONS (1992) (highlighting that the issue was brought to the CDC's attention by lawyers); *see also* Mireya Navarro, *Conversations: Katrina Haslip; An AIDS Activist Who Helped Women Get Help Earlier*, N.Y. TIMES (November 15, 1992), bit.ly/3FDpkt9. ("But by last month, when the Federal Centers for Disease Control announced plans to expand the AIDS definition, Ms. Haslip had nothing to hide … she has talked about her infection at conferences, protests and in one-on-one outreach work. She has met with C.D.C officials in private, and berated them in public, as she doggedly pushed for the new definition that she says will help get women tested and the disease diagnosed early, when treatment is more effective.")

116. Centers for Disease Control, *1993 Revised Classification System for HIV Infection and Expanded Surveillance Case Definition for AIDS among Adolescents and Adults* (1993), www.cdc.gov/mmwr/preview/mmwrhtml/00018871.htm.
117. Statement by Katrina Haslip, Read by Barbara Goodman, The Expansion of the CDC Definition Press Conference, October 28, 1992 (on file with author from personal files of Terry McGovern).
118. Mireya Navarro, *Conversations: Katrina Haslip; An AIDS Activist Who Helped Women Get Help Earlier*, N.Y. Times (November 15, 1992), bit.ly/3FDpkt9; Obituary, *Katrina Haslip Dies; AIDS Worker Was 33*, N.Y. Times (December 3, 1992), bit.ly/41XzcFx.
119. Note that the CDC clarified that "The revised HIV classification system and the AIDS surveillance case definition are intended for use in conducting public health surveillance. The CDC's AIDS surveillance case definition was not developed to determine whether statutory or other legal requirements for entitlement to Federal disability or other benefits are met. Consequently, this revised surveillance case definition does not alter the criteria used by the Social Security Administration in evaluating claims based on HIV infection under the Social Security disability insurance and Supplemental Security Income programs. Other organizations and agencies providing medical and social services should develop eligibility criteria appropriate to the services provided and local needs." Centers for Disease Control, *1993 Revised Classification System for HIV Infection and Expanded Surveillance Case Definition for AIDS among Adolescents and Adults* (1993), www.cdc.gov/mmwr/preview/mmwrhtml/00018871.htm.
120. Statement of Katrina Haslip read by Brenda Goodman, The Expansion of the CDC Definition Press Conference, Oct. 28, 1992. Terry McGovern, Eulogy for Katrina Haslip, n.d.
121. Unlike in the United States, where blood tests were rolled out in the mid 1990s, the WHO definition was crafted for international use, in settings where serological testing was not available. The WHO didn't require blood tests for HIV diagnosis globally until 2013 given the unavailability of tests.
122. World Health Organization, *Weekly Epidemiological Record* (1994). The *Weekly Epidemiological Record* highlights that the change followed a meeting convened by the WHO Global Programme on AIDS with the intended purpose of reviewing current case definitions for AIDS surveillance.

## 3 EXPERIMENTS IN RISK: CLINICAL TRIALS AND WOMEN

1. For an in-depth discussion on the political and scientific questions that surrounded AZT see Steven Epstein, Impure Science: AIDS, Activism, and the Politics of Knowledge 198–199 (1996).
2. Name was changed to protect privacy.

3. *See* Memorandum on the FDA's Proposed Guideline for the Study and Evaluation of Gender Differences in the Clinical Evaluation of Drugs from Theresa M. McGovern, Martha S. Jones, and Martha Davis, The HIV Law Project et al. 2 (Oct. 18, 1993) (on file with author).
4. *See generally* Jennifer Nelson, More than Medicine (2015); Wendy Kline, Bodies of Knowledge: Sexuality, Reproduction and Women's Health in the Second Wave (2010).
5. Steven Epstein, Inclusion: The Politics of Difference in Medical Research 17 (2007). Epstein introduces the inclusion-and-difference paradigm as an example of what he terms a biopolitical paradigm. He describes this paradigm as building on "Peter Hall's concept of the policy paradigm and Michel Foucault's characterization of biopolitics, I define biopolitical paradigms and frameworks of ideas, standards, formal procedures, and unarticulated understandings that specify how concerns about health, medicine, and the body are made the simultaneous focus of biomedicine and state policy." Epstein further argues that we cannot presume that "[k]nowledge doesn't travel across categories of identity" even as we appreciate the positive effect of "improving medical research by making it more inclusive." *See* Steven Epstein, Inclusion: The Politics of Difference in Medical Research 2 (2007). Epstein's work is helpful to understand how an identitarian approach to knowledge production meant that feminists were making the claim that "social identities correspond to relatively distinct kinds of bodies" which required seeing these sexed and raced bodies were, in their "embodied states," medically incommensurable.
6. *See generally* Rebecca Dresser, *Wanted Single, White Male for Medical Research*, 22 (1) The Hastings Center Report 24–29 (1992).
7. *See* Marion Banzhaf et al., *The Politics and Practice of the Feminist Health Movement and How It Relates to the AIDS Movement*, The ACT UP Women's Caucus Women and AIDS Handbook or a Reassessment of Reality (1990) (on file with author) (describing how feminist activism in AIDS stems from the feminist movement prior to do actions specifically focused on women and to incorporate a perspective on women into other actions you might organize).
8. *See generally* Raymond A. Smith & Patricia D. Siplon, Drugs into Bodies: Global AIDS Treatment Activism (2006); Lewis Grossman, Choose Your Medicine: Freedom of Therapeutic Choice in America (2021).
9. As documented by many scholarly accounts, in some of their most famous actions, ACT UP demanded treatments, conducted die-ins, and were arrested targeting agency officials. For descriptions of AIDS activism, see Deborah Gould, Moving Politics: Emotion and ACT UP's Fight against AIDS (2009).
10. FDA, bit.ly/4jtPqgY.

11. *See* Ruth Merkatz et al., *Women in Clinical Trials of New Drugs: A Change in Food and Drug Administration Policy*, 329 NEW ENGLAND J. MEDICINE 292–293 (1998).
12. *See* Guideline for the Study and Evaluation of Gender Differences in the Clinical Evaluation of Drugs, 58 Fed. Reg. 39406 (July 22, 1993), www.fda.gov/media/75648/download.
13. LEWIS GROSSMAN, CHOOSE YOUR MEDICINE: FREEDOM OF THERAPEUTIC CHOICE IN AMERICA (2021).
14. Guideline for the Study and Evaluation of Gender Differences in the Clinical Evaluation of Drugs, 58(139) Fed. Reg. 39406–39416 (July 22, 1993).
15. *West German Thalidomide Maker Offers $27-Million Settlement*, N.Y. TIMES (Jan. 27, 1970), www.nytimes.com/1970/01/27/archives/west-german-thalidomide-maker-offers-27million-settlement.html; *see, e.g.*, *Thalidomide: Britons Launch Legal Case*, BBC (June 5, 2014), www.bbc.com/news/uk-27708295; Ben Hirschler, *Thalidomide Victims Seek Compensation, 50 Years on*, REUTERS (Apr. 3, 2008), http://bit.ly/3RbRH4o.
16. Placing the clinical trial in a political and economic context, see generally MELINDA COOPER & CATHERINE WALDBY, CLINICAL LABOR: TISSUE DONORS AND RESEARCH SUBJECTS IN THE GLOBAL BIOECONOMY (2014). On the role of tort litigation in the context of clinical trial litigation, see generally E. Haavi Morreim, *Litigation in Clinical Research: Malpractice Doctrines versus Research Realities*, 32 J. L. MED. & ETHICS 474 (2004).
17. *See* SARAH SCHULMAN, LET THE RECORD SHOW: A POLITICAL HISTORY OF ACT UP NEW YORK, 1987–1993 564 (2021). *See* LEWIS GROSSMAN, CHOOSE YOUR MEDICINE: FREEDOM OF THERAPEUTIC CHOICE IN AMERICA 162–186 (2021); *see also* Michael Specter, *How ACT UP Changed America*, NEW YORKER (June 21, 2021), www.newyorker.com/magazine/2021/06/14/how-act-up-changed-america.
18. *See* Rita Rubin, *Collaboration and Conflict: Looking Back at the 30-Year History of the AIDS Clinical Trial Groups*, 314 J. AM. MED. ASS'N 2604 (2015).
19. *See* LEWIS GROSSMAN, CHOOSE YOUR MEDICINE: FREEDOM OF THERAPEUTIC CHOICE IN AMERICA 162 (2021).
20. STEVEN EPSTEIN, INCLUSION: THE POLITICS OF DIFFERENCE IN MEDICAL RESEARCH (2007).
21. *See* STEVEN EPSTEIN, INCLUSION: THE POLITICS OF DIFFERENCE IN MEDICAL RESEARCH (2007) (on the fight to include women and minorities in clinical trial research); *see also* Marcia Inhorn & K. Lisa Whittle, *Feminism Meets the "New" Epidemiologies: Toward an Appraisal of Antifeminist Biases in Epidemiological Research on Women's Health*, 53 SOC. SCI. & MED. 553 (2001); *see generally* WOMEN'S HEALTH, POLITICS, AND POWER (Elizabeth Fee & Nancy Krieger eds., 1994).

22. Nancy Krieger & Glen Margo, *Women and AIDS: Introduction*, 21 (1) Int'l J. Health Servs. 127–130 (1991); *see also* Nancy Krieger & Glen Margo, AIDS: The Politics of Survival (1994).
23. *See* Ruth Merkatz, *Inclusion of Women in Clinical Trials: A Historical Overview of Scientific and Ethical Issues*, 27 J. Obstetric, Gynecologic & Neonatal Nursing 78 (1998).
24. Maxine Wolfe & Iris Long, *Women and Clinical Trials*, in The ACT UP Women's Caucus Women and AIDS Handbook or a Reassessment of Reality 48 (Illith Rosenblum and Maria Maggenti, and the ACT UP Organization, 1998) (on file with author). Maxine Wolfe writes: "We hope this handbook has provided useful information about the situation in the AIDS crisis. We also hope the information will motivate you to do actions specifically focused on women and to incorporate a perspective on women into other actions you might organize."
25. 1988 FDA ACT UP Pamphlet (on file with author).
26. 1988 FDA ACT UP Pamphlet (on file with author).
27. Maxine Wolfe & Iris Long, *Women and Clinical Trials*, in The ACT UP Women's Caucus Women and AIDS Handbook or a Reassessment of Reality 48 (Illith Rosenblum and Maria Maggenti, and the ACT UP Organization, 1998) (on file with author).
28. Maxine Wolfe & Iris Long, *Women and Clinical Trials*, in The ACT UP Women's Caucus Women and AIDS Handbook or a Reassessment of Reality 48 (Illith Rosenblum and Maria Maggenti, and the ACT UP Organization, 1998) (on file with author). ("Women may be excluded, de facto, because no support services are provided. Many women with AIDS are the sole support and caretaker of their children … As far as we know, there are no drug trials which provide child-care or money to obtain childcare services.")
29. Maxine Wolfe & Iris Long, *Women and Clinical Trials*, in The ACT UP Women's Caucus Women and AIDS Handbook or a Reassessment of Reality 51 (Illith Rosenblum and Maria Maggenti, and the ACT UP Organization, 1998) (on file with author).
30. Gina Kolata, *AIDS Research on New Drugs Bypasses Addicts and Women*, N.Y. Times (Jan. 5, 1988).
31. FDA, *Center for Drug Evaluation and Research, Guideline for the Format and Content of the Clinical and Statistical Sections of an Application* (July 1988), www.fda.gov/media/71436/download.
32. FDA, *Center for Drug Evaluation and Research, Guideline for the Format and Content of the Clinical and Statistical Sections of an Application* (July 1988), www.fda.gov/media/71436/download.
33. The ACT UP Network Women's Issues Committee at the December ACTG Meetings (Jan. 31, 1992) (on file with Lesbian Herstory Archive, Maxine Wolfe Collection, Box 2, Folder 1).

34. The ACT UP Network Women's Issues Committee at the December ACTG Meetings (Jan. 31, 1992) (on file with Lesbian Herstory Archive, Maxine Wolfe Collection, Box 2, Folder 1).
35. Maxine Wolfe & Iris Long, *Through the Eye of a Needle: Women's Access to Drug Treatments through Clinical Trials*, in THE ACT UP WOMEN'S CAUCUS WOMEN AND AIDS HANDBOOK OR A REASSESSMENT OF REALITY 48 (Illith Rosenblum and Maria Maggenti, and the ACT UP Organization, 1998) (on file with author).
36. Maxine Wolfe wrote that a "staff person told us it finally happened, 10 years into this epidemic, because '25 AIDS activists sat in his office and he got scared to death.'" The ACT UP Network Women's Issues Committee at the December ACTG Meetings (Jan. 31, 1992) (on file with Lesbian Herstory Archive, Maxine Wolfe Collection, Box 2, Folder 1). *See* Maxine Wolf, ACT UP Network Women's Issues Committee Meetings with NIAID (National Institutes of Allergy and Infectious Diseases) Epidemiology Branch (Dec. 3 and 6, 1991) (on file with author).
37. *See* Ruth Merkatz, *Inclusion of Women in Clinical Trials: A Historical Overview of Scientific and Ethical Issues*, 27 J. OBSTETRIC, GYNECOLOGIC & NEONATAL NURSING 78 (1998).
38. Barbara Mikulski, for example, inspired numerous congresspeople to take up the cause of clinical trial inclusion and proposed the Women's Health Equity Act of 1990 S.2961 101st Congress (1989–1990).
39. FDA Oral History Program, Final Edited Transcript, Oral History Interview with Ruth B. Merkatz, PhD, RN, FAAN (Oct. 16, 2019), www.fda.gov/media/165295/download?attachment at 14. ("The men with HIV were very well organized, and they had a lot of money. The women with HIV, for the most part, were very poor women who were … contracting HIV through sharing needles and through sexual transmission. There was one group however, that was organized and headed by a very dynamic woman by the name of Terry McGovern – this was the HIV Law Project – and they started demanding that there be changes made in getting women into clinical trials.")
40. *See* Ruth Merkatz et al., *Women in Clinical Trials of New Drugs: A Change in Food and Drug Administration Policy*, 329 NEW ENGLAND J. MED. 292, 292–293 (1998); *see also* M. Pearl et al., *Women in US Government Clinical Trials*, 3866 8TH INT'L CONF. ON AIDS (1992).
41. The FDA and GAO reports frequently interchange sex and gender.
42. Government Accountability Office, Women's Health: FDA Needs to Ensure More Study of Gender Differences in Prescription Drugs, GAO HRD 93–17, Oct. 29, 1992.
43. *See* Stephen W. Nicholas & Elaine J. Abrams, *Boarder Babies with AIDS in Harlem: Lessons in Applied Public Health*, 92 AM. J. PUB. HEALTH 163 (2002); *see also* Jane Gross, *Babies to Have AIDS Center in Harlem*,

N.Y. Times B1 (May 8, 1987), www.nytimes.com/1987/05/08/nyregion/babies-to-have-aids-center-in-harlem.html.

44. *See* Carole A. Campbell, Women, Families, and HIV/AIDS: A Sociological Perspective on the Epidemic in America 39 (1999).
45. *See* Carole A. Campbell, Women, Families, and HIV/AIDS: A Sociological Perspective on the Epidemic in America 39 (1999).
46. *See* Carole A. Campbell, Women, Families, and HIV/AIDS: A Sociological Perspective on the Epidemic in America 39 (1999).
47. Sarah Schulman, Let the Record Show: A Political History of ACT UP New York, 1987–1993 564–565 (2021).
48. Laurie Garrett, *AZT Treatment for Babies*, Newsday (Oct. 17 [ND]). On the question of race and clinical trials at the FDA, see Jonathan Kahn, Race in a Bottle: The Story of BiDil and Racialized Medicine in a Post-Genomic Age (2014); Dorothy Roberts, *What's Wrong with Race-Based Medicine?: Genes, Drugs, and Health Disparities*, 12 (1) Minn. J. L., Sci. & Tech. 1–21 (2011); *see also* Steven Epstein, Inclusion: The Politics of Difference in Medical Research 203–232 (2007). See generally Dorothy Roberts, What's Wrong with Race-Based Medicine?: Genes, Drugs, and Health Disparities 12 Minn. J.L. Sci & Tech 1 (2011).
49. *See* Sarah Schulman, Let the Record Show: A Political History of ACT UP New York, 1987–1993 564–565 (2021).
50. Interview by Sarah Schulman with Tracy Morgan, activist, ACT UP Oral History Project, in New York, NY at 44–45 (May 25, 2007).
51. Sarah Schulman, Let the Record Show: A Political History of ACT UP New York, 1987–1993 564–565 (2021) (Interview with Marion Banzhaf).
52. Sarah Schulman, Let the Record Show: A Political History of ACT UP New York, 1987–1993 564–565 (2021) (Interview with Marion Banzhaf).
53. Interview by Sarah Schulman with Tracy Morgan, activist, ACT UP Oral History Project, in New York, NY at 44–45 (May 25, 2007).
54. Sarah Schulman, Let the Record Show: A Political History of ACT UP New York, 1987–1993 564–565 (2021) (Interview with Tracy Morgan).
55. *See* Steven Epstein, Impure Science: AIDS, Activism, and the Politics of Knowledge 291 (1996). As noted by Steven Epstein in his writing on the ACTG 076 trial, the contestation brought to the fore questions of what kinds of expertise should matter. In the context of ACTG 076, competing claims to expertise were being made: AIDS activists – members of ACT UP's Treatment and Data Committee – had become sophisticated in the science of AIDS.

56. Sarah Schulman, Let the Record Show: A Political History of ACT UP New York, 1987–1993 568 (2021).
57. *See generally* Steven Epstein, Impure Science: AIDS, Activism, and the Politics of Knowledge 291 (1996).
58. Terry McGovern (HIV Law Project), Martha Davis (NOW Legal Defense) and Alma Gomez (American Civil Liberties Union), Citizen's Petition, Dec. 15, 1992 (on file with author).
59. Citing to *Mississippi University for Women v. Hogan*, 458 U.S. 718, 724 (1982).
60. *See* Lewis Grossman, Choose Your Medicine: Freedom of Therapeutic Choice in America 19 (2021); *see also* Lewis Grossman, *AIDS Activists, FDA Regulation, and the Amendment of America's Drug Constitution*, 42 (4) Am. J. L. and Med. 1 (2016).
61. The choice framing that took hold in feminism would be later critiqued by scholars including Dorothy Roberts, *Reproductive Justice, Not Just Rights*, Dissent (Fall 2015), www.dissentmagazine.org/article/reproductive-justice-not-just-rights/.
62. FDA Oral History Program, Final Edited Transcript, Oral History Interview with Ruth B. Merkatz, PhD, RN, FAAN (Oct. 16, 2019), www.fda.gov/media/165295/download?attachment. ("I wasn't angry at them – I empathized with them, but I was angry at the system. For me, it didn't require that kind of action to make me realize we had to do something because the facts were obvious, but still, it was very dramatic.")
63. FDA Oral History Program, Final Edited Transcript, Oral History Interview with Ruth B. Merkatz, PhD, RN, FAAN (Oct. 16, 2019), www.fda.gov/media/165295/download?attachment.
64. *See* Guideline for the Study and Evaluation of Gender Differences in the Clinical Evaluation of Drugs, 58 Fed. Reg. 39406 (July 22, 1993).
65. *See* Guideline for the Study and Evaluation of Gender Differences in the Clinical Evaluation of Drugs, 58 Fed. Reg. 39406 (July 22, 1993).
66. *See* Ruth Merkatz et al., *Women in Clinical Trials of New Drugs: A Change in Food and Drug Administration Policy*, 329 New England J. Med. 292–293 (1998) ("The most likely causes of differences in pharmacokinetics between women and men and among women are variations in body size and composition and the effects of hormones"); *see also* Lori Allesee & Colleen M. Gallagher, *Pregnancy and Protection: The Ethics of Limiting a Pregnant Woman's Participation in Clinical Trials*, 2 J. Clinical Rsch. & Bioethics 1 (Aug. 2011), www.ncbi.nlm.nih.gov/pmc/articles/PMC3158978/.
67. Ruth Merkatz et al., *Women in Clinical Trials of New Drugs: A Change in Food and Drug Administration Policy*, 329 New England J. Med. 292, 293 (1998).

68. Ruth Merkatz et al., *Women in Clinical Trials of New Drugs: A Change in Food and Drug Administration Policy*, 329 New England J. Med. 294 (1998).
69. FDA Oral History Program, Final Edited Transcript, Oral History Interview with Ruth B. Merkatz, PhD, RN, FAAN (Oct. 16, 2019), www.fda.gov/media/165295/download?attachment.
70. FDA Oral History Program, Final Edited Transcript, Oral History Interview with Ruth B. Merkatz, PhD, RN, FAAN (Oct. 16, 2019), www.fda.gov/media/165295/download?attachment.
71. *See* Memorandum on the FDA's Proposed Guideline for the Study and Evaluation of Gender Differences in the Clinical Evaluation of Drugs from Theresa M. McGovern, Martha S. Jones, and Martha Davis, The HIV Law Project et al. 6 (Oct. 18, 1993) (on file with author).
72. Memorandum on the FDA's Proposed Guideline for the Study and Evaluation of Gender Differences in the Clinical Evaluation of Drugs from Theresa M. McGovern, Martha S. Jones, and Martha Davis, The HIV Law Project et al. 6–7 (Oct. 18, 1993) (on file with author).
73. Memorandum on the FDA's Proposed Guideline for the Study and Evaluation of Gender Differences in the Clinical Evaluation of Drugs from Theresa M. McGovern, Martha S. Jones, and Martha Davis, The HIV Law Project et al. 7 (Oct. 18, 1993) (on file with author).
74. *See* Guideline for the Study and Evaluation of Gender Differences in the Clinical Evaluation of Drugs, 58 Fed. Reg. 39406 (July 22, 1993). ("[E]xcept in the case of trials intended for the study of drug effects during pregnancy, clinical protocols should include measures that will minimize the possibility of fetal exposure to the investigational drug. These would ordinarily include providing for the use of a reliable method of contraception (or abstinence) for the duration of drug exposure (which may exceed the length of the study), use of pregnancy testing (beta HCG) to detect unsuspected pregnancy prior to initiation of study treatment, and timing of studies (easier with studies of short duration) to coincide with, or immediately follow, menstruation.")
75. *See* Memorandum on the FDA's Proposed Guideline for the Study and Evaluation of Gender Differences in the Clinical Evaluation of Drugs from Theresa M. McGovern, Martha S. Jones, and Martha Davis, The HIV Law Project et al. 2, 16 (Oct. 18, 1993) (on file with author). ("[T]he 1993 Guideline is not an adequate response to the Citizen's petition, as it fails to mandate the inclusion of women in clinical trials; it fails to mandate a by-gender analysis of drug response; it fails to eliminate gender specific protocol criteria and, in fact, encourages the use of such criteria; it fails to mandate the completion of animal reproduction studies prior to human testing; it fails to identify the criteria used in determining fetal toxicity; it fails to mandate an adequate

analysis of male mediated effects; it fails to require the FDA to halt trials restricting the access of women and it fails, in totality, to change the FDA policy of discriminating against women in the clinical trial process.")

76. Letter from Ruth B. Merkatz, Director of the Office of Women's Health, U.S. Food and Drug Admin. & Theresa Toigo, Deputy Director of the Office of AIDS and Special Health Issues, U.S. Food and Drug Admin., to Mary Lucey, ACT UP Women's Caucus (Oct. 12, 1994) (on file with author).
77. *See* Memorandum from Theresa M. McGovern, Nat'l Task Force on AIDs Drug Development to Donna Shalala, Secretary, U.S. Depart. Of Health and Human Services (July 19, 1994) (on file with author) ("The Department of Health and Human Services, the National Institutes of Health (NIH), and the Food and Drug Administration (FDA) all discriminate against women with HIV in the research setting").
78. *See* Ruth Merkatz et al., *Women in Clinical Trials of New Drugs: A Change in Food and Drug Administration Policy*, 329 NEW ENGLAND J. MED. 292, 293 (1998). ("We recognize and are very concerned by the lack of full participation of HIV-infected women in trials of drugs for HIV/AIDS. This underrepresentation cannot be attributed to FDA restrictions because FDA has never recommended gender-based restrictions in life-threatening illnesses.")
79. Letter from Linda A. Suydam, Interim Deputy Commissioner for Operations, U.S. Food & Drug Admin. to Theresa M. McGovern, AIDS Service Center HIV Law Project et al., at 17 (Oct. 27, 1994), RE Docket No. 92P-0494 (on file with author).
80. *See* Letter from Linda A. Suydam, Interim Deputy Commissioner for Operations, U.S. Food & Drug Admin. to Theresa M. McGovern, AIDS Service Center HIV Law Project et al. (Oct. 27, 1994), RE Docket No. 92P-0494 (on file with author).
81. *See* Letter from Linda A. Suydam, Interim Deputy Commissioner for Operations, U.S. Food & Drug Admin. to Theresa M. McGovern, AIDS Service Center HIV Law Project et al. (Oct. 27, 1994), RE Docket No. 92P-0494 at 6 (on file with author).
82. *See* Letter from Linda A. Suydam, Interim Deputy Commissioner for Operations, U.S. Food & Drug Admin. to Theresa M. McGovern, AIDS Service Center HIV Law Project et al. (Oct. 27, 1994), RE Docket No. 92P-0494 (on file with author).
83. *See* Letter from Linda A. Suydam, Interim Deputy Commissioner for Operations, U.S. Food & Drug Admin. to Theresa M. McGovern, AIDS Service Center HIV Law Project et al. (Oct. 27, 1994), RE Docket No. 92P-0494 at 15 (on file with author).

84. *See* Letter from Linda A. Suydam, Interim Deputy Commissioner for Operations, U.S. Food & Drug Admin. to Theresa M. McGovern, AIDS Service Center HIV Law Project et al. (Oct. 27, 1994), RE Docket No. 92P-0494 at 9 (on file with author).
85. *See* Letter from Linda A. Suydam, Interim Deputy Commissioner for Operations, U.S. Food & Drug Admin. to Theresa M. McGovern, AIDS Service Center HIV Law Project et al. (Oct. 27, 1994), RE Docket No. 92P-0494 (on file with author).
86. Report on Meeting with David Kessler, Sept. 9, 1994. The meeting included David Kessler, representatives from ACT UP NY, Los Angeles, Philadelphia, Karyn Pena from Housingworks, Michelle Lopez from the Community Constituency Group, and Virge Parks from San Francisco.
87. Centers for Disease Control, Mortality and Morbidity Weekly, Recommendations of the U.S. Public Health Service Task Force on the Use of Zidovudine to Reduce Perinatal Transmission of Human Immunodeficiency Virus (Aug. 5, 1994).
88. *See also* STEVEN EPSTEIN, INCLUSION: THE POLITICS OF DIFFERENCE IN MEDICAL RESEARCH 85 (2007) (discussing the use of *International Union, United Automobile Workers v. Johnson Controls* in the citizen's petition). For a discussion of clinical research and gender see also Karen H. Rothenberg, *Gender Matters: Implications for Clinical Research and Women's Health Care*, 32 HOUS. L. REV. 1201 (1996).
89. J. R. Steinberg, B. E. Turner, B. T. Weeks et al., *Analysis of Female Enrollment and Participant Sex by Burden of Disease in US Clinical Trials between 2000 and 2020*, 4 (6) J. AM. MED. ASS'N NETWORK OPEN e2113749 (2021).

## 4 SEX BARGAINS

1. For a discussion on the role of gender in law reform strategies at the World Bank, see Kerry Rittich, *The Future of Law and Development: Second-Generation Reforms and the Incorporation of the Social*, in THE NEW LAW AND ECONOMIC DEVELOPMENT (David M. Trubek & Alvaro Santos eds., 2006).
2. Richard A. Posner & Tomas J. Philipson, *Optimal Regulation of AIDS* 1 (Coase-Sandor Inst. for L. & Econ., Working Paper No. 6, 1992).
3. Marcia C. Inhorn & K. Lisa Whittle, *Feminism Meets the "New" Epidemiologies: Toward an Appraisal of Antifeminist Biases in Epidemiological Research on Women's Health*, 53 SOC. SCI. & MED. 553–567 (2001).
4. JANET HALLEY, SPLIT DECISIONS: HOW AND WHY TO TAKE A BREAK FROM FEMINISM 28 (2008) (describing feminist theories of sex and sexuality).

5. For a description of this moment, see generally Alice Echols, Daring to Be Bad: Radical Feminism in America, 1967–1975 (1989).
6. For a description of this moment, see generally Alice Echols, Daring to Be Bad: Radical Feminism in America, 1967–1975 (1989).
7. The reasons for this success, however, are contested. Two questions dominate this discussion. Was feminism absorbed, changed, and spit out by a broader social and economic system that prioritized individual responsibility and liberal values at the cost of structural solutions? In this telling, feminists were innocent bystanders. Or were feminists active participants in a broader social and economic project that would come to disenfranchise so many?
8. Kristin Bumiller, In an Abusive State: How Neoliberalism Appropriated the Feminist Movement against Sexual Violence (Kindle Location 328). Kindle Edition. (2008).
9. Catharine A. MacKinnon, *Feminism, Marxism, Method, and the State: An Agenda for Theory*, 7 Feminist Theory 515 (1982). ("Sexual objectification is the primary process of the subjection of women. It unites act with word, construction with expression, perception with enforcement, myth and reality. Man fucks woman. Subject verb object.") Discussing the role of sexual violence in the feminist movement, see generally Kristin Bumiller, In an Abusive State: How Neoliberalism Appropriated the Feminist Movement against Sexual Violence (Kindle Location 380). Kindle Edition. (2008).
10. Kristin Bumiller, In an Abusive State: How Neoliberalism Appropriated the Feminist Movement against Sexual Violence (Kindle Location 329). Kindle Edition. (2008). Later, MacKinnon would use the war metaphor to describe partner violence "as a form of domestic captivity or sexual terrorism." Catharine A. MacKinnon, *Women's September 11th: Rethinking the International Law of Conflict*, 47 Harv. Int'l L. J. 1 (2006).
11. National Organization of Women, History of Marches and Mass Actions, www.now.org/history/history-of-marches-and-mass-actions.
12. Kristin Bumiller, In an Abusive State: How Neoliberalism Appropriated the Feminist Movement against Sexual Violence (Kindle Location 305). Kindle Edition. (2008).
13. Alice Echols, Daring to Be Bad: Radical Feminism in America, 1967–1975 (1989).
14. For a discussion on the turn toward criminal law to address social issues, see generally Jonathan Simon, Governing through Crime: How the War on Crime Transformed American Democracy and Created a Culture of Fear (2007).

15. Mimi Kim, *Dancing the Carceral Creep: The Anti-Domestic Violence Movement and the Paradoxical Pursuit of Criminalization, 1973–1986* (Inst. for the Study of Societal Issues, Working Paper, Oct. 14, 2015).
16. Violent Crime Control and Law Enforcement Act of 1994, H.R. 3355, 103rd Congress (1993–1994).
17. Aya Gruber, The Feminist War on Crime: The Unexpected Role of Women's Liberation in Mass Incarceration (2021).
18. Duncan Kennedy, *Three Globalizations of Law and Legal Thought: 1880–2000*, in The New Law and Economic Development: A Critical Appraisal (David Trubek & Alvaro Santos eds., 2006). The women's rights movement was one of many identity-based struggles that emerged inside of what Duncan Kennedy describes as the Third Globalization in which an "identity/rights complex" that was distinctly "Unitedstatesean" in character began to emerge globally.
19. Sally Engle Merry, Human Rights and Gender Violence: Translating International Law into Local Justice (2006); *see also* Peggy Antrobus, The Global Women's Movement (2006); U.N. Secretary-General, *Report of the World Conference of the International Women's Year*, U.N. Doc. E/CONF.66/34 (1976).
20. *See generally* Jean Quartaert, Advocating Dignity: Human Rights Mobilizations in Global Politics (2010).
21. For a history of feminist organizing on sexual violence in international law and the consequences of this activism, see Jutta M. Joachim, Agenda Setting, the UN, and NGOs: Gender Violence and Reproductive Rights (2007); Karen Engle, The Grip of Sexual Violence in Conflict (2020); *see also* Ali Miller, *Sexuality, Violence against Women, and Human Rights: Women Make Demands and Ladies Get Protection*, 7 (2) Health and Human Rights 16–47 (2004).
22. Jutta M. Joachim, Agenda Setting, the UN, and NGOs: Gender Violence and Reproductive Rights (Kindle Location 96). Kindle Edition. (2007).
23. A key movement at the center of debates on law and health was the burgeoning literature on health and human rights. *See generally* Sofia Gruskin, *What Are Health and Human Rights?*, 363 Lancet 329 (2004); Jonathan Mann et al., 1 Health and Human Rights 6 (1994); Daniel Tarantola & Sofia Gruskin, *The Recognition and Evolution of the HIV and Human Rights Interface: 1981–2017*, in Research Handbook on Global Health Law (Gian Luca Burci & Brigit Toebes eds., 2018).
24. Tomas J. Philipson & Richard A. Posner, Private Choices and Public Health: The AIDS Epidemic in an Economic Perspective 3–4 (1993). It was not the first time law and economics

had taken on sex. RICHARD A. POSNER, SEX AND REASON (Kindle Location 1304). Kindle Edition. (1992). ("The model of rational sexual behavior emphasizes the varied goals of sex, the costs of sexual search, and the nature of marriage – whether companionate or noncompanionate – as critical determinants of sexual practices and attitudes, along with urbanization and, above all, the occupational and financial situation of women. Sex, in other words, is the product of cost-benefit analysis, albeit as costs and benefits are understood in the context of marriage cultures (i.e., whether people are in love when they marry) and the broader cultural context. Loving one's spouse, in the case of companionate marriage, for example, could alter the demand for extramarital sex.") The publication of *Sex and Reason* and *Private Choices and Public Health* produced commentary from legal scholars, particularly feminist and gender scholars. *See* Martha Albertson Fineman, *The Hermeneutics of Reason: A Commentary on Sex and Reason*, 25 CONN. L. REV. 503 (1992); William Eskridge Jr., *A Social Constructionist Critique of Posner's Sex and Reason: Steps toward a Gaylegal Agenda*, 102 YALE L. J. 333 (1992). Posner replied to some of these commentators in several articles including this one, Richard Posner, *The Radical Feminist Critique of Sex and Reason*, 25 CONN. L. REV. 515 (1992). There were also feminist reviews of *Private Choices and Public Health*, see, for example Kimberly Christensen, *Economics without Money; Sex without Gender: A Critique of Philipson and Posner's Private Choices and Public Health: The AIDS Epidemic in an Economic Perspective*, 4 (2) FEMINIST ECONOMICS 1–24 (1998) (drawing on feminist economics to show that the "neoclassical assumptions of their model are erroneous").

25. TOMAS J. PHILIPSON & RICHARD A. POSNER, PRIVATE CHOICES AND PUBLIC HEALTH: THE AIDS EPIDEMIC IN AN ECONOMIC PERSPECTIVE 16 (1993).
26. RICHARD A. POSNER, SEX AND REASON (Kindle Location 83). Kindle Edition. (1992).
27. Richard A. Posner & Tomas J. Philipson, *Optimal Regulation of AIDS* 1 (Coase-Sandor Inst. for L. & Econ., Working Paper No. 6, 1992) at 1.
28. TOMAS J. PHILIPSON & RICHARD A. POSNER, PRIVATE CHOICES AND PUBLIC HEALTH: THE AIDS EPIDEMIC IN AN ECONOMIC PERSPECTIVE 31 (1993).
29. TOMAS J. PHILIPSON & RICHARD A. POSNER, PRIVATE CHOICES AND PUBLIC HEALTH: THE AIDS EPIDEMIC IN AN ECONOMIC PERSPECTIVE (1993).
30. Posner and Philipson define utility maximization: "'[U]tility' refers to the subjective welfare of the actor and 'expected' to the presence of uncertainty, which may make the choice – for example, unsafe sex – that

was best ex ante (that is, when made) a poor choice ex post (after it is made). Rationality implies nothing more, really, that suiting means to ends, whatever those ends may be." TOMAS J. PHILIPSON & RICHARD A. POSNER, PRIVATE CHOICES AND PUBLIC HEALTH: THE AIDS EPIDEMIC IN AN ECONOMIC PERSPECTIVE 8 (1993).

31. In turn, the epidemic "although not exclusively, [is] the consequence of voluntary decisions by persons of different HIV infection status to have unshielded sexual intercourse with each other." TOMAS J. PHILIPSON & RICHARD A. POSNER, PRIVATE CHOICES AND PUBLIC HEALTH: THE AIDS EPIDEMIC IN AN ECONOMIC PERSPECTIVE 31 (1993).
32. As opposed to what they call voluntary "partner observed" HIV testing. TOMAS J. PHILIPSON & RICHARD A. POSNER, PRIVATE CHOICES AND PUBLIC HEALTH: THE AIDS EPIDEMIC IN AN ECONOMIC PERSPECTIVE 94 (1993).
33. TOMAS J. PHILIPSON & RICHARD A. POSNER, PRIVATE CHOICES AND PUBLIC HEALTH: THE AIDS EPIDEMIC IN AN ECONOMIC PERSPECTIVE 89 93 (1993).
34. TOMAS J. PHILIPSON & RICHARD A. POSNER, PRIVATE CHOICES AND PUBLIC HEALTH: THE AIDS EPIDEMIC IN AN ECONOMIC PERSPECTIVE 89 (1993).
35. TOMAS J. PHILIPSON & RICHARD A. POSNER, PRIVATE CHOICES AND PUBLIC HEALTH: THE AIDS EPIDEMIC IN AN ECONOMIC PERSPECTIVE 88–89, 147 (1993) ("All things considered, the prudent conclusion is that testing, whether voluntary or mandatory, is, unless universal or close to it, as likely to increase the spread of AIDS as to curtail it").
36. Nan Hunter, *Complications of Gender: Women and HIV Disease*, in AIDS AGENDA: EMERGING ISSUES IN CIVIL RIGHTS 7 (NAN HUNTER & WILLIAM B. RUBENSTEIN EDS. 1992).
37. For a description of the dominance frame in feminism, see Kathy Abrams, *Sex Wars Redux: Agency and Coercion in Feminist Legal Theory*, 95 COLUM. L. REV. 305–376 (1995).
38. RICHARD POSNER, SEX AND REASON (Kindle Location 411). Kindle Edition. (1992).
39. RICHARD POSNER, SEX AND REASON (Kindle Location 418). Kindle Edition. (1992).
40. TOMAS J. PHILIPSON & RICHARD A. POSNER, PRIVATE CHOICES AND PUBLIC HEALTH: THE AIDS EPIDEMIC IN AN ECONOMIC PERSPECTIVE 76–77 (1993). ("We expect the relative preference for safe sex by women compared to men to be greater among blacks than among whites, since black men, constituting the pool from which black women choose the vast majority of their sexual partners, have a higher infection rate than white men. If, however, a woman has few alternatives in the market for sexual relationships, a man may be able to compensate

her at very low cost to himself – perhaps just by being willing to have a relationship with her – for acceding to his request for risky sex. Because black women have poorer options in the dating and marriage markets than white women, we expect black women to be more willing to accept such compensation.")

41. Tomas J. Philipson & Richard A. Posner, Private Choices and Public Health: The AIDS Epidemic in an Economic Perspective 98 (1993).

42. Tomas J. Philipson & Richard A. Posner, *The Microeconomics of the AIDS Epidemic in Africa*, 12 Population and Dev. Rev. 836 842–843 (1995). ("We have been discussing the demand for safe sex chiefly among men and must now consider more carefully the demand conditions on the other side of the sexual exchange. In our book we ascribed the very high prevalence of AIDS among black compared to white women in the United States (almost ten times higher) to the poor bargaining position of black women vis-a-vis black men. The ratio of marriageable black men to marriageable black women is abnormally low in the United States, implying that a black woman will often have to offer a net transfer to a black man to induce marriage or any other form of long-term sexual relationship. That net transfer might take the form of forgoing insistence that the man use a condom, a use to which many men are averse. Superficially, the bargaining position of African women might seem more favorable. Polygyny increases the effective demand for women as wives; and as a result of the prevalence of migrant labor, many African cities and towns have a very high ratio of men to women. Nevertheless, because of legal disabilities and pervasive discrimination, the African woman's bargaining position appears on balance to be very poor. For example, migrant workers are not looking for wives since they often will have left a wife at home, and restrictions on women's employment may largely confine unmarried women's job opportunities to prostitution. The prevalence of prostitution may provide an additional explanation for why, even though women are more susceptible to becoming infected with the AIDS virus in heterosexual intercourse than men, and even though male homosexual intercourse and (mostly male) intravenous drug use are not important sources of HIV transmission in Africa, as many African men as African women are HIV-positive. Since prostitutes have a much larger number of sexual partners on average than do promiscuous men, a small number of prostitutes can infect a large number of men even though the disease is more easily transmitted from men to women than vice versa.")

43. Tomas J. Philipson & Richard A. Posner, *The Microeconomics of the AIDS Epidemic in Africa*, 12 Population and Dev. Rev. 835–848 (1995).

44. Tomas J. Philipson & Richard A. Posner, *The Microeconomics of the AIDS Epidemic in Africa*, 12 Population and Dev. Rev. 843 (1995).

45. Martha Ainsworth & A. Mead Over, *Confronting AIDS: Public Priorities in a Global Epidemic* (World Bank Report No. 17285, Oct. 31, 1997) at 105–106. Emphasis added.
46. Tomas J. Philipson & Richard A. Posner, Private Choices and Public Health: The AIDS Epidemic in an Economic Perspective 6 (1993).
47. For an example of this type of study, see Omar Galárraga et al., *The Disproportionate Burden of HIV and STIs among Male Sex Workers in Mexico City and the Rationale for Economic Incentives to Reduce Risks*, 17 (1) J. Int'l AIDS Soc'y 19218 (2014).
48. Jason Jackson & Aziza Ahmed, *Race, Risk and Personal Responsibility in the Response to COVID-19*, 121 Colum. L. Rev. 57–58 (2021). ("As the sub-fields of information economics and behavioral economics grew in the 1980s and 1990s, so did the idea that an alternative approach to addressing public health crises, like obesity or diabetes, would be to improve the decision-making ability of individuals. Behavioral economics challenged the idea of a purely rational individual, instead arguing that people were rational within certain bounds shaped by social factors including systematic bias or the interplay of psychological forces. Taking behavioral economics seriously meant challenging the notion of a purely rational individual and rethinking the role of regulation in helping people make optimal decisions.") *See also* Lindsay F. Wiley et al., *Health Reform Reconstruction*, 55 UC Davis L. Rev. 657 (2021) (identifying individualism, fiscal fragmentation, privatization, and federalism as fixtures in healthcare reform that have undermined a social-justice-oriented vision of healthcare).
49. Frances E. Olsen, *The Myth of State Intervention in the Family*, in Law and Families (Helen Rhoades ed., 2006).
50. Marcia C. Inhorn, *Feminism Meets the "New" Epidemiologies: Toward an Appraisal of Antifeminist Biases in Epidemiological Research on Women's Health*, 53 Soc. Sci. & Med. 553 (2001); *see generally* Women's Health, Politics, and Power (Elizabeth Fee & Nancy Krieger eds., 1994).
51. Jeanette Ickovics & Judith Rodin, *Women and Aids in the United States: Epidemiology, Natural History, and Mediating Mechanisms*, 1 Health Psych. 11, 1 (1992).
52. Jeanette Ickovics & Judith Rodin, *Women and Aids in the United States: Epidemiology, Natural History, and Mediating Mechanisms*, 1 Health Psych. 11, 1 (1992).
53. Priscilla Ulin, *African Women and Aids: Negotiating Behavioral Change*, 34 Soc. Sci. & Med. 63–73 (1992).
54. Suzanne Maman et al., *The Intersections of HIV and Violence: Directions for Future Research and Interventions*, 50 Soc. Sci. & Med. 459 (2000).

55. *See, e.g.*, Charlotte. Watts et al., *Women, Violence and HIV/AIDS in Zimbabwe*, 5 SAfAIDS News 2 (1997); Suzanne Maman et al., *The Intersections of HIV and Violence: Directions for Future Research and Interventions*, 50 Soc. Sci. & Med. 459 (2000); Kyung-Hee Choi et al., *Sexual Harassment, Sexual Coercion, and HIV Risk among U.S. Adults 18–49 Years*, 2 AIDS and Behavior 2, 33–40 (1998).
56. D. Durevall & A. Lindskog, *Intimate Partner Violence and HIV in Ten Sub-Saharan African Countries: What Do the Demographic and Health Surveys Tell Us?*, 3 Lancet Global Health e34–e43 (2015).
57. The stakes were described in a *Lancet* editorial by Sunita Kishor, then Director of the Demographic Health Surveys Program, a US Agency for International Development-funded population data collection initiative. Kishor described the reaction of gender-based advocates to a published study by Guy Harling and co-researchers that found no significant association between HIV status and experience of intimate partner violence:

> When [Guy] Harling and colleagues' article was first published in 2010, the equivalent of a shocked silence fell across the gender-based violence community. The study had found no significant association between women's HIV status and their experience of intimate partner violence in all of the sub-Saharan African and three other countries for which Demographic and Health Survey data were available. The timing of publication of the report could not have been worse. *Despite strong evidence of the negative effects of intimate partner violence on several aspects of women's reproductive health, it was not until intimate partner violence was judged to be a risk factor for HIV that the gender-based violence community had finally gained traction in obtaining international commitment for the elimination of intimate partner violence*. In fact, it was during this period that the community had finally been able to propose to the UNAIDS-led HIV Monitoring and Evaluation Reference Group that intimate partner violence in the past 12 months become the UN General Assembly Special Sessions indicator to monitor the goal of gender inequality reduction. Although the proposed indicator was finally accepted, Harling and colleagues' report had very nearly derailed these efforts.

The Kishor editorial demonstrates the material importance of retaining the link between VAW and HIV as central to feminists in order to gain support of the international community. The necessity of proving an association between gender-based violence (GBV) and HIV not only validated the feminist project, but also legitimated the interests of anti-GBV advocates as a broader human rights and development issue. *See* Sunita Kishor, *Intimate Partner Violence and HIV: Clearing Up the Confusion*, 3 Lancet E4-E5 (2015).

58. For an example of how women were treated as vectors in the biological literature, see Markus W. Vogt et al., *Isolation of HTLV-III/LAV from Cervical Secretions of Women at Risk for Aids*, 327 LANCET 525 (1986); C. B. Wofsy et al., *Isolation of AIDS-Associated Retrovirus from Genital Secretions of Women with Antibodies to the Virus*, 1 LANCET 527 (1986).
59. As later described by Jennifer Higgins, the idea of women's increased vulnerability grew as it was analogized to other sexually transmitted infections which were known to have different rates of transmission between men and women. Jennifer A. Higgins, Susie Hoffman & Shari L. Dworkin, *Rethinking Gender, Heterosexual Men, and Women's Vulnerability to HIV/AIDS*, 100 AM. J. PUB. HEALTH 435 (2010).
60. *See generally* ROYAL TROPICAL INSTITUTE, South Africa AIDS Information Dissemination Service, and World Health Organization, FACING HIV, AIDS, STDS: A GENDER BASED RESPONSE 10 (1995).
61. U.N. Secretary-General, *Report of the Fourth World Conference on Women*, U.N. Doc. A/CONF.177/20/Rev.1 (1996). Italics added.
62. U.N. Secretary-General, *Declaration of Commitment on HIV/AIDS: Global Crisis – Global Action* (June 25–27, 2001).
63. U.N. Secretary-General, *Declaration of Commitment on HIV/AIDS: Global Crisis – Global Action*, (June 25–27, 2001).
64. G.A. Res. S-26/2 (Aug. 2, 2001).
65. Thomas C. Quinn & Julie Overbaugh, *HIV/AIDS in Women: An Expanding Epidemic*, SCIENCE (2005). doi: 10.1126/science.1112489. Italics added.
66. Writing on how feminist ideas travel between countries and within human rights discourse includes SALLY ENGLE MERRY, HUMAN RIGHTS AND GENDER VIOLENCE: TRANSLATING INTERNATIONAL LAW INTO LOCAL JUSTICE (2006); MARGARET E. KECK & KATHRYN SIKKINK, ACTIVISTS BEYOND BORDERS: ADVOCACY NETWORKS IN INTERNATIONAL POLITICS (1998); Karen Engle, *Feminism and Its (Dis) contents: Criminalizing Wartime Rape in Bosnia Herzegovina*, 99 AM. J. INT'L L. 778–816 (2005); INDERPAL GREWAL, Transnational America: Feminism, Diaspora, Neoliberalisms (2005); *see generally* Ali Miller, *Sexuality, Violence against Women, and Human Rights: Women Make Demands and Ladies Get Protection*, 7 (2) HEALTH AND HUM. RTS. 16–47 (2004).
67. Examples of cost–benefit analysis of HIV include: USAID, COST-BENEFIT ANALYSIS OF HIV WORKPLACE PROGRAMMES IN ZAMBIA (2007), http://pdf.usaid.gov/pdf_docs/PNADK430.pdf; Steven D. Pinkerton, David R. Holtgrave, & Frederick R. Bloom, *Cost-Effectiveness of Post-Exposure Prophylaxis Following Sexual Exposure to HIV*, 12 AIDS 1067 (1998); Andrew Creese et al., *Cost-Effectiveness of HIV/AIDS*

*Interventions in Africa: A Systematic Review of the Evidence*, 359 LANCET 1635–1642 (2002).

68. As described by Shari Dworkin, a researcher at the Institute for Development Studies, the dominance feminist AIDS narrative produced a specific idea about women and AIDS: "She is the leading lady in the AIDS epidemic. She was under the surface, hidden, but finally emerged, rushed forward with newfound breath, born into existence with twin shoves: first, feminism; next epidemiological fathomability and visibility. She appeared in 1993 as vulnerable." Shari Dworkin, *Commentary: Who Is Epidemiologically Fathomable in the HIV/AIDS Epidemic? Gender, Sexuality, and Intersectionality in Public Health*, 6 CULTURE, HEALTH & SEXUALITY 615 (2005).
69. Elizabeth Fee & Nancy Krieger, *Understanding AIDS: Historical Interpretations and the Limits of Biomedical Individualism*, 83 AM. J. PUB. HEALTH 1477–1486 (1993).
70. For critical perspectives on feminism, see Ratna Kapur, *The Tragedy of Victimization Rhetoric: Resurrecting the "Native" Subject in International/Post-Colonial Feminist Legal Politics*, 15 HARV. HUM. RTS. J. 1 (2002). For additional writing on feminism, feminist debates, and the domestic violence movement, see Aya Gruber, *The Feminist War on Crime*, 92 (3) IOWA L. REV. 741 (2006); Donna Coker, *Crime Control and Feminist Law Reform in Domestic Violence Law: A Critical Review*, 4 BUFFALO CRIM. L. REV. 801–860 (2001); Leigh Goodmark, *Should Domestic Violence Be Decriminalized?*, 40 HARV. J. L. GENDER 53 (2017); Deborah Weissman, *VAWA @ 20: The Politics of Pretext: VAWA Goes Global*, 18 CUNY L. REV. 37 (2014); RASHMI GOEL & LEIGH GOODMARK, COMPARATIVE PERSPECTIVES ON GENDER VIOLENCE: LESSONS FROM EFFORTS WORLDWIDE (2015); Patricia Erwin, *Exporting U.S. Domestic Violence Reforms: An Analysis of Human Rights Frameworks and U.S. "Best Practices"*, 3 FEMINIST CRIMINOLOGY 188–206 (2006). For a critical perspective on legal reforms in the context of sexual violence in conflict, see KAREN ENGLE, THE GRIP OF SEXUAL VIOLENCE IN CONFLICT: FEMINIST INTERVENTIONS IN INTERNATIONAL LAW (2022). For critical perspectives on criminal law in reproductive rights, see DOROTHY ROBERTS, KILLING THE BLACK BODY: RACE, REPRODUCTION AND THE MEANING OF LIBERTY (1997); MICHELE GOODWIN, POLICING THE WOMB: INVISIBLE WOMEN AND THE CRIMINALIZATION OF MOTHERHOOD (2020).
71. For a discussion on how framing issues as bad actors and aggrieved victims undermines structural responses, see Allegra McLeod, *Exporting U.S. Criminal Justice*, 29 YALE L. & POL'Y REV. 83, 92 (2010). McLeod is drawing on JONATHAN SIMON, GOVERNING THROUGH CRIME: HOW THE WAR ON CRIME TRANSFORMED AMERICAN DEMOCRACY AND CREATED A CULTURE OF FEAR (2007).

72. Human Rights Watch, Just Die Quietly: Domestic Violence and Women's Vulnerability to HIV in Uganda (2003), www.hrw.org/reports/2003/uganda0803/uganda0803.pdf.
73. For a discussion on the production of identity in the context of AIDS, see Shari Dworkin, *Commentary: Who Is Epidemiologically Fathomable in the HIV/AIDS Epidemic? Gender, Sexuality, and Intersectionality in Public Health*, 7 (6) Culture, Health & Sexuality 7 615–623 (2005).
74. Violent Crime Control and Law Enforcement Act of 1994, Pub. L. No. 103–322, 1089 Stat. 1796 Section 40503(c) (1994).
75. *See, e.g.*, Nicholas Kristof, *Moonshine or the Kids?*, N.Y. Times (May 22, 2010), www.nytimes.com/2010/05/23/opinion/23kristof.html; Nicholas Kristof and Sheryl WuDunn, *The Women's Crusade*, N.Y. Times (Aug. 17, 2009), www.nytimes.com/2009/08/23/magazine/23Women-t.html.
76. Donna Coker, *Shifting Power for Battered Women: Law, Material Resources, and Poor Women of Color*, 33 U.C. Davis L. Rev. 1009 (2000).
77. Mimi Kim, *Dancing the Carceral Creep: The Anti-Domestic Violence Movement and the Paradoxical Pursuit of Criminalization, 1973–1986* (Inst. for the Study of Societal Issues, Working Paper, Oct. 14, 2015). Kimberlé Crenshaw notes the disconnect from the police, see Kimberlé Crenshaw, *Mapping the Margins: Intersectionality, Identity Politics, and Violence against Women of Color*, 43 Stan. L. Rev. 1241–1299, 1257 (1991); Donna Coker, *Shifting Power for Battered Women: Law, Material Resources, and Poor Women of Color*, 33 U.C. Davis L. Rev. 1009 (2000). Kimberlé Crenshaw noted that it was necessary to acknowledge tensions within communities of color – including those between anti-racist organizing and advocacy on violence against women – given that anti-racist advocacy produced outcomes that could worsen the situation of women. *See* Kimberlé Crenshaw, *Mapping the Margins: Intersectionality, Identity Politics, and Violence against Women of Color*, 43 Stan. L. Rev. 1241–1299, 1257 (1991).
78. *See* Aya Gruber, The Feminist War on Crime: The Unexpected Role of Women's Liberation in Mass Incarceration (2021).
79. Carole S. Vance, *Pleasure and Danger: Toward a Politics of Sexuality*, in Pleasure and Danger (Carole S. Vance ed., 1984).
80. For a description of competing feminist views on sexuality and their origins, see Ummni Khan, Vicarious Kinks (2014); Gayle S. Rubin, Deviations: A Gayle Rubin Reader (2011).
81. *See generally* Ali Miller, *Sexuality, Violence against Women, and Human Rights: Women Make Demands and Ladies Get Protection*, 7 (2) Health and Hum. Rts. 16–47 (2004) (describing how women's vulnerability to violence became an accepted feature of human rights activism while economic justice as a means of addressing violence against women was sidelined).

82. Angela Harris, *Race and Essentialism in Feminist Legal Theory*, 42 Stan. L. Rev 581, 585 (1990). ("I argue that their work, though powerful and brilliant in many ways, relies on what I call essentialism – the notion that a unitary, 'essential' women's experience can be isolated and described independently of race, class, sexual orientation, and other realities of experience. The result of tendency toward gender essentialism, I argue, is not only that some are silenced in order to privilege others (for this is an inevitable of categorization, which is necessary both for human community and political movement), but that the voices that are silenced to be the same voices silenced by the mainstream legal voice of People – among them, the voices of black women.")
83. Nina Harawa, *Incarceration, African Americans, and HIV: Advancing a Research Agenda*, 100 J. Nat'l Med. Ass'n 57 (2008).
84. Cathy Cohen, The Boundaries of Blackness: AIDS and the Breakdown of Black Politics (1999).
85. Paula Braveman & Sofia Gruskin, *Poverty, Equity, Human Rights and Health*, 81 Bulletin of the World Health Organization 539–545 (2003).
86. Many of the critiques by feminists levied against the AIDS response came from outside of AIDS organizing. In global advocacy this was exemplified by the women's group DAWN (Development Alternatives for Women in a New Era). DAWN theorized gender with specific attention to "class, race, and nation." It sought to fight oppression on a global scale with an emphasis on critiquing dominant economic policies, but with specific attention to location and its impact on poor women. *See, generally*, Gita Sen & Caren Grown, Development, Crisis, and Alternative Visions (1985).
87. Celeste Watkins-Hayes, Remaking a Life: How Women Living with HIV Confront Inequality (2019) (describing the ways in which women living with HIV and AIDS activists created a social safety net against an environment hostile to health).

## 5 THE SEX WARS COME TO AIDS: RISK AND CONSENT

1. The story of Ashabai is taken from an article by Aziza Ahmed & Meena Seshu, *We Have the Right Not to Be Rescued*, 1 Anti-Trafficking Rev. 149 (2012). Names were changed to protect privacy. Parts of this chapter reproduce and draw on Aziza Ahmed, *Feminism, Power, and Sex Work in the Context of HIV/AIDS*, 34 Harvard Journal of Law and Gender 225 (2011); Aziza Ahmed & Meena Seshu, *We Have the Right Not to Be Rescued*, 1 Anti-Trafficking Rev. 149 (2012); Aziza Ahmed, Trafficked? *AIDS, Criminal Law and the Politics of Measurement*, 70 U. Mia. L. Rev. 96 (2015); Aziza Ahmed, *Addressing HIV/AIDS at the*

*Intersection of Anti-Trafficking and Health Law and Policy*, in REVISITING THE LAW AND GOVERNANCE OF TRAFFICKING, FORCED LABOR, AND MODERN DAY SLAVERY (Prabha Kotiswaran ed., 2017); Aziza Ahmed, *Transnational Legal Orders and Global Health*, in THE HANDBOOK OF TRANSNATIONAL LAW (Peer Zumbansen ed., 2021).

2. Janie Chuang, *Rescuing Trafficking from Ideological Capture: Prostitution Reform and Anti-Trafficking Law and Policy*, 158 U. PA. L. REV. 1655, 1664 (2010).
3. Michael L. Rekart, *Sex-Work Harm Reduction*, 366 LANCET 2123, 2123 (2005).
4. For a description of feminist positions on criminal law, sex work, and trafficking, see Janet Halley et al., *From the International to the Local in Feminist Legal Responses to Rape, Prostitution/Sex Work, and Sex Trafficking: Four Studies in Contemporary Governance Feminism*, 29 HARV. J. L. & GENDER 335, 338 (2006).
5. Janet Halley et al., *From the International to the Local in Feminist Legal Responses to Rape, Prostitution/Sex Work, and Sex Trafficking: Four Studies in Contemporary Governance Feminism*, 29 HARV. J. L. & GENDER 335, 338 (2006). (Abolitionist feminists do not support the prosecution of sex workers.)
6. The driving rationales behind the Acts shifted over time and are difficult to isolate. As argued by Judith Walkowitz, the Acts may have been driven by concerns over sexuality in the Victorian period as well as venereal disease. JUDITH WALKOWITZ, PROSTITUTION AND VICTORIAN SOCIETY: WOMEN, CLASS, AND THE STATE 70 (1980).
7. The Acts applied to "military stations, garrison and seaport towns." Margaret Hamilton, *Opposition to the Contagious Diseases Acts, 1864–1888*, 10 (1) ALBION: A QUARTERLY JOURNAL CONCERNED WITH BRITISH STUDIES 14–27, 14 (1978); The Contagious Diseases Prevention Act 1864, 27 & 28 Vict. c. 84 & 85, §§ 12–14 (U.K.). The Contagious Diseases Acts, 1866/1869 Sections 15–16 (where the 1866 Act states: "Where an information on oath is laid before a justice by a superintendent of police, charging to the effect that the informant has good cause to believe that a woman therein named is a common prostitute … The justice present, on oath being made before him substantiating the matter of the information to his satisfaction, may, if he thinks fit, order that the woman be subject to periodical medical examinations … for the purpose of ascertaining at the time of each such examination whether she is affected with a contagious disease").
8. Margaret Hamilton, *Opposition to the Contagious Diseases Acts, 1864–1888*, 10 ALBION: A QUARTERLY JOURNAL CONCERNED WITH BRITISH STUDIES 14–27, 14 (1978).
9. As argued by Walkowitz, statistics produced about venereal disease amongst soldiers played a large role in justifying the CDAs. JUDITH

WALKOWITZ, PROSTITUTION AND VICTORIAN SOCIETY: WOMEN, CLASS, AND THE STATE 75 (1980).

10. Margaret Hamilton, *Opposition to the Contagious Diseases Acts, 1864–1886*, 10 ALBION: A Q. J. CONCERNED WITH BRIT. STUD. 14, 16 (1978); *see* ASHWINI TAMBE, CODES OF MISCONDUCT: REGULATING PROSTITUTION IN LATE COLONIAL BOMBAY 52 (2009).
11. Margaret Hamilton, *Opposition to the Contagious Diseases Acts, 1864–1886*, 10 ALBION: Q. J. CONCERNED WITH BRIT. STUD. 14, 16 (1978); *see* ASHWINI TAMBE, CODES OF MISCONDUCT: REGULATING PROSTITUTION IN LATE COLONIAL BOMBAY 52 (2009).
12. JESSICA R. PLILEY, POLICING SEXUALITY: THE MANN ACT AND THE MAKING OF THE FBI 13 (2014).
13. Jeremy Waldron, *Mill on Liberty and on the Contagious Diseases Acts*, J. S. MILL'S POLITICAL THOUGHT 14 (Nadia Urbinati & Alex Zakaras eds., 2007) (quoting Josephine Butler).
14. JESSICA R. PLILEY, POLICING SEXUALITY: THE MANN ACT AND THE MAKING OF THE FBI 14 (2014).
15. JESSICA R. PLILEY, POLICING SEXUALITY: THE MANN ACT AND THE MAKING OF THE FBI (2014) (explaining that although there was common ground between the Christian Purity movement and Butler's LNA, the religious actors were motivated by the desire to protect female innocence rather than to enact a feminist politics); *see also* JUDITH WALKOWITZ, PROSTITUTION AND VICTORIAN SOCIETY: WOMEN, CLASS, AND THE STATE 34 (1980).
16. JESSICA R. PLILEY, POLICING SEXUALITY: THE MANN ACT AND THE MAKING OF THE FBI 16 (2014) (exploring how Mill's opposition to the CDAs mandates a closer examination of Mill's harm principle).
17. ASHWINI TAMBE, CODES OF MISCONDUCT: REGULATING PROSTITUTION IN LATE COLONIAL BOMBAY 31 (2009).
18. ALLAN BRANDT, NO MAGIC BULLET: A SOCIAL HISTORY OF VENEREAL DISEASE IN THE UNITED STATES SINCE 1880 35 (1985).
19. Kerry Abrams, *Polygamy, Prostitution, and the Federalization of Immigration*, 105 COLUM. L. REV. 641, 661 (2005); Pub. L. No. 43–141, 18 Stat. 477 (1875).
20. ASHWINI TAMBE, CODES OF MISCONDUCT: REGULATING PROSTITUTION IN LATE COLONIAL BOMBAY 52 (2009). ("In Europe and North America, the turn of the twentieth century was marked by a moral panic about white women being transported to brothels in colonies. This panic was expressed first through the idiom of 'white slavery' and then through laws against 'trafficking.' The antitrafficking measures in Europe and North America such as the 1910 Mann Act gained emotive weight from the image of violated white women.") Tambe further notes that much of the anxiety around white slavery rooted in sex work

in the colonies, including the migration of women to India to earn money from British settlers and military stationed in the country. *See* ASHWINI TAMBE, CODES OF MISCONDUCT: REGULATING PROSTITUTION IN LATE COLONIAL BOMBAY 53 (2009). *see also* JESSICA R. PLILEY, POLICING SEXUALITY: THE MANN ACT AND THE MAKING OF THE FBI 15 (2014).

21. *See* JESSICA R. PLILEY, POLICING SEXUALITY: THE MANN ACT AND THE MAKING OF THE FBI 2 (2014); ASHWINI TAMBE, CODES OF MISCONDUCT: REGULATING PROSTITUTION IN LATE COLONIAL BOMBAY 52 (2009).
22. 18 U.S. Code § 2421 Mann Act. For a critical history of the Mann Act see JESSICA R. PLILEY, POLICING SEXUALITY: THE MANN ACT AND THE MAKING OF THE FBI 13 (2014).
23. International Convention for the Suppression of the White Slave Traffic, May 4, 1910, 98 U.N.T.S. 101, *amended by* the Protocol signed at Lake Success, New York, May 4, 1949 [hereinafter Convention for Suppression of White Slave Traffic].
24. International Convention for the Suppression of Traffic in Women and Children, Sept. 30, 1921, 9 L.N.T.S. 415, *amended by* a Protocol approved by the General Assembly on Oct. 20, 1947, 53 U.N.T.S. 13 [hereinafter Traffic in Women and Children Convention]. The conventions increasingly emphasized the welfare of the victims, controlling crime, and immorality.
25. ALLAN BRANDT, NO MAGIC BULLET: A SOCIAL HISTORY OF VENEREAL DISEASE IN THE UNITED STATES SINCE 1880 37 (1987); *see also* Alex Smolak, *White Slavery, Whorehouse Riots, Venereal Disease, and Saving Women: Historical Context of Prostitution Interventions and Harm Reduction in New York City during the Progressive Era*, 28 (5) SOCIAL WORK IN PUBLIC HEALTH 496–508 (2013).
26. ALLAN BRANDT, NO MAGIC BULLET: A SOCIAL HISTORY OF VENEREAL DISEASE IN THE UNITED STATES SINCE 1880 74–75 (1987).
27. For a sampling of books on the ideas, disagreements, and politics of feminist organizing, see ALICE ECHOLS, DARING TO BE BAD: RADICAL FEMINISM IN AMERICA 1967–1975 (2019); JANET HALLEY, SPLIT DECISIONS: HOW AND WHY TO TAKE A BREAK FROM FEMINISM (2006); PATRICIA HILL COLLINS, BLACK FEMINIST THOUGHT: KNOWLEDGE, CONSCIOUSNESS AND THE POLITICS OF EMPOWERMENT (2002); WENDY KLINE, BODIES OF KNOWLEDGE: SEXUALITY, REPRODUCTION AND WOMEN'S HEALTH IN THE SECOND WAVE (2010); SERENA MAYERI, REASONING FROM RACE: FEMINISM, LAW, AND THE CIVIL RIGHTS REVOLUTION (2011).
28. For a history of debates on agency and coercion in feminist legal theory, see generally Kathy Abrams, *Sex Wars Redux: Agency and Coercion in Feminist Legal Theory*, 95 COLUM. L. REV. 326–330 (1995); *see also* Carole

S. Vance, *Pleasure and Danger: Toward a Politics of Sexuality*, in PLEASURE AND DANGER (Carole S. Vance ed., 1984); UMMNI KHAN, VICARIOUS KINKS: S/M IN THE SOCIO-LEGAL IMAGINARY (2014).

29. Some, like Andrea Dworkin, felt that prostitution could only be abusive. Andrea Dworkin, *Prostitution and Male Supremacy*, 1 MICH. J. GENDER AND L. 1, 3 (1993) ("I am talking to you about prostitution per se, without more violence, without extra violence, without a woman being hit, without a woman being pushed. Prostitution in and of itself is an abuse of a woman's body"). Catharine MacKinnon, a leading feminist legal theorist, wrote in this period that "investigations reveal … pornography, and prostitution as not primarily abuses of physical force, violence, authority, or economics … they are abuses of women; they are abuses of sex." CATHARINE MACKINNON, TOWARD A FEMINIST THEORY OF THE STATE 113 (1989). In her book *Female Sexual Slavery* Kathleen Barry writes of women in prostitution: "These women and girls are victims of female sexual slavery. Some have escaped; others have not. When it is organized, female sexual slavery is a highly profitable business that merchandises women's bodies to brothels and harems around the world." KATHLEEN BARRY, FEMALE SEXUAL SLAVERY 41 (1984).
30. UMMNI KHAN, VICARIOUS KINKS: S/M IN THE SOCIO-LEGAL IMAGINARY (2014).
31. In *The New York Times*, Kathleen Barry declared: "[Prostitution is] like Black slavery in the nineteenth century, you have to begin to imagine that it would not exist … and eventually you get rid of it." Judy Klemserud, *A Personal Crusade against Prostitution*, N.Y. TIMES (June 24, 1985), bit.ly/3Ym9YQe.
32. Charlotte Bunch on Behalf of herself, Kathleen Barry, and Shirley Castley to Priscilla Alexander (Nov. 2, 1982) (Harvard Schlesinger Archive, COYOTE Archives, Series XIV, Forder 765).
33. Letter from Charlotte Bunch on behalf of herself, Kathleen Barry, and Shirley Castley to Priscilla Alexander (Nov 2, 1982) (Harvard Schlesinger Archive, COYOTE Archives, Margo St. James Files, Series XIV, Folder 765). The dates and references in the letters suggest that some are missing from the archive, though the conversation is continuous.
34. Carole S. Vance, *Pleasure and Danger: Toward a Politics of Sexuality*, in PLEASURE AND DANGER (Carole S. Vance ed., 1984); Heather Love, *Diary of a Conference on Sexuality, 1982*, 17 GLQ: J. GAY AND LESBIAN STUD. 49–51 (2011).
35. Letter from Charlotte Bunch on behalf of herself, Kathleen Barry, and Shirley Castle to Margo St. (1982) (Harvard Schlesinger Archive, COYOTE Archives, Margo St. James Files, Series XIV, Folder 765). The dates and references in the letters suggest that some are missing, though the conversation is continuous.

36. Kathy Abrams, *Sex Wars Redux: Agency and Coercion in Feminist Legal Theory*, 95 COLUM. L. REV. 326–330 (1995); *see also* Carole S. Vance, *Pleasure and Danger: Toward a Politics of Sexuality*, in PLEASURE AND DANGER (Carole S. Vance ed., 1984) (Vance challenges dominance feminist thinking on sex and sexuality in *Pleasure and Danger*). UMMNI KHAN, VICARIOUS KINKS: S/M IN THE SOCIO-LEGAL IMAGINARY (2014).
37. Presentation by Gail Pheterson and Margo St. James, Sex Workers Make History: 1985 & 1986 – The World Whores' Congress, www.walnet.org/csis/groups/icrse/brussels-2005/SWRights-History.pdf.
38. Presentation by Gail Pheterson and Margo St. James, *Sex Workers Make History: 1985 & 1986 – The World Whores' Congress*, www.walnet.org/csis/groups/icrse/brussels-2005/SWRights-History.pdf.
39. Presentation by Margo St. James and Gail Pheterson, *Sex Workers Make History: 1985 & 1986 – The World Whores' Congress*, www.walnet.org/csis/groups/icrse/brussels-2005/SWRights-History.pdf (describing how Priscilla Alexander attended the conference in Rotterdam).
40. Kathleen Barry, Charlotte Bunch, and Shirley Castley, *International Feminism: Networking against Female Sexual Slavery: Report of the Global Feminist Workshop to Organize against Traffic in Women*, Rotterdam, the Netherlands, Apr.6–15, 1983 at 29.
41. International Committee for Prostitutes' Rights, *World Charter for Prostitutes' Rights: International Committee for Prostitutes' Rights February 1985, Amsterdam*, 37 SOCIAL TEXT 183–185 (1993).
42. Presentation by Margo St. James and Gail Pheterson, *Sex Workers Make History: 1985 & 1986 – The World Whores' Congress*, available at www.walnet.org/csis/groups/icrse/brussels-2005/SWRights-History.pdf.
43. International Committee for Prostitutes' Rights, *World Charter for Prostitutes' Rights: International Committee for Prostitutes' Rights February 1985, Amsterdam*, 37 SOCIAL TEXT 183–185 (1993).
44. *See*, for example, William Rubenstein, *Law and Empowerment: The Idea of Order in the Time of AIDS*, 98 YALE LJ, 982 (1988) (exploring the legal dimensions of HIV/AIDS).
45. CRIMINAL LAW, PHILOSOPHY AND PUBLIC HEALTH PRACTICE (Adrian M. Viens, John Coggon, & Anthony S. Kessel eds., 2013).
46. J. Stan Lehman et al., *Prevalence and Public Health Implications of State Laws that Criminalize Potential HIV Exposure in the United States*, 18 AIDS & BEHAVIOR 997, 998, 1002 (2014).
47. Larry Rohter, *Haitians with H.I.V. Leave Cuba Base for Lives in U.S.*, N.Y. TIMES (June 15, 1993), www.nytimes.com/1993/06/15/us/haitians-with-hiv-leave-cuba-base-for-lives-in-us.html.
48. *See, e.g.*, David Robinson, Jr., *AIDS and the Criminal Law: Traditional Approaches and a New Statutory Proposal*, 14 HOFSTRA L. REV. 91, 99 (1985–1986). ("Prostitution may be a more efficient mode of transferring

the AIDS virus than most noncommercialized sexual encounters; prostitutes are often intravenous drug abusers, and multiple partners of prostitutes present greater opportunities for spreading the prostitutes' infections. Moreover, previously-deposited semen may itself be contacted by subsequent male patrons in the course of a prostitute's work. Thus, deterrence of some behavior which risks spreading AIDS could be attempted through vigorous enforcement of laws against prostitution and patronizing prostitutes.")

49. *See* Robert D. Benford & David A. Snow, *Framing Processes and Social Movements: An Overview and Assessment*, 26 Ann. Rev. Soc. 611, 614–615 (2000) (explaining that the use of the verb "framing" "denotes an active, processual phenomenon that implies agency and contention at the level of reality construction." In turn collective action frames are partly constructed to "negotiate a shared understanding of some problematic condition or situation … in need of change").
50. Melissa Hope Ditmore, When Sex Work and Drug Use Overlap: Considerations for Advocacy and Practice 9 (2013).
51. G. Alan Marlatt, *Harm Reduction: Come as You Are*, 21 (6) Addictive Behaviors 779 (1996).
52. G. Alan Marlatt, *Harm Reduction: Come as You Are*, 21 (6) Addictive Behaviors 779, 782 (1996); Laura Flanders, *Dr. Jocelyn Elders: Marijuana, Masturbation and Medicine*, Nation: Healthcare Policy (Oct. 20, 2010), www.thenation.com/blog/155500/dr-joycelyn-elders-marijuana-masturbation-and-medicine#.
53. Philip J. Hilts, *Jonathan Mann, AIDS Pioneer, Is Dead at 51*, N.Y. Times (Sept. 4, 1998), www.nytimes.com/1998/09/04/us/jonathan-mann-aids-pioneer-is-dead-at-51.html.
54. Jonathan M. Mann & Kathleen Kay, *Confronting the Pandemic: The World Health Organization's Global Programme on AIDS, 1986–1989*, 5 AIDS S221, S226 (1991).
55. Gail Pheterson, *Not Repeating History*, in A Vindication of the Rights of Whores 3, 4–5 (Gail Pheterson ed., 1989).
56. Michael L. Rekart, *Sex-Work Harm Reduction*, 366 Lancet 2123, 2123 (2005).
57. *See* Melissa Hope Ditmore, When Sex Work and Drug Use Overlap: Considerations for Advocacy and Practice 9 (2013).
58. *See generally* Melissa Hope Ditmore, When Sex Work and Drug Use Overlap: Considerations for Advocacy and Practice (2013) (applying harm-reduction principles to address the harms of sex work).
59. Michael L. Rekart, *Sex-Work Harm Reduction*, 366 Lancet 2124–2125 (2005).
60. *See* Melissa Ditmore, *Sex Work, Trafficking and HIV: How Development Is Compromising Sex Workers' Human Rights*, in Development with a Body:

Sexuality, Human Rights & Development (Andrea Cornwall, Sonia Corrêa & Susan Jolly eds., 2008). This support resulted in a deep alliance between sex positive feminists and sex workers, providing a movement based on theory and lived experience.

61. *See, e.g.*, Network for Sex Worker Projects, www.nswp.org.
62. *Making Sex Work Safe*, NSWP, www.nswp.org/page/making-sex-work-safe.
63. *Making Sex Work Safe*, NSWP, www.nswp.org/page/making-sex-work-safe.
64. Kathleen Barry, The Prostitution of Sexuality: The Global Exploitation of Women 99 (1995). ("At the time, Butler was not only the first woman but also the most radical, in a feminist sense, to challenge prostitution .... The weakness of Butler's campaign lay not in her outrage nor in her organizing skills but in her strategy. Instead of campaigning against prostitution as customer abuse of women, Butler confined her campaigns to action against third-party coercion by pimps and state regulation. In opposing state regulation, she refrained from action in relation to 'freely chosen' prostitution at a time when its industrialization made the women and the sex an ordinary commodity. Instead, by accepting the emerging concept of 'forced prostitution,' which referred to the young girls and women found on the street and forced to undergo medical exams only to be registered as prostitutes, Josephine Butler in her campaigns also had to implicitly accept that there was a prostitution that was not 'forced.' At that time, most of society considered prostitution to be harmful. Therefore, Butler's position likely seemed to be making inconsequential distinctions between free and forced prostitution in the 1860s, a century before Western society became so thoroughly sexualized through pornography and the media.")
65. Kathleen Barry, The Prostitution of Sexuality: The Global Exploitation of Women (Kindle Location 1595). Kindle edition. (1995).
66. Kathleen Barry, The Prostitution of Sexuality: The Global Exploitation of Women (Kindle Location 1602). Kindle edition. (1995).
67. Kathleen Barry, The Prostitution of Sexuality: The Global Exploitation of Women (Kindle Location 153). Kindle edition. (1995).
68. Janie Chuang, *Rescuing Trafficking from Ideological Capture: Prostitution Reform and Anti-Trafficking Law and Policy*, 158 U. Pa. L. Rev. 1655, 1664 (2010).
69. Kathleen Barry, The Prostitution of Sexuality: The Global Exploitation of Women (Kindle Location 236). Kindle edition. (1995).
70. For writing on carceral feminism, see Elizabeth Bernstein, *Militarized Humanitarianism Meets Carceral Feminism: The Politics of Sex, Rights, and Freedom in Contemporary Antitrafficking Campaigns*, 36 (1) Signs:

J. WOMEN IN CULTURE AND SOC'Y 45–71 (2010) (coining the term); *see generally* AYA GRUBER, THE FEMINIST WAR ON CRIME: THE UNEXPECTED ROLE OF WOMEN'S LIBERATION IN MASS INCARCERATION (2020).

71. Aya Gruber, *The Feminist War on Crime*, 92 IOWA L. REV. 741, 750 (2007).
72. Victims of Trafficking and Violence Protection Act of 2000, Pub. L. No. 106–386, 114 Stat. 1464 (2000).
73. Victims of Trafficking and Violence Protection Act of 2000, Pub. L. No. 106–386, 114 Stat. 1470 (2000) Sec. 103(9).
74. The general definition of sex trafficking includes all commercial sex work. In order to qualify for services, however, you must be a victim of a severe form of sex trafficking defined to include force, fraud, or coercion. Victims of Trafficking and Violence Protection Act of 2000 §103(8)(A) & (B). (A) sex trafficking in which a commercial sex act is induced by force, fraud, or coercion, or in which the person induced to perform such act has not attained 18 years of age; or (B) the recruitment, harboring, transportation, provision, or obtaining of a person for labor or services, through the use of force, fraud, or coercion for the purpose of subjection to involuntary servitude, peonage, debt bondage, or slavery. Victims of Trafficking and Violence Protection Act of 2000, Pub. L. No. 106–386, 114 Stat. 1470 (2000) Sec. 103(8)–(9).
75. Victims of Trafficking and Violence Protection Act of 2000, Pub. L. No. 106–386, 114 Stat. 1481 (2000) Sec. 108(2).
76. Protocol to Prevent, Suppress and Punish Trafficking in Persons, Especially Women and Children, Supplementing the United Nations Convention Against Transnational Organized Crime, Dec. 23, 2003, 2237 U.N.T.S. 319, 343–45, 349. ("'Trafficking in persons' shall mean the recruitment, transportation, transfer, harbouring or receipt of persons, by means of the threat or use of force or other forms of coercion, of abduction, of fraud, of deception, of the abuse of power or of a position of vulnerability or of the giving or receiving of payments or benefits to achieve the consent of a person having control over another person, for the purpose of exploitation. Exploitation shall include, at a minimum, the exploitation of the prostitution of others or other forms of sexual exploitation, forced labour or services, slavery or practices similar to slavery, servitude or the removal of organs.")
77. For a description of the negotiations, see generally Janet Halley et al., *From the International to the Local in Feminist Legal Responses to Rape, Prostitution/Sex Work, and Sex Trafficking: Four Studies in Contemporary Governance Feminism*, 29 HARV. J. L. AND GENDER 335 (2006); Jo Doezema, *Now You See Her, Now You Don't: Sex Workers at the UN Trafficking Protocol Negotiation*, 14 (1) SOC. & LEGAL STUD. 61–89 (2005); ANNE GALLAGHER, THE INTERNATIONAL LAW OF HUMAN

TRAFFICKING (2010); Marjan Wijers, *How We Got Here: The Story of the Palermo Protocol on Trafficking*, OPEN DEMOCRACY (Feb. 11, 2021), www.opendemocracy.net/en/beyond-trafficking-and-slavery/how-we-got-here-story-palermo-protocol-trafficking/. For an analysis of the language of the protocol and its interpretation, see Hila Shamir, *A Labor Paradigm for Human Trafficking*, 60 UCLA L. REV. 76 (2012); GLOBAL ALLIANCE AGAINST TRAFFIC IN WOMEN, HUMAN RIGHTS STANDARDS FOR THE TREATMENT OF TRAFFICKED PERSONS (1999).

78. Jo Doezema, *Now You See Her, Now You Don't: Sex Workers at the UN Trafficking Protocol Negotiation*, 14 (1) SOC. & LEGAL STUD. 61, 80 (2005).
79. Kathleen Barry here discusses her evolution: "[T]he abolitionist position does not concern itself with prostitution as long as women are not forced. In 1979, in *Female Sexual Slavery*, I took an abolitionist position regarding *individual* women in prostitution, recommending policy that would recognize that as long [as] a woman can freely leave prostitution at any time she chooses, neither individuals nor the state should interfere with her personally. In 1983, I argued that it is possible to 'accept the abolitionist position for individuals but feminism requires that in exposing patriarchal power we must separate the individual from the institution which controls her, and that we examine the institution of prostitution as a product of male domination, of sexual violence and enslavement.' However, individuals cannot be separated from the institutions. More importantly, this position perpetuates the false distinction between 'free' and 'forced' prostitution, which assumes that prostitution itself is not damaging to women and therefore is not a form of sexual exploitation. By the mid 1980s, I had reformulated my position on prostitution law, having recognized that decriminalization is necessary and appropriate only for prostitute women, not customers." KATHLEEN BARRY, THE PROSTITUTION OF SEXUALITY 238 (1995).
80. United States Leadership Against HIV/AIDS, Tuberculosis, and Malaria Act of 2003 (Leadership Act), P.L. 108–25 (2003).
81. Penelope Saunders, *Prohibiting Sex Work Projects, Restricting Women's Rights: The International Impact of the 2003 U.S. Global AIDS Act*, 7 HEALTH & HUM. RTS. 179, 182 (2004).
82. Penelope Saunders, *Prohibiting Sex Work Projects, Restricting Women's Rights: The International Impact of the 2003 U.S. Global AIDS Act*, 7 HEALTH & HUM. RTS. 179, 182 (2004).
83. Penelope Saunders, *Prohibiting Sex Work Projects, Restricting Women's Rights: The International Impact of the 2003 U.S. Global AIDS Act*, 7 HEALTH & HUM. RTS. 179, 182 (2004).
84. Jonathan Cohen & Tony Tate, *The Less They Know the Better: Abstinence-Only HIV/AIDS Programs in Uganda*, 14 REPROD. HEALTH MATTERS 174, 174–178 (2006).

85. John W. Dietrich, *The Politics of PEPFAR: The President's Emergency Plan for AIDS Relief*, 21 ETHICS & INT'L AFF. 277, 289 (2007). Advocates and AIDS activists advocated to reverse these amendments. They succeeded in removing the application of the global gag rule, but the remainder of the restrictions were applied to AIDS funding.
86. Penelope Saunders, *Prohibiting Sex Work Projects, Restricting Women's Rights: The International Impact of the 2003 U.S. Global AIDS Act*, 7 HEALTH & HUM. RTS. 179, 186 (2004).
87. Janie Chuang, *Rescuing Trafficking from Ideological Capture: Prostitution Reform and Anti-Trafficking Law and Policy*, 158 U. PA. L. REV. 1655, 1664 (2010).
88. United States Leadership Against HIV/AIDS, Tuberculosis, and Malaria Act of 2003 (Leadership Act), P.L. 108–25 (2003). ("The sex industry, the trafficking of individuals into such industry, and sexual violence are additional causes of and factors in the spread of the HIV/AIDS epidemic. One in nine South Africans is living with AIDS, and sexual assault is rampant, at a victimization rate of one in three women. Meanwhile in Cambodia, as many as 40 percent of prostitutes are infected with HIV and the country has the highest rate of increase of HIV infection in all of Southeast Asia. Victims of coercive sexual encounters do not get to make choices about their sexual activities.") The Act exempted the Global Fund to Fight AIDS, Tuberculosis and Malaria; the WHO, International AIDS Vaccine Initiative; and any "United Nations agency" from its requirements.
89. Michael L. Rekart, *Sex-Work Harm Reduction*, 366 LANCET 2123, 2123 (2005).
90. *See* World Health Organization et al., *Prevention and Treatment of HIV and Other Sexually Transmitted Infections for Sex Workers in Low- and Middle-Income Countries: Recommendations for a Public Health Approach*, 16 (Dec. 2012), https://tinyurl.com/3vwhn57k.
91. *See* World Health Organization et al., *Prevention and Treatment of HIV and Other Sexually Transmitted Infections for Sex Workers in Low- and Middle-Income Countries: Recommendations for a Public Health Approach*, 16 (Dec. 2012), https://iris.who.int/bitstream/handle/10665/77745/9789241504744_eng.pdf?sequence=1.
92. Letter from the Christian Dental and Med. Ass'n to Former President George W. Bush (Aug. 4, 2005) (on file with author).
93. *See* Noy Thrupkaew, *Beyond Rescue: The Campaign against Forced Prostitution Works When It Addresses Victims' Needs*, NATION (Oct. 8, 2009), www.thenation.com/article/archive/beyond-rescue/; *see, e.g.*, Priya Shetty, *Profile: Meena Saraswathi Seshu: Tackling HIV for India's Sex Workers*, 376 LANCET 17, 17 (2010); *see also* Joanna Busza, *Having the Rug Pulled from under Your Feet: One Project's Experience of the US Policy Reversal on Sex Work*, 21 HEALTH POL'Y PLAN 329, 329 (2006).

94. USAID Reply Brief, Case 1:05-cv-01604-EGS.
95. Parts of this analysis are pulled from Aziza Ahmed, *Transnational Legal Orders and Global Health*, in THE HANDBOOK OF TRANSNATIONAL LAW (Peer Zumbansen ed., 2021).
96. Brief for AIDS Action et al. as Amici Curiae, *DKT v. USAID*, 477 F.3d 758 (D.C. 2007) (No. 05-01604).
97. Janie Chuang, *Rescuing Trafficking from Ideological Capture: Prostitution Reform and Anti-Trafficking Law and Policy*, 158 U. PA. L. REV. 1655, 1664 (2010).
98. *Trafficking of Women and Children in E. Asia and Beyond: A Review of U.S. Pol'y: Hearing before the S. Subcomm. on East Asian and Pacific Affairs of the S. Comm. on Foreign Relations*, 108th Cong. 1 (2003) (statement of Donna Hughes, Professor and Carlson Endowed Chair in Women's Studies, Univ. of Rhode Island).
99. *Trafficking of Women and Children in E. Asia and Beyond: A Review of U.S. Pol'y: Hearing before the S. Subcomm. on East Asian and Pacific Affairs of the S. Comm. on Foreign Relations*, 108th Cong. 1 (2003) (statement of Donna Hughes, Professor and Carlson Endowed Chair in Women's Studies, Univ. of Rhode Island) at 2–3 ("In the House, Representative Chris Smith has been successful in adding an amendment to the Global HIV/AIDS bill (H.S. 1298) that will prevent funds from this Act being used to provide assistance to any group that does not have a policy explicitly opposing prostitution and sex trafficking").
100. Government's Reply Brief in Support of Motion to Dismiss, *DKT v. USAID*, 477 F.3d 758 (D.C. 2005) (No. 05-01604).
101. Brief for Coal. Against Trafficking in Women et al. as Amici Curiae Supporting Respondents, *AOSI v. USAID*, 430 F. Supp. 2d 222 (S.D.N.Y. 2006) (No. 05-8209).
102. Brief for Coal. Against Trafficking in Women et al. as Amici Curiae Supporting Respondents, *AOSI v. USAID*, 430 F. Supp. 2d 222 (S.D.N.Y. 2006) (No. 05-8209) at 2 ("The United States has compelling reasons to decide that its funds are better spent on organizations whose approach will in the long run be far more effective").
103. Brief for Coal. Against Trafficking in Women et al. as Amici Curiae Supporting Respondents, *AOSI v. USAID*, 430 F. Supp. 2d 222 (S.D.N.Y. 2006) (No. 05-8209) at 5.
104. Brief for Coal. Against Trafficking in Women et al. as Amici Curiae Supporting Respondents, *AOSI v. USAID*, 430 F. Supp. 2d 222 (S.D.N.Y. 2006) (No. 05-8209) at 3. The brief includes other examples of abolitionist feminist reasoning: "The prostitution and sex trafficking industry, whether legal or illegal, brings physical and mental devastation upon the persons – mostly female, and mostly young – whose bodies are bought and sold for sexual use. Individuals living in prostitution or emerging

from prostitution exhibit symptoms of mental and emotional trauma at levels that are comparable to the mental health injuries sustained by survivors of combat or rape. This harm to mental health, typically accompanied by serious harm to physical health, is readily explained upon examination of conditions in the sex industry. Prostitution within that industry is an experience that is saturated in violence and coercion, both physical and sexual."

105. Brief for AIDS Action et al. as Amici Curiae Supporting Plaintiff-Appellees, *AOSI v. USAID*, 430 F. Supp. 2d 222 (S.D.N.Y. 2006) (No. 05-8209).
106. *AOSI v. USAID*, 430 F. Supp. 2d 222 (S.D.N.Y. 2006).
107. *AOSI v. USAID*, 430 F. Supp. 2d 222 (S.D.N.Y. 2006).
108. United States Agency for International Development, *Acquisition and Assistance Policy Directive*, 72 Fed. Reg. 41,076 (July 26, 2007).
109. Henry Waxman and Barbara Lee, *Comments on RIN-0991-AB60 Organizational Integrity of Entities Implementing Leadership Act Programs and Activities, Notice of Proposed Rulemaking* (Dec. 22, 2009).
110. 74 Fed. Reg. 61096 (November 23, 2009).
111. Letter from the Ctr. for Health and Gender Equity and Hum. Rights Watch to Kathleen Sebelius, Secretary, U.S. Dep't of Health and Hum. Srvs., *Comments on Office of Global Health Affairs' Regulation on the Organizational Integrity of Entities Implementing Leadership Act Programs and Activities, Notice of Proposed Rulemaking* (Dec. 23, 2009) (on file at www.pledgechallenge.org/documents/commentary/20091223.CHANGE_HRW_Comments.pdf).
112. Letter from 21 Humanitarian, Public Health, and Human Rights Organizations to Kathleen Sebelius, Secretary, U.S. Dep't of Health and Hum. Srvs., *Comments on Office of Global Health Affairs; Reg. on the Organizational Integrity of Entities Implementing Leadership Act Programs and Activities, Notice of Proposed Rulemaking* (Dec. 23, 2009) (on file at www.brennancenter.org/page/-/Justice/AJLawsuits/20091223.Groups_Comments.pdf).
113. Letter from 21 Humanitarian, Public Health, and Human Rights Organizations to Kathleen Sebelius, Secretary, U.S. Dep't of Health and Hum. Srvs., *Comments on Office of Global Health Affairs; Reg. on the Organizational Integrity of Entities Implementing Leadership Act Programs and Activities, Notice of Proposed Rulemaking* (Dec. 23, 2009) (on file at www.brennancenter.org/page/-/Justice/AJLawsuits/20091223.Groups_Comments.pdf).
114. Letter from 170+ Individuals and Grassroots Orgs. to Kathleen Sebelius, Secretary, U.S. Dep't of Health and Hum. Srvs., *Comments on Office of Global Health Affairs' Reg. on the Organizational Integrity of Entities Implementing Leadership Act Programs and Activities, Notice of Proposed*

*Rulemaking* (Dec. 23, 2009) (on file at www.brennancenter.org/page/-/Justice/CourtCases/20091223.Grassroots_comments.pdf).

115. Organizational Integrity of Entities That Are Implementing Programs and Activities Under the Leadership Act, 75 Fed. Reg. 18, 760 (Apr. 13, 2010) (codified at 45 C.F.R. pt. 89).
116. "Given the numerous factual situations that may arise, the Department has deliberately adopted a case-by-case approach in this area, recognizing that circumstances in some countries may make it difficult for organizations to satisfy some of the factors demonstrating objective integrity and independence. The Department also plans to work with recipients to address individual questions regarding the separation criteria, and to help remedy violations before taking enforcement action. We believe these steps will ensure recipients have adequate channels for engaging in protected speech while still adhering to the requirement of the Leadership Act that recipient organizations be opposed to the practices of prostitution and sex trafficking because of the psychological and physical risks they pose for women, men and children." Organizational Integrity of Entities That Are Implementing Programs and Activities Under the Leadership Act, 75 Fed. Reg. 18, 760 (Apr. 13, 2010) (codified at 45 C.F.R. pt. 89).
117. *See Alliance for 13 Open Soc. Int'l, Inc. v. U.S. Agency for Int'l Dev.*, 651 F.3d 218 (2d Cir. 2011).
118. Brief for UNAIDS as Amicus Curiae Supporting Petitioners, *Alliance for the Open Society Institute v. United States Agency for International Development*, 133 S. Ct. 2321 (2013).
119. Brief for UNAIDS as Amicus Curiae Supporting Petitioners, *Alliance for the Open Society Institute v. United States Agency for International Development*, 133 S. Ct. 2321 (2013). The layering of international and national law both on the side of the aid-giving and aid-receiving countries is an example of transnational law. Peer Zumbansen, *Where the Wild Things Are: Journeys to Transnational Legal Order, and Back*, 1 UC IRVINE J. OF INT'L TRANSNAT'L AND COMPAR. L. 161 (2016). In their book, Terence Halliday and Gregory Shaffer define transnational legal order as a "collection of formalized legal norms and associated organizations and actors that authoritatively order the understanding and practice of law across national jurisdictions." They describe transnational legal orders as having the following three characteristics: "(1) seek to produce order in an issue area that relevant actors construe as a 'problem'; (2) are legal insofar as they adopt legal form to address the problem, their norms are produced or conveyed in connection with a transnational body or network, and they directly or indirectly engage national legal bodies; and (3) are transnational insofar as they transcend and permeate state boundaries in one way or another." TERENCE HALLIDAY & GREGORY

Shaffer, Transnational Legal Orders (2015). I have developed this further in Aziza Ahmed, *Transnational Legal Orders and Global Health*, in The Oxford Handbook of Transnational Law (Peer Zumbansen ed., 2021).

120. Brief for Coalition Against Trafficking in Women and Others as Amicus Curiae Supporting Petitioners, *Alliance for the Open Society Institute v. United States Agency for International Development*, 133 S. Ct. 2321 (2013).
121. 45 C.F.R. Part 89 (2014). ("U.S. organizations that are prime recipients or sub recipients of Leadership Act HIV/AIDS funds are not required to have a policy explicitly opposing prostitution and sex trafficking. The Department of Health and Human Services applies the requirement of the Leadership Act that organizations have a policy explicitly opposing prostitution and sex trafficking only to foreign organizations, including foreign affiliates of United States organizations, whether prime recipients or subrecipients, unless exempted by the Act or implementing regulations.")
122. *Sex Work and HIV/AIDS: UNAIDS Technical Update*, UNAIDS 10, 15 (2002), http://data.unaids.org/publications/IRC-pub02/jc705-sexwork-tu_en.pdf.
123. *Sex Work and HIV/AIDS: UNAIDS Technical Update*, UNAIDS 10, 15 (2002), http://data.unaids.org/publications/IRC-pub02/jc705-sexwork-tu_en.pdf. Emphasis added.
124. *Sex Work Tool Kit*, WHO, http://who.arvkit.net/sw/en/contentdetail.jsp?ID=204&d=sw.11; *Context: Key Principles*, WHO (Nov. 7, 2010), www.who.int/hiv/topics/vct/sw_toolkit/context/en/index4.html; *New Online Tool Kit on HIV/AIDS Prevention for Sex Workers: GTZ, WHO and Sex Work Networks Share Information and Lessons Learned*, WHO (Nov. 11, 2004), www.who.int/mediacentre/news/releases/2004/pr80/en/print.html.
125. *Context: Key Principles*, WHO (Nov. 7, 2010) www.who.int/hiv/topics/vct/sw_toolkit/context/en/index4.html.
126. *See generally* Avni Amin, Cheryl Overs, & Penelope Saunders, *Violence against Women and HIV/AIDS: Critical Intersections – Violence against Sex Workers and HIV Prevention*, World Health Organization 3 (2005), https://shorturl.at/frRR3 ("Criminalization of sex work contributes to an environment in which, violence against sex workers is tolerated, leaving them less likely to be protected from it").
127. *International Guidelines on HIV/AIDS and Human Rights*, Office of U.N. High Comm'r for Hum. Rts. & UNAIDS 30 (2006), https://shorturl.at/HJwfz.
128. *International Guidelines on HIV/AIDS and Human Rights*, Office of U.N. High Comm'r for Hum. Rts. & UNAIDS 238 (2006), http://data.unaids.org/Publications/IRC-pub07/jc1252-internguidelines_en.pdf.

129. *See Rep. of the Global Technical Consultation on HIV and Sex Work*, UNAIDS, U.N. Population fund ("UNFPA") & Nat'l STD/AIDS Programme of the Ministry of Health of Brazil (2006) (on file with author).
130. *See Rep. of the Global Technical Consultation on HIV and Sex Work*, UNAIDS, U.N. Population fund ("UNFPA") & Nat'l STD/AIDS Programme of the Ministry of Health of Brazil, at 17–18 (2006) (on file with author).
131. *See Rep. of the Global Technical Consultation on HIV and Sex Work*, UNAIDS, U.N. Population fund ("UNFPA") & Nat'l STD/AIDS Programme of the Ministry of Health of Brazil (2006) (on file with author).
132. Anna-Louise Crago, *The Curious Sex Worker's Guide to the UNAIDS Guidance Note on HIV and Sex Work*, https://swannet.org/the-curi ous-sex-workers-guide-to-the-unaids-guidance-note-on-hiv-and-sex-work/.
133. Anna Louise Crago, *The Curious Sex Worker's Guide to the UNAIDS Guidance Note on HIV and Sex Work*, https://swannet.org/the-curious-sex-workers-guide-to-the-unaids-guidance-note-on-hiv-and-sex-work/.
134. *See UNAIDS Guidance Note on HIV and Sex Work* (2007), www.unaids .org/sites/default/files/media_asset/JC2306_UNAIDS-guidance-note-HIV-sex-work_en_0.pdf.
135. *UNAIDS Guidance Note on HIV and Sex Work* (2007), www.unaids.org/ sites/default/files/media_asset/JC2306_UNAIDS-guidance-note-HIV-sex-work_en_0.pdf.
136. Joint U.N. Programme on HIV/AIDS (UNAIDS), *UNAIDS Guidance Note on HIV and Sex Work*, at 8 (Mar. 2009), https://shorturl.at/rqHGT.
137. *UNAIDS Guidance Note on HIV and Sex Work*, at 5 (2009), www.unaids .org/sites/default/files/media_asset/JC2306_UNAIDS-guidance-note-HIV-sex-work_en_0.pdf.
138. *UNAIDS Advisory Group on HIV and Sex Work & Global Working Group on HIV and Sex Work Policy*, Global Network of Sex Work Projects, www.nswp.org/unaids-advisory-group.
139. *UNAIDS Advisory Group on HIV and Sex Work & Global Working Group on HIV and Sex Work Policy*, Global Network of Sex Work Projects, www.nswp.org/unaids-advisory-group.
140. *UNAIDS Advisory Group on HIV and Sex Work*, Paolo Longo Research Initiative, www.plri.org/story/unaids-advisory-group-hiv-and-sex-work.
141. *UNAIDS Guidance Note on HIV and Sex Work* (2012), www.unaids.org/ sites/default/files/media_asset/JC2306_UNAIDS-guidance-note-HIV-sex-work_en_0.pdf.

142. *UNAIDS Guidance Note on HIV and Sex Work*, at 6 (2012), www.unaids.org/sites/default/files/media_asset/JC2306_UNAIDS-guidance-note-HIV-sex-work_en_0.pdf.
143. *UNAIDS Guidance Note on HIV and Sex Work*, at 6 (2012), www.unaids.org/sites/default/files/media_asset/JC2306_UNAIDS-guidance-note-HIV-sex-work_en_0.pdf.
144. *UNAIDS Guidance Note on HIV and Sex Work*, at 6 (2012), www.unaids.org/sites/default/files/media_asset/JC2306_UNAIDS-guidance-note-HIV-sex-work_en_0.pdf.
145. *UNAIDS Guidance Note on HIV and Sex Work*, at 15 (2012).
146. *Special Rapporteur on the Right of Everyone to the Enjoyment of the Highest Attainable Standard of Physical and Mental Health*, U.N. Hum. Rights Off. of the High Commissioner for Hum. Rights, www.ohchr.org/EN/Issues/Health/Pages/SRRightHealthIndex.aspx.
147. Anand Grover (Special Rapporteur on the Right of Everyone to the Enjoyment of the Highest Attainable Standard of Physical and Mental Health), *Promotion and Protection of All Human Rights, Civil, Political, Economic, Social and Cultural Rights, Including the Right to Development*, U.N. Doc. A/HRC/14/20 at 29 (Apr. 27, 2010). ("Historically, sex work has been criminalized in two major ways. First, through the criminalization of the selling of sexual services, with the imposition of penalties upon sex workers themselves. Second, through the criminalization of various practices around sex work: these include, but are not limited to, keeping a brothel; recruiting for or arranging the prostitution of others; living off the proceeds of sex work; solicitation; and facilitating sex work through the provision of information or assistance. Although the former is not directly criminalized in many States worldwide, sex workers are nonetheless treated as criminals where activities around sex work are criminalized, or through the use of other pre-existing laws (not specific to sex work) to harass, intimidate or justify the use of force against sex workers. Examples include the use of vagrancy or public nuisance laws to detain or arrest street sex workers, or the use of laws prohibiting homosexual acts in relation to male and transgender sex workers.")
148. I served on the Technical Advisory Group to the Commission.
149. United Nations Development Program, Global Commission on HIV and the Law, available at https://hivlawcommission.org/report/.
150. UNAIDS Programme Coordinating Board, *Report of the Thirty-Fifth Meeting of the Programme Coordinating Board*, UNAIDS/PCB (35)/14.24 rev. 1, at 79 (Dec. 11, 2014), www.unaids.org/sites/default/files/media_asset/20141211_35PCB%20_StigmaDiscrimination_rev.pdf.
151. UNAIDS Programme Coordinating Board, *Report of the Thirty-Fifth Meeting of the Programme Coordinating Board*, UNAIDS/PCB (35)/14.24

rev. 1, at 79 (Dec. 11, 2014), www.unaids.org/sites/default/files/media_asset/20141211_35PCB%20_StigmaDiscrimination_rev.pdf.

152. United Nations Development Program, Global Commission on HIV and the Law, 99, available at https://hivlawcommission.org/report/.
153. World Health Organization, *Prevention and Treatment of HIV and Other Sexually Transmitted Infections for Sex Workers in Low- and Middle-Income Countries: Recommendations for a Public Health Approach*, at 8 (Dec. 2012), bit.ly/3En4yOc.
154. World Health Organization, *Prevention and Treatment of HIV and Other Sexually Transmitted Infections for Sex Workers in Low- and Middle-Income Countries: Recommendations for a Public Health Approach*, at 8 (Dec. 2012), http://apps.who.int/iris/bitstream/10665/77745/1/9789241504744_eng.pdf.
155. World Health Organization, *Prevention and Treatment of HIV and Other Sexually Transmitted Infections for Sex Workers in Low- and Middle-Income Countries: Recommendations for a Public Health Approach*, at 8 (Dec. 2012), http://apps.who.int/iris/bitstream/10665/77745/1/9789241504744_eng.pdf.
156. World Health Organization, *Prevention and Treatment of HIV and Other Sexually Transmitted Infections for Sex Workers in Low- and Middle-Income Countries: Recommendations for a Public Health Approach*, at 8 (Dec. 2012), http://apps.who.int/iris/bitstream/10665/77745/1/9789241504744_eng.pdf.
157. World Health Organization, *Prevention and Treatment of HIV and Other Sexually Transmitted Infections for Sex Workers in Low- and Middle-Income Countries: Recommendations for a Public Health Approach*, at 8 (Dec. 2012), http://apps.who.int/iris/bitstream/10665/77745/1/9789241504744_eng.pdf.
158. Melissa Ditmore & Penelope Saunders, *Sex Work and Sex Trafficking*, 1 Sexual Health Exchange 15 (1998).
159. *See, e.g.*, J. Gupta et al., *History of Sex Trafficking, Recent Experiences of Violence, and HIV Vulnerability among Female Sex Workers in Coastal Andhra Pradesh, India*, 114 (2) Int'l J. Gynaecology and Obstetrics 101–105 (2011); Jay Silverman et al., *HIV Prevalence and Predictors of Infection in Sex-Trafficking Nepalese Girls and Women*, 298 (5) J. Am. Med. Ass'n 536–542 (2007).
160. J. Silverman et al., *HIV Prevalence and Predictors among Rescued Sex-Trafficked Women and Girls in Mumbai, India*, 43 J. Acquired Immune Deficiency Syndrome 588 (2006); J. Gupta et al., *History of Sex Trafficking, Recent Experiences of Violence, and HIV Vulnerability among Female Sex Workers in Coastal Andhra Pradesh, India*, 114 (2) Int'l J. Gynaecology and Obstetrics 101–105 (2011).
161. J. Gupta et al., *History of Sex Trafficking, Recent Experiences of Violence, and HIV Vulnerability among Female Sex Workers in Coastal Andhra Pradesh, India*, 114 (2) Int'l J. Gynaecology and Obstetrics 101–105 (2011).

162. J. Silverman et al., *HIV Prevalence and Predictors among Rescued Sex-Trafficked Women and Girls in Mumbai, India*, 43 J. Acquired Immune Deficiency Syndrome 588 (2006).
163. S. Goldenberg et al., *Exploring the Context of Trafficking and Adolescent Sex Industry Involvement in Tijuana, Mexico: Consequences of HIV Risk and Prevention*, 21 (4).
164. J. Silverman et al., *Associations of Sex Trafficking History with Recent Sexual Risk among HIV-Infected FSWs in India*, 18 (3) AIDS and Behav. 555–561 (2014).
165. *HIV and Sex Workers*, Lancet (July 23, 2014), www.thelancet.com/series/hiv-and-sex-workers; Kate Shannon et al., *Global Epidemiology of HIV among Female Sex Workers: Influence of Structural Determinants*, 385 Lancet 55, 63, 65, 66 (2015) (explaining that decriminalizing sex work in Vancouver, India, and Kenya "would have the greatest effect on the course of HIV epidemics across all settings, averting 33–46% of HIV infections in the next decade").
166. The Lancet, *Sex Workers and HIV – Forgotten and Ostracized*, 380 Lancet 188 (2012).
167. Lucy Platt et al., *Associations between Sex Work Laws and Sex Workers' Health: A Systematic Review and Meta-analysis of Quantitative and Qualitative Studies*, 15 (12) PLOS Medicine (Dec. 11, 2018), 10.1371/journal.pmed.1002680.

## CONCLUSION: GOVERNING THE UNKNOWN: LEGAL–SCIENTIFIC SETTLEMENTS

1. *See generally* Ulrich Beck, Risk Society: Towards a New Modernity (1992) (discussing risk, knowledge, and governance).
2. The idea of "political settlements" is discussed in development studies scholarship. In his work on the governance of economic development, for example, Mushtaq Khan writes of political settlements: "A political settlement emerges when the distribution of benefits supported by its institutions is consistent with the distribution of power in society, and the economic and political outcomes of these institutions are sustainable over time." Mushtaq H. Khan, *Political Settlements and the Governance of Growth-Enhancing Institutions*, https://eprints.soas.ac.uk/9968/1/Political_Settlements_internet.pdf. Khan further elaborates on the concept of political settlements describing that the framework addresses the differences in how "policies and institutions that worked well in some contexts appeared to achieve much poorer results in others" in the first instance and how "different policies and institutions appeared to be effective in solving similar problems in different contexts." The idea of political settlements "addresses these questions by

arguing that the way institutions work in practice depends on the responses of the organizations operating under these institutions." Mushtaq H. Khan, *Introduction: Political Settlements and the Analysis of Institutions*, 120 AFR. AFFS. 509 (2018). The idea of political settlement is resonant with the idea of "institutional settlements" introduced by Henry Hart and Albie Sacks. *See* HENRY M. HART, JR. & ALBERT M. SACKS, THE LEGAL PROCESS 4 (William N. Eskridge, Jr. & Philip P. Frickey eds., 1994). Hart and Sacks understand an institutional settlement as "express[ing] the judgment that decisions which are the duly arrived at result of duly established procedures of this kind ought to be accepted as binding upon the whole society unless and until they are duly changed." An institutional settlement, as described by John Manning, "presumes that in order to avoid 'chaos' and 'advance the larger purposes' of the polity, society 'establish[es] … regularized and peaceable methods of decision.'" John Manning, *Without the Pretense of Legislative Intent* 130 HARV. L. REV. 2397, 2413 (2017). Later Manning describes institutional settlements as the "proposition that fights about interpretation theory are really fights about the different actors' complex institutional roles and relationships." John Manning, *Without the Pretense of Legislative Intent* 130 HARV. L. REV. 2397 (2017). For additional discussion on institutional settlements, see Richard H. Fallon, *Arguing in Good Faith about the Constitution: Ideology, Methodology, and Reflective Equilibrium*, 84 U. CHI. L. REV. 125, 126–127 (2017); *see also* Charles L. Barzun, *The Forgotten Foundations of Hart and Sacks*, 99 VA. L. REV. 1 (2013) (discussing the foundations of legal process theory). Legal process theory developed by Hart and Sacks and within which the idea of institutional settlements emerges has been subject to many critiques. *See, e.g.*, Duncan Kennedy, *Utopian Rationalism in American Legal Thought: A Critique of the Hart & Sacks Legal Process Materials* (Harv. Pub. L., Working Paper No. 23–44, 2023).

3. *See generally* Sheila Jasanoff, *The Idiom of Co-production*, in STATES OF KNOWLEDGE: THE CO-PRODUCTION OF SCIENCE AND SOCIAL ORDER (Sheila Jasanoff ed., 2004).
4. Janet Halley, *Distribution and Decision: Assessing Governance Feminism*, in GOVERNANCE FEMINISM: AN INTRODUCTION (Janet Halley et al. eds., 2018) (describing how to do a distributional analysis).
5. To understand how law and economics contributed to the push toward individual responsibility, see Aziza Ahmed & Jason Jackson, *Race, Risk and Personal Responsibility in the Response to COVID-19*, 121 COLUMBIA L. REV. 57 (2021). For writing on state responsibility during COVID, see Gregg Gonsalves, *Welcome to the You Do You Pandemic*, NATION (Sept. 1, 2023), www.thenation.com/article/society/covid-surge-response-ignored/; Amy Kapczynki & Gregg Gonsalves, *The New Politics of Care*, BOS. REV. (Apr. 27, 2020), www.bostonreview.net/articles/gregg-gon

salves-amy-kapczynski-new-deal-public-health-we-need/; Elizabeth Fee & Nancy Krieger, *Understanding AIDS: Historical Interpretations and the Limits of Biomedical Individualism*, 83 (10) AM. J. PUB. HEALTH 1477–1486 (1993) (discussing how the biomedical model furthers individualism in the AIDS response).

6. On the shift toward criminal law, see generally JONATHAN SIMON, GOVERNING THROUGH CRIME: HOW THE WAR ON CRIME TRANSFORMED AMERICAN DEMOCRACY AND CREATED A CULTURE OF FEAR (2007). Discussing the role of the courts in furthering "penal welfare," see Aya Gruber, Amy J. Cohen, & Kate Mogulescu, *Penal Welfare and the New Human Trafficking Intervention Courts*, 68 FLA. L. REV. 1333 (2016). On the demise of the welfare state and rise of the law and order society, see Stuart Hall, *Drifting into a Law and Order Society: The 1979 Cobden Trust Human Rights Day Lecture [1980]*, in SELECTED WRITINGS ON RACE AND DIFFERENCE (Paul Gilroy & Ruth Wilson Gilmore eds., 2021).
7. For discussion on the impact of feminism inside of institutions, see generally JANET HALLEY ET AL., GOVERNANCE FEMINISM: AN INTRODUCTION (2018); JANET HALLEY ET AL., GOVERNANCE FEMINISM: NOTES FROM THE FIELD (2019).
8. *See generally* Donna Haraway, *Situated Knowledges: The Science Question in Feminism and the Privilege of Partial Perspective*, 14 FEMINIST STUD. 581 (1988) (describing feminist engagement in critiques of science and knowledge).
9. Ian Hacking, *Making Up People*, in RECONSTRUCTING INDIVIDUALISM: AUTONOMY, INDIVIDUALITY, AND THE SELF IN WESTERN THOUGHT 165 (Thomas C. Heller, Morton Sosna, & David Willbery eds., 1985); *see also* GOWRI VIJAYAKUMAR, AT RISK: INDIAN SEXUAL POLITICS AND THE GLOBAL AIDS CRISIS (2021) (thinking about the question of sexual identity in the AIDS response and the stakes of being defined as "at risk").
10. Stephen Phillips & Michelle Williams, *Confronting Our Next National Health Disaster – Long Haul COVID*, 385 NEW ENGLAND J. MED. (2021); Felicity Callard & Elisa Perego, *How and Why patients Made Long Covid*, 268 SOC. SCI. & MED. 11342 (2021). On the question of race and COVID, see Patricia Williams, *The Endless Looping of Public Health and Scientific Racism*, in ASSESSING LEGAL RESPONSES TO COVID-19 (Scott Burris et al. eds., 2020).
11. Alex Rushforth et al., *Long Covid – The Illness Narratives*, 286 SOC. SCI. & MED. 11432 (2021); Kenton Kaplan & Emily Mendenhall, *Framing Long Covid through Patient Activism in the United States: Patient, Provider, Academic, and Policymaker Views*, 350 SOC. SCI. & MED. 116901 (2024); Elisa Perego & Felicity Callard, *Patient-Made Long Covid Changed COVID-19 (and the Production of Science, Too)* (Feb. 9, 2021), https://osf.io/preprints/socarxiv/n8yp6.

12. Fiona Lowenstein & Ryan Prior, *The Long COVID Revolution*, NATION (Apr. 11, 2023), www.thenation.com/article/society/long-covid-disability-policy/. For an example of the types of benefits of the Long Covid designation, see U.S. Dept. of Health & Hum. Servs., Guidance on "Long COVID" as a Disability under the ADA, Section 504, and Section 1557 (2021); The BMJ Podcast, *Anthony Fauci on Covid-19*, BRIT. MED. J. (Sept. 23, 2020), www.bmj.com/content/370/bmj.m3703; Peter S. Kim, Sarah W. Read, & Anthony S. Fauci, *Therapy for Early COVID-19: A Critical Need*, 324 J. AM. MED. ASS'N 2149 (2020); Ctrs. for Disease Control and Prevention, Long COVID Basics (2024).
13. Donna Lu, *They Can't Ignore Us Anymore: Five Women on Long COVID and Medical Misogyny*, GUARDIAN (Oct. 18, 2022), www.theguardian.com/society/2022/oct/18/long-covid-women-symptoms-medical-misogyny; Catherine Villanueva Gardner, *Feminist Bioethics Perspectives on "Long-COVID Syndrome"*, 15 (1) IJFAB: INT'L J. FEMINIST APPROACHES TO BIOETHICS 189–191 (2022).
14. Letter from Delta Airlines to Rochelle Walensky, Director, Ctrs. for Disease Control and Prevention (Dec. 21, 2021) (on file with author).
15. Niraj Chokshi & Lauren Hirsch, Delta Air Lines and a Union Spar over Isolation Periods for Sick Workers, N.Y. TIMES (Jan. 12, 2022), at B6-L., www.nytimes.com/2022/01/11/business/delta-flight-attendants-union-isolation-covid.html?searchResultPosition=1.
16. Lawrence Gostin, I. Glenn Cohen, & Jeffrey P. Koplan, *Universal Masking in the United States: The Role of Mandates, Health Education, and the CDC*, 324 (9) J. AM. MED. ASS'N 837–838 (2020) (describing the patchwork of masking laws and regulation of masks); Dannagal Young et al., *The Politics of Mask-Wearing: Political Preferences, Reactance, and Conflict Aversion during COVID*, 298 SOC. SCI. & MED. 114836 (2022) (discussing the politics of masking).
17. In 2003, concern about the Bush administration pandering to its base led Representative Henry Waxman to investigate. *See* Minority Staff of H.R. Comm. on Gov't Reform, 108th Cong., Rep. on Content of Federally Funded Abstinence-Only Education Programs (2004); Advocate.com Editors, *Bush Administration Slammed for Deleting Info from CDC Condom Fact Sheet*, ADVOCATE (Dec. 20, 2002), www.advocate.com/health/health-news/2002/12/20/bush-administration-slammed-deleting-info-cdc-condom-fact-sheet-7264; *Editorials Address Controversy over Bush Administration's Deletion, Alteration of Condom, Abortion Information on Government Web Sites*, KFF HEALTH NEWS (Jan. 7, 2003), https://kffhealthnews.org/morning-breakout/dr00015363/; Robert Walgate, *Bush's AIDS Plan Criticised for Emphasising Abstinence and Forbidding Condoms*, 329 BRIT. MED. J. 192 (2004).

# INDEX

CAMBRIDGE STUDIES IN LAW AND SOCIETY

*Books in the Series*

*Diseases of the Will: Alcohol and the Dilemmas of Freedom*
Mariana Valverde

*The Politics of Truth and Reconciliation in South Africa: Legitimizing the Post-Apartheid State*
Richard A. Wilson

*Modernism and the Grounds of Law*
Peter Fitzpatrick

*Unemployment and Government: Genealogies of the Social*
William Walters

*Autonomy and Ethnicity: Negotiating Competing Claims in Multi-Ethnic States*
Yash Ghai

*Constituting Democracy: Law, Globalism and South Africa's Political Reconstruction*
Heinz Klug

*The Ritual of Rights in Japan: Law, Society, and Health Policy*
Eric A. Feldman

*Governing Morals: A Social History of Moral Regulation*
Alan Hunt

*The Colonies of Law: Colonialism, Zionism and Law in Early Mandate Palestine*
Ronen Shamir

*Law and Nature*
David Delaney

*Social Citizenship and Workfare in the United States and Western Europe: The Paradox of Inclusion*
Joel F. Handler

*Law, Anthropology, and the Constitution of the Social: Making Persons and Things*
Edited by Alain Pottage and Martha Mundy

*Judicial Review and Bureaucratic Impact: International and Interdisciplinary Perspectives*
Edited by Marc Hertogh and Simon Halliday

*Immigrants at the Margins: Law, Race, and Exclusion in Southern Europe*
Kitty Calavita

*Lawyers and Regulation: The Politics of the Administrative Process*
Patrick Schmidt

*Law and Globalization from Below: Towards a Cosmopolitan Legality*
Edited by Boaventura de Sousa Santos and César A. Rodríguez-Garavito

*Public Accountability: Designs, Dilemmas and Experiences*
Edited by Michael W. Dowdle

*Law, Violence and Sovereignty among West Bank Palestinians*
Tobias Kelly

*Legal Reform and Administrative Detention Powers in China*
Sarah Biddulph

*The Practice of Human Rights: Tracking Law between the Global and the Local*
Edited by Mark Goodale and Sally Engle Merry

*Judges beyond Politics in Democracy and Dictatorship: Lessons from Chile*
Lisa Hilbink

*Paths to International Justice: Social and Legal Perspectives*
Edited by Marie-Bénédicte Dembour and Tobias Kelly

*Law and Society in Vietnam: The Transition from Socialism in Comparative Perspective*
Mark Sidel

*Constitutionalizing Economic Globalization: Investment Rules and Democracy's Promise*
David Schneiderman

*The New World Trade Organization Knowledge Agreements: Second Edition*
Christopher Arup

*Justice and Reconciliation in Post-Apartheid South Africa*
Edited by François du Bois and Antje du Bois-Pedain

*Militarization and Violence against Women in Conflict Zones in the Middle East: A Palestinian Case-Study*
Nadera Shalhoub-Kevorkian

*Child Pornography and Sexual Grooming: Legal and Societal Responses*
Suzanne Ost

*Darfur and the Crime of Genocide*
John Hagan and Wenona Rymond-Richmond

*Fictions of Justice: The International Criminal Court and the Challenge of Legal Pluralism in Sub-Saharan Africa*
Kamari Maxine Clarke

*Conducting Law and Society Research: Reflections on Methods and Practices*
Simon Halliday and Patrick Schmidt

*Planted Flags: Trees, Land, and Law in Israel/Palestine*
Irus Braverman

*Culture under Cross-Examination: International Justice and the Special Court for Sierra Leone*
Tim Kelsall

*Cultures of Legality: Judicialization and Political Activism in Latin America*
Javier Couso, Alexandra Huneeus, and Rachel Sieder

*Courting Democracy in Bosnia and Herzegovina: The Hague Tribunal's Impact in a Postwar State*
Lara J. Nettelfield

*The Gacaca Courts, Post-Genocide Justice and Reconciliation in Rwanda: Justice without Lawyers*
Phil Clark

*Law, Society, and History: Themes in the Legal Sociology and Legal History of Lawrence M. Friedman*
Edited by Robert W. Gordon and Morton J. Horwitz

*After Abu Ghraib: Exploring Human Rights in America and the Middle East*
Shadi Mokhtari

*Adjudication in Religious Family Laws: Cultural Accommodation, Legal Pluralism, and Gender Equality in India*
Gopika Solanki

*Water on Tap: Rights and Regulation in the Transnational Governance of Urban Water Services*
Bronwen Morgan

*Elements of Moral Cognition: Rawls' Linguistic Analogy and the Cognitive Science of Moral and Legal Judgment*
John Mikhail

*Mitigation and Aggravation at Sentencing*
Edited by Julian V. Roberts

*Institutional Inequality and the Mobilization of the Family and Medical Leave Act: Rights on Leave*
Catherine R. Albiston

*Authoritarian Rule of Law: Legislation, Discourse and Legitimacy in Singapore*
Jothie Rajah

*Law and Development and the Global Discourses of Legal Transfers*
Edited by John Gillespie and Pip Nicholson

*Law against the State: Ethnographic Forays into Law's Transformations*
Edited by Julia Eckert, Brian Donahoe, Christian Strümpell, and Zerrin Özlem Biner

*Transnational Legal Ordering and State Change*
Edited by Gregory C. Shaffer

*Legal Mobilization under Authoritarianism: The Case of Post-Colonial Hong Kong*
Waikeung Tam

*Complementarity in the Line of Fire: The Catalysing Effect of the International Criminal Court in Uganda and Sudan*
Sarah M. H. Nouwen

*Political and Legal Transformations of an Indonesian Polity: The Nagari from Colonisation to Decentralisation*
Franz von Benda-Beckmann and Keebet von Benda-Beckmann

*Pakistan's Experience with Formal Law: An Alien Justice*
Osama Siddique

*Human Rights under State-Enforced Religious Family Laws in Israel, Egypt, and India*
Yüksel Sezgin

*Why Prison?*
Edited by David Scott

*Law's Fragile State: Colonial, Authoritarian, and Humanitarian Legacies in Sudan*
Mark Fathi Massoud

*Rights for Others: The Slow Home-Coming of Human Rights in the Netherlands*
Barbara Oomen

*European States and Their Muslim Citizens: The Impact of Institutions on Perceptions and Boundaries*
Edited by John R. Bowen, Christophe Bertossi, Jan Willem Duyvendak, and Mona Lena Krook

*Environmental Litigation in China: A Study in Political Ambivalence*
Rachel E. Stern

*Indigeneity and Legal Pluralism in India: Claims, Histories, Meanings*
Pooja Parmar

*Paper Tiger: Law, Bureaucracy and the Developmental State in Himalayan India*
Nayanika Mathur

*Religion, Law and Society*
Russell Sandberg

*The Experiences of Face Veil Wearers in Europe and the Law*
Edited by Eva Brems

*The Contentious History of the International Bill of Human Rights*
Christopher N. J. Roberts

*Transnational Legal Orders*
Edited by Terence C. Halliday and Gregory Shaffer

*Lost in China? Law, Culture and Society in Post-1997 Hong Kong*
Carol A. G. Jones

*Security Theology, Surveillance and the Politics of Fear*
Nadera Shalhoub-Kevorkian

*Opposing the Rule of Law: How Myanmar's Courts Make Law and Order*
Nick Cheesman

*Ironies of Colonial Governance: Law, Custom and Justice in Colonial India*
James Jaffe

*The Clinic and the Court: Law, Medicine and Anthropology*
Edited by Ian Harper, Tobias Kelly, and Akshay Khanna

*The World of Indicators: The Making of Government Knowledge through Quantification*
Edited by Richard Rottenburg, Sally E. Merry, Sung-Joon Park, and Johanna Mugler

*Contesting Immigration Policy in Court: Legal Activism and Its Radiating Effects in the United States and France*
Leila Kawar

*The Quiet Power of Indicators: Measuring Governance, Corruption, and Rule of Law*
Edited by Sally Engle Merry, Kevin E. Davis, and Benedict Kingsbury

*Investing in Authoritarian Rule: Punishment and Patronage in Rwanda's Gacaca Courts for Genocide Crimes*
Anuradha Chakravarty

*Contractual Knowledge: One Hundred Years of Legal Experimentation in Global Markets*
Edited by Grégoire Mallard and Jérôme Sgard

*Iraq and the Crimes of Aggressive War: The Legal Cynicism of Criminal Militarism*
John Hagan, Joshua Kaiser, and Anna Hanson

*Culture in the Domains of Law*
Edited by René Provost

*China and Islam: The Prophet, the Party, and Law*
Matthew S. Erie

*Diversity in Practice: Race, Gender, and Class in Legal and Professional Careers*
Edited by Spencer Headworth, Robert L. Nelson, Ronit Dinovitzer, and David B. Wilkins

*A Sociology of Constitutions: Constitutions and State Legitimacy in Historical-Sociological Perspective*
Chris Thornhill

*A Sociology of Transnational Constitutions: Social Foundations of the Post-National Legal Structure*
Chris Thornhill

*Genocide Never Sleeps: Living Law at the International Criminal Tribunal for Rwanda*
Nigel Eltringham

*Shifting Legal Visions: Judicial Change and Human Rights Trials in Latin America*
Ezequiel A. González-Ocantos

*The Demographic Transformations of Citizenship*
Heli Askola

*Criminal Defense in China: The Politics of Lawyers at Work*
Sida Liu and Terence C. Halliday

*Contesting Economic and Social Rights in Ireland: Constitution, State and Society, 1848–2016*
Thomas Murray

*Buried in the Heart: Women, Complex Victimhood and the War in Northern Uganda*
Erin Baines

*Palaces of Hope: The Anthropology of Global Organizations*
Edited by Ronald Niezen and Maria Sapignoli

*The Politics of Bureaucratic Corruption in Post-Transitional Eastern Europe*
Marina Zaloznaya

*Revisiting the Law and Governance of Trafficking, Forced Labor and Modern Slavery*
Edited by Prabha Kotiswaran

*Incitement on Trial: Prosecuting International Speech Crimes*
Richard Ashby Wilson

*Criminalizing Children: Welfare and the State in Australia*
David McCallum

*Global Lawmakers: International Organizations in the Crafting of World Markets*
Susan Block-Lieb and Terence C. Halliday

*Duties to Care: Dementia, Relationality and Law*
Rosie Harding

*Insiders, Outsiders, Injuries, and Law: Revisiting "The Oven Bird's Song"*
Edited by Mary Nell Trautner

*Hunting Justice: Displacement, Law, and Activism in the Kalahari*
Maria Sapignoli

*Injury and Injustice: The Cultural Politics of Harm and Redress*
Edited by Anne Bloom, David M. Engel, and Michael McCann

*Ruling Before the Law: The Politics of Legal Regimes in China and Indonesia*
William Hurst

*The Powers of Law: A Comparative Analysis of Sociopolitical Legal Studies*
Mauricio García-Villegas

*A Sociology of Justice in Russia*
Edited by Marina Kurkchiyan and Agnieszka Kubal

*Constituting Religion: Islam, Liberal Rights, and the Malaysian State*
Tamir Moustafa

*The Invention of the Passport: Surveillance, Citizenship and the State, Second Edition*
John C. Torpey

*Law's Trials: The Performance of Legal Institutions in the US "War on Terror"*
Richard L. Abel

*Law's Wars: The Fate of the Rule of Law in the US "War on Terror"*
Richard L. Abel

*Transforming Gender Citizenship: The Irresistible Rise of Gender Quotas in Europe*
Edited by Eléonore Lépinard and Ruth Rubio-Marín

*Muslim Women's Quest for Justice: Gender, Law and Activism in India*
Mengia Hong Tschalaer

*Children as 'Risk': Sexual Exploitation and Abuse by Children and Young People*
Anne-Marie McAlinden

*The Legal Process and the Promise of Justice: Studies Inspired by the Work of Malcolm Feeley*
Jonathan Simon, Rosann Greenspan, Hadar Aviram

*Gift Exchanges: The Transnational History of a Political Idea*
Grégoire Mallard

*Measuring Justice: Quantitative Accountability and the National Prosecuting Authority in South Africa*
Johanna Mugler

*Negotiating the Power of NGOs: Women's Legal Rights in South Africa*
Reem Wael

*Indigenous Water Rights in Law and Regulation: Lessons from Comparative Experience*
Elizabeth Jane Macpherson

*The Edge of Law: Legal Geographies of a War Crimes Court*
Alex Jeffrey

*Everyday Justice: Law, Ethnography, and Injustice*
Sandra Brunnegger

*The Uncounted: Politics of Data in Global Health*
Sara L. M. Davis

*Transnational Legal Ordering of Criminal Justice*
Gregory Shaffer and Ely Aaronson

*Five Republics and One Tradition*
Pablo Ruiz-Tagle

*The Law Multiple: Judgment and Knowledge in Practice*
Irene van Oorschot

*Health as a Human Right: The Politics and Judicialisation of Health in Brazil*
Octávio Luiz Motta Ferraz

*Shari'a, Inshallah: Finding God in Somali Legal Politics*
Mark Fathi Massoud

*Policing for Peace: Institutions, Expectations, and Security in Divided Societies*
Matthew Nanes

*Rule of Law Intermediaries: Brokering Influence in Myanmar*
Kristina Simion

*Lactation at Work: Expressed Milk, Expressing Beliefs, and the Expressive Value of Law*
Elizabeth A. Hoffmann

*The Archival Politics of International Courts*
Henry Redwood

*Global Pro Bono: Causes, Context, and Contestation*
Edited by Scott L. Cummings, Fabio de Sa e Silva, and Louise G. Trubek

*The Practice and Problems of Transnational Counter-Terrorism*
Fiona de Londras

*Decoupling: Gender Injustice in China's Divorce Courts*
Ethan Michelson

*Anti-constitutional Populism*
Martin Krygier, Adam Czarnota, and Wojciech Sadurski

*Lawyers in Conflict and Transition*
Kieran McEvoy, Louse Mallinder, and Anna Bryson

*The Ghostwriters: Lawyers and the Politics behind the Judicial Construction of Europe*
Tommaso Pavone

*The Sentimental Court: The Affective Life of International Criminal Justice*
Jonas Bens

*Practices of Reparations in International Criminal Justice*
Christoph Sperfeldt

*Seeking Supremacy: The Pursuit of Judicial Power in Pakistan*
Yasser Kureshi

*The Power of the Jury: Transforming Citizens into Jurors*
Nancy S. Marder

*Undue Process: Persecution and Punishment in Autocratic Courts*
Fiona Feiang Shen-Bayh

*Discounting Life: Necropolitical Law, Culture, and the Long War on Terror*
Jothie Rajah

*Clean Air at What Cost? The Rise of Blunt Force Regulation in China*
Denise Sienli van der Kamp

*Law and Precarity: Legal Consciousness and Daily Survival in Vietnam*
Tu Phuong Nguyen

*Prosecutors, Voters and the Criminalization of Corruption in Latin America: The Case of Lava Jato*
Ezequiel A. Gonzalez-Ocantos and Paula Muñoz Chirinos

*Entangled Domains: Empire, Law and Religion in Northern Nigeria*
Rabiat Akande

*The Social Constitution: Embedding Social Rights Through Legal Mobilization*
Whitney K. Taylor

*Out of Place: Fieldwork and Positionality in Law and Society*
Edited by Lynette J. Chua and Mark Fathi Massoud

*Negotiating Legality: Chinese Companies in the U.S. Legal System*
Ji Li

*Law and Jewish Difference: Ambivalent Encounters*
Mareike Riedel

*A Sociology of Post-Imperial Constitutions: Suppressed Civil War and Colonized Citizens*
Chris Thornhill

*The Regulation of Prostitution in China: Law in the Everyday Lives of Sex Workers, Police Officers, and Public Health Officials*
Margaret L. Boittin

*Immoral Traffic: An Ethnography of Law, NGOs, and the Governance of Prostitution in India*
Vibhuti Ramachandran

*From Manners to Rules: Advocating for Legalism in South Korea and Japan*
Celeste L. Arrington

For EU product safety concerns, contact us at Calle de José Abascal, 56–1°, 28003 Madrid, Spain or eugpsr@cambridge.org.

www.ingramcontent.com/pod-product-compliance
Lightning Source LLC
LaVergne TN
LVHW011812200926
848484LV00005B/1159

* 9 7 8 1 1 0 8 4 8 5 5 0 0 *